COMMUNITY COLLEGE LEADERSHIP

# COMMUNITY COLLEGE LEADERSHIP

## A Multidimensional Model for Leading Change

*Pamela L. Eddy*

Foreword by George R. Boggs

STERLING, VIRGINIA

Sty/us

COPYRIGHT © 2010 BY STYLUS PUBLISHING, LLC.

Published by Stylus Publishing, LLC
22883 Quicksilver Drive
Sterling, Virginia 20166-2102

**Library of Congress Cataloging-in-Publication-Data**
Eddy, Pamela Lynn.
   Community college leadership : a multidimensional
model for leading change / Pamela L. Eddy, foreword by
George R. Boggs.
      p.   cm.
   Includes bibliographical references and index.
   ISBN 978-1-57922-415-8 (cloth : alk. paper)
   ISBN 978-1-57922-416-5 (pbk. : alk. paper)
   1. Community college presidents.   2. Community
colleges—Administration.   3. Educational leadership.
4. Educational change.   I. Boggs, George R.   II. Title.
LB2341.E33   2010
378.1′11—dc22

                                          2010005186

13-digit ISBN: 978-1-57922-415-8 (cloth)
13-digit ISBN: 978-1-57922-416-5 (paper)

Printed in the United States of America

All first editions printed on acid free paper that meets the
American National Standards Institute Z39-48 Standard.

Bulk Purchases

Quantity discounts are available for use in workshops
and for staff development.
Call 1-800-232-0223

First Edition, 2010

10   9   8   7   6   5   4   3   2   1

*To my husband, David,*
*and children,*
*Andrew, Jeffrey, and Laura.*

# CONTENTS

# ACKNOWLEDGMENTS

All scholarship results from an interaction with others and their ideas. I am grateful for sharing thinking space with Marilyn Amey, Regina Garza Mitchell, and Sharon McDade. My work has been enhanced by those who have paved the way for research in and about community colleges, including Barbara Townsend and Susan Twombly, John Levin, Berta Virgil Laden, and Art Cohen and Florence Brawer. Research by these scholars provides a foundation on which others can build. In particular, my work serves as an important reminder of the legacy of Barbara Townsend and all she did for community college research and for the mentorship she provided to emerging scholars. She was with me in spirit as I wrote this book. Carrie Kisker provided her well-honed copy editing skills to this book and pushed my thinking to achieve better clarity. I am appreciative of the contributions of George Boggs for his foreword and for the reminder his participation held for me to make this book matter for those leading community colleges. Nan Ottenritter provided helpful insights regarding the multidimensional model to move me past concepts to the creation of a product that others may find useful. My thanks go to John von Knorring, who followed this project through from conception to reality. It is important that I acknowledge the college leaders and campus members who participated in this research. These individuals cared deeply about their colleges and the mission to educate students who might not have a chance elsewhere and to contribute to their community. I feel fortunate to have shared time with them and to be welcome on their campuses. Finally, I acknowledge the Fulbright Commission for providing me support that allowed me the thinking space to complete this writing. Despite all the help I have had in this project, any errors or gaps are my responsibility.

# FOREWORD

*George R. Boggs*

Community College Leadership: A Multidimensional Model for Leading Change is a significant contribution to the field of community college leadership. Through the use of case studies and vignettes, Pamela Eddy relates classical and new theories of leadership and the consensus on leadership competencies to leadership practice. She has written a book that will prove to be useful to current leaders as they continue to learn and to improve their effectiveness. However, the audience also includes aspiring leaders who want to learn more about career pathways and how to overcome barriers. Scholars of leadership development, policy makers, and, in general, those who are concerned about the future of America's community colleges and who will lead them will find this book valuable and thought-provoking.

America's community colleges are undergoing leadership turnover at a time of significant change and challenge. Enrollment pressure on the colleges continues to increase while funding support continues to decrease. At the same time, there are increasing demands from the federal government and from states and local communities to respond to educational and workforce needs. Campus constituents seek strong leadership but also leadership that is collaborative and understanding of their situations and challenges. Increasing calls for accountability on the part of government, accrediting agencies, and the public in general add to the increasing complexity of leadership. Dr. Eddy makes the case that today's community colleges are complex and multidimensional organizations. As such, they need complex and multidimensional leadership.

When viewed from a multidimensional perspective, a community college leader requires a variety of competencies, some skill based, some personality based, and others learned through experience. The book discusses the six leadership competencies that were developed with coordination from the

---

Dr. Boggs is President and CEO of the American Association of Community Colleges in Washington, DC, and Superintendent/President Emeritus of Palomar College in California.

American Association of Community Colleges and funded by the W. K. Kellogg Foundation. Although a review of competencies is helpful, we know that individuals generally lead based on how they have learned to lead, mainly through experience and trial and error. They learn from their own mistakes and those they have observed in others. Dr. Eddy points out that leaders have developed a cognitive schema or map, based on their experiences, that allows them to interpret situations quickly and to act accordingly. However, a danger is that a leader's schema may also serve as a blinder to reality. Anything that conflicts with a leader's schema will be ignored or recast to fit it—unless the leader is adept at making adjustments.

Leaders who see themselves as learners can tap into resources for making necessary adjustments and handling new situations more appropriately. Learning from books such as this one provides one source for broadening an individual's schema. Engaging in professional development activities that are offered through state and national associations is also an important investment in success. Presidents can participate in the many activities of the Presidents Academy of the American Association of Community Colleges; aspiring leaders can participate in several institutes sponsored by a variety of associations and councils. An added, and most important, benefit is that participation in institutes and workshops helps leaders develop a network of support, a network of people who are living the same lives and facing the same challenges and opportunities. Participants often form lifelong friendships, and these colleagues are valuable sources of advice.

The case studies in this book, along with those often studied at leadership institutes, provide opportunities for leaders and aspiring leaders to gain perspective and to move beyond their own leadership experiences to role-play how they would handle different situations.

Community college leadership has evolved and continues to do so. Top-down leadership practices that may have worked in earlier years are no longer effective. New concepts of leadership focus on collaborative relationships, team building, and participatory governance. The author presents a model of multidimensional leadership with five tenets that point out how leaders must and do respond to the complex organizations they lead. The "fit" between a leader's skills and the institution's needs is one of the most critical factors for a successful leadership experience. Dr. Eddy discusses how important it is for a presidential candidate to find out about the difficulties facing a college before accepting a presidency. Fit, however, is not static; the needs of institutions change over time, and leaders must change and grow—or they themselves will be changed. One current example of change is the movement for institutions to be responsible and accountable for the success of their students. In the past, community college leaders were concerned, almost exclusively, about student access. Success was generally the responsibility of the student. Now, we recognize that access is not enough and, if we are to maintain our national standard of living, more of our population will have to complete college programs, and leaders will be held accountable for improving student success rates.

The author also gives the reader perspectives from female leaders and leaders of color. How they lead and how they are perceived as leaders is important to understand, especially for the boards of trustees who employ them and who need to support them. These leaders often face challenges based on perceptions and expectations that may not be realistic. Even though men and women do not necessarily follow the prescribed styles for their gender, assumptions and norms based on gender often create challenges for leaders. However, we cannot assume that today's White men lead in the same way as past leaders or that they are all the same in their leadership styles. All leaders must see themselves as learners, as mentors for aspiring leaders, and as supporters for their colleagues. Increasing the diversity of community college leadership is an important goal that was recently endorsed by both the American Association of Community Colleges and the Association of Community College Trustees.

Dr. Eddy also discusses the important leadership role of institutional "sensemaking." The leader has the opportunity to frame situations and challenges through a variety of tools. Communicating, leading by example, and appropriate use of symbols and traditions are powerful methods that can be used by leaders. Being available and visible on campus is critical to building the trust necessary to frame situations. Visionary framing is especially useful in turbulent and uncertain times as the leader focuses on the college's possibilities rather than its realities. Although the leader as team builder is not a focus of this book, the author does point out the importance of having administrators who can represent the leader accurately in communications and who can keep the leader informed.

The book also explores career paths for those who are interested in moving into more responsible leadership positions in community colleges. Many community college leaders did not begin their careers with the aspirations of being a president. Community college professionals develop career goals over time and take advantage of opportunities as they arise. Developing a career plan, getting the necessary degrees and credentials, getting the necessary experience, participating in professional development programs, working with a mentor, and developing a network of support are all important components of a successful strategy to move into a more advanced leadership position. The book points out that lack of mobility can be a significant barrier to advancement. Most often, it is necessary to move to a different college, sometimes in another city or state, to accept a new position. Women and leaders of color may be most affected by the expectation that leaders must be geographically flexible. The difficulties inherent in balancing one's career with the demands of raising a family or of accommodating the professional needs of a spouse may keep some aspiring leaders from seeking higher-level positions—or at least delay plans for advancement.

Chapter 7 outlines some helpful suggestions for aspiring leaders, in particular for women and leaders of color. There are also valuable suggestions for current leaders and trustees about the importance of supporting the development of leaders, mentoring, and grow-your-own leadership development programs. Last, there are suggestions for the profession in general about the need to share best practices, to create support networks, and to expand leadership research.

A lot of attention is always paid to the challenges of leadership, how demanding it is, and how vulnerable leaders are. However, leading others is also one of the most rewarding things a person can do. Leaders have transformed institutions and communities—and they most often take great pleasure in the successes of their faculty, staff, students, and alumni. *Community College Leadership: A Multidimensional Model for Leading Change* provides a valuable set of tools that can help our leaders and future leaders to be even more effective.

# THE NEED TO RE-ENVISION COMMUNITY COLLEGE LEADERSHIP

If your actions inspire others to dream more,
learn more, do more and become more, you are
a leader.

John Quincy Adams

Higher education leadership is a popular topic for research and discussion and has inspired numerous books and articles over the years. An electronic search on the phrase *community college leadership* alone yields close to 3,000 hits. Heightened interest in the subject has been spurred recently by predictions that as many as 84% of community college presidents will retire over the next 10 years (Shults, 2001; Weisman & Vaughan, 2007). These pending retirements, as well as severe cuts in state funding and other external pressures, mean that community colleges currently face leadership changes and challenges not seen since the massive expansion of 2-year colleges in the 1960s.

As community colleges prepare for a mass changing of the leadership guard, several questions emerge. Who will make up the next generation of community college leaders? What new ideas and experiences will they bring with them? How can community colleges prepare for new leaders who may break with traditional, male-dominated leadership models? What sort of training and leadership development programs should be put in place to prepare future community college leaders? The current period of transition provides an opportune time to re-envision community college leadership.

Given these changes and challenges, today's community college leaders, including presidents, chief academic officers, vice presidents, deans, and chairs, as well as those seeking such positions, continuously seek guidance on how to improve their leadership skills and effectiveness. Some borrow from industry and attempt to apply business-based theories to a collegiate setting, but for various reasons, these efforts are not always successful (Birnbaum, 2000). Within the community college sector, several sources of support for leaders have emerged. In 2005, the American Association of Community Colleges (AACC) released *Competencies for Community College Leaders*. This monograph was the result of a 2-year effort to provide a set of competencies that can guide future leaders. In particular, the AACC hoped that emerging leaders would use the framework to measure their development and prepare for high-level leadership positions in community colleges.

In addition, many professional organizations, state associations, and individual colleges have created formal leadership development programs. Some of these specifically target the AACC's leadership competencies, whereas others focus on developing leaders to meet the contextual needs of their college (Eddy, 2009; Jeandron, 2006). Although developing leaders by measuring specific competencies and emphasizing the importance of context and culture in leadership development are not mutually exclusive, the two approaches are based on differing conceptions of what a leader is and should be, and perhaps on competing ideas of who should be recruited to campus leadership positions. The emphasis on competencies underscores a set of skills acquired irrespective of the particular needs of a community college. For instance, the specific traits of communication and resource management focus on becoming adept at the process of relationships and the balancing of competing needs for resource allocation. Attention to contextual needs, on the other hand, focuses on the specific culture, history, and challenges facing a particular college. The unique constellation of an individual campus's situation means that communication and resource managements operate within contextual boundaries. It is important for leaders to understand their college's situation to best meet challenges.

This book is based on the premise that leadership is not composed of a prescribed list of traits or skills. Rather, leadership is multidimensional, with the various dimensions existing on continua that reflect the evolution of a leader's understanding of what it means to lead, as well as his or her ability to respond to leadership opportunities in new ways. Key to a multidimensional understanding of leadership is recognition of the fact that all leaders rely to some extent on their core beliefs and underlying schemas (i.e., ways of understanding the world) in making leadership decisions. However, leaders also possess a variety of other leadership dimensions, which interact in ways that are obscured or oversimplified by traditional, two-dimensional theories and models of leadership. Intended as a foundation to the ideas presented throughout the book, this chapter describes the challenges of community college leadership, briefly details the evolution of leadership philosophies, and provides background information on the nine case studies from which empirical data were drawn. The chapter concludes with an overview of the rest of the book.

## Challenges of Community College Leadership

Scholars and policy makers often talk about the community college's historic tripartite mission of transfer education, vocational training, and community service. Yet this idea often oversimplifies the many functions of community colleges. True, the colleges serve as points of access to higher education and lower-cost paths to a bachelor's degree for students who cannot or choose not to matriculate directly at 4-year universities. And yes, community colleges offer vocational training and apprenticeship programs that lead to direct employment, as well as courses that fulfill local community desires and needs. However, in recent years community colleges have also become the primary institutions responsible for providing remedial education to students who are unprepared for college-level work. In addition, they increasingly offer contract training for employees of local businesses, as well as a wide range of adult learning programs. Furthermore, because of their literal and figurative locations between high schools and 4-year universities, community colleges have become the nexus of educational partnerships forming what policy makers envision as seamless educational pathways from kindergarten through the baccalaureate (Amey, Eddy, Campbell, & Watson, 2008; Cherry Commission, 2004; U.S. Department of Education, 2006). Even with serving all of these functions, many community colleges have sought to confer applied bachelor's degrees in areas such as teacher education, nursing, and technology (Floyd, Skolnik, & Walker, 2005; Townsend & Ignash, 2003).

The central challenge of community college leadership is thus balancing these multiple missions and functions in a way that best meets the demands of the community, the state, and the nation. In doing so, leaders must be responsive to changing regional needs and business demands, as well as student aspirations and limitations. Gumport (2003) frames this balancing act as a continuous struggle by community college leaders (as well as those at other public institutions of higher education) to straddle an industry logic that puts a premium on economic priorities and a social logic that prioritizes meeting students' educational needs. This balance is clearly a difficult task, and some believe that it may be impossible to give equal weight to each mission. Boggs (as cited in Evelyn, 2004) argues that community college leaders must navigate internal and external demands and prioritize some institutional goals over others. Such leadership decisions necessarily mean that certain college functions go unfilled. However, by connecting college priorities to community needs and enacting specific strategies to fulfill institutional objectives, leaders can help campus constituents make meaning of their roles at the institution as they focus on improving college outcomes (Eddy, 2003; Neumann, 1995).

The ways in which community colleges are funded provide another leadership challenge. Historically, local taxes were the primary source of revenue to the colleges, which meant that leaders often prioritized regional needs and demands in order to secure a steady stream of funds. However, since the early 1960s state apportionments have outpaced local contributions; in 2000 the states provided 45% of public community college revenues, compared to 20% from local sources (Cohen & Brawer, 2008). This dependence on state apportionments not only complicates the ways in which college leaders make decisions about institutional priorities, but also means that cutbacks in state funding have disproportionately affected 2-year colleges (U.S. Department of Education, 1980, 1995, 2007). In an attempt to stabilize revenues, community colleges have increasingly sought investments from business and industry, particularly in vocational programs. However, most community colleges derive less than 10% of their income from private sources, and thus contributions from local businesses go only so far in easing the institutions' financial woes. Moreover, some argue that greater collaboration with business and industry puts pressure on college leaders to prioritize narrowly tailored vocational courses and workforce development programs over transfer education. Needless to say, dependence on state apportionments, variable funding streams, and variable expectations from businesses and local communities complicate planning and make budgeting difficult.

Student demographics at 2-year colleges also pose a leadership challenge. The average community college student differs greatly from the traditional 4-year university student. Perhaps most important, community college students are older; the average age of a community college student is 27, compared to an average age of 24 at 4-year institutions (U.S. Department of Education, 2007). Community college students are in various life stages and often must balance multiple work, school, and family responsibilities. The mission of community colleges as institutions of second chances and open access creates additional challenges for community college leaders. Public community colleges enroll a full 45% of students in the lowest household income quartile (Bailey, Jenkins, & Leinbach, 2005). Low-income students are constantly pressed by financial concerns, which often results in their placing a premium on work over class attendance. Thus, community college leaders must consider providing flexible scheduling, accelerated degree programs, alternative content delivery options, on-campus child care, and financial support systems to help bridge the funding gap for students.

The vast number of community college students requiring remedial coursework also presents a challenge to community college leaders. Nationwide, 44% of first-time community college students enroll in at least one developmental course (Cohen & Brawer, 2008). Moreover, the percentage of public 4-year institutions that provide remedial education dropped from 85% in 1994 to 76% in 2007, thus pushing a greater number of students who are unprepared for college-level work to community colleges (U.S. Department of Education, 2007). Successfully moving students through remedial courses and into transfer and vocational programs presents a significant pressure for community college leaders, as does the growing percentage of operating budgets necessarily devoted to remediation.

Clearly, community college leadership requires a delicate balancing act. Today's leaders must navigate multiple demands from college and community constituents, uncertain funding streams, challenging and changing student demographics, and increased demands for accountability. Furthermore, an increasing number of community college presidents face these challenges on their own, as a vast number of faculty retirements and a greater reliance on part-time faculty diminishes collegial governance. Contemporary community college leaders thus require skill sets and life experiences that differ from those needed in the past and that allow them to successfully navigate 21st-century challenges.

## Traditional Thoughts on Leadership

Leadership theories have become more complex as the contexts in which leadership occurs has evolved. At the inception of the industrial revolution, when researchers were grappling with understanding organizational and corporate structures, classical leadership theory centered on the concept of a "great man" who could rely on his inherent talents and skills to direct others in newly formed organizations (Heifetz, 1994). As leadership philosophies were expanded beyond large industrial models, the limitations of a one-size-fits-all mode of leading gave way to a more humanistic approach to leadership in which relationships between leaders and followers were acknowledged and valued (Lewin, Lippitt, & White, 1939; Stogdill & Coons, 1957).

As different types of people began to enter the leadership ranks—women and minorities, for example—leadership theorists began to consider how the culture of an organization affects the ways leaders lead. Critical to this expanded understanding of leadership were the ways in which leaders helped followers make meaning of culture and changes (Smircich & Morgan, 1982; Weick, 1995). This perspective emphasized how leaders learn to lead (Amey, 2005; Davis, 2003) and highlighted how leaders' underlying mental maps influence their actions (Senge, 1990). Recently, higher education scholars have called for a different way of thinking about leadership that calls attention to ethics, globalization, and accountability (Kezar, Carducci, & Contreras-McGavin, 2006).

Although philosophies of leadership have evolved and become more nuanced in response to changing organizational structures and the addition of female and non-White leaders, a reliance on trait-based and hierarchical models of leadership remains. Recent research on emerging conceptions of leadership at community colleges underscores this reliance (Eddy & VanDer-Linden, 2006). Nonetheless, some leaders—in both industry and institutions of higher education—are beginning to demonstrate different conceptions of leadership that focus on collaborative relationships, team building, and shared governance. As community colleges face replacing their leadership ranks, search committees should identify the specific needs of their campus to obtain the best fit. Those desiring a more collaborative leader can focus on questioning potential applicants about specific instances that portray the candidates' leadership approach. These types of conversations are telling because past behavior and experiences predict what to expect when the leader arrives on campus.

The ways in which individuals construct their own understanding of leadership (Amey, 1992, 2005) may help further expand philosophies of leadership and may put into practice new conceptions of leadership that are not oriented toward individual leaders. This book uses this broader philosophy of leadership as its starting point and relies on the voices and experiences of current community college leaders to untangle some of the complexity surrounding concepts of leadership.

## Case Studies and Methods

To understand better the challenges of leadership in the field, a variety of community colleges were studied and supplemental individual interviews conducted. These case studies serve as examples of leadership in action and offer individuals an opportunity to see how others dealt with common campus issues, including missteps and learning from these mistakes. Aspiring leaders can learn from these examples and contemplate how they would have responded under similar circumstances. Likewise, students in graduate programs can analyze these cases using the theories they acquire in their classes and what they bring to their understanding from their own practice.

Colleges were selected based on change efforts underway on campus and the presence of a new president—one who had been on campus less than 5 years. Additional minority presidents were interviewed to provide a broader appreciation of issues emanating because of race and color. All of the names used in this text for individuals and colleges are pseudonyms. The logic for the selection criteria was twofold. First, new leaders bring to campus fresh ideas and practices. Observation and study of these early initiatives can provide insight into the influence of leadership development on actions and campus reactions to shifts in leadership. Second, change, by its very nature, destabilizes the existing equilibrium of the culture. How campus members react to these changes and, in turn, how the new president considers this feedback can provide examples for best practices and critical elements leading to success. Campus selection also included a variety of regional locations throughout the United States. The range of locales included rural, suburban, and urban colleges, as well as colleges of various sizes. A detailed outline of the methodology underpinning the information reported here is located in Appendix A.

The following is a brief overview of all the case sites included in this study. The cases presented embody a good cross section of institutions that readers may encounter or lead. Appendix B contains expanded versions of the case studies for the sites; each case includes a series of questions at the end for use in reflection regarding how to handle the given situations and prompts for tactics to frame understanding of the complex scenarios facing the case study presidents. These questions provide an opportunity for readers to reflect on their responses to the same challenges the site presidents faced. Additionally, each case intersects with the six competencies put forth by the AACC as important for leadership development and provides a mechanism for contemplating possible solutions and actions.

## Technology Community College

Technology Community College (TCC), located in the Northeast, is a residential 2-year technical college that serves as the de facto community college for the region. The main campus is in a rural part of the state, and there is a branch campus 35 miles away. Because TCC draws students from a broad swath of the state, the student body is more diverse than either the faculty or the local population. TCC has received national recognition for its use of technology.

Before taking the helm at TCC, President Chris Jones was president of a 2-year college in the Midwest. Before that, Jones taught in and led a community college manufacturing engineering technologies department, as well as a computer-aided design department. He also brought to TCC experience as a business consultant, designer, small-business owner, and Vietnam veteran. Jones's main focus since arriving at TCC was the initiation of Think-Pad University at the college, a college program in which each entering student was required to purchase a ThinkPad computer for use in his or her college program. Financial aid was available to underwrite the costs for the computers; because the students owned the computers, they kept their laptops after graduation or transfer from the college.

## Hunkering Down Community College

Like TCC, Hunkering Down Community College (HDCC) is a residential 2-year campus located in a rural area of the Northeast. It, too, is the only 2-year college in the region. The campus is situated on 625 acres of land and offers targeted courses tied to the needs of area businesses. HDCC's premier academic programs include golf management, hospitality, and veterinary technology curricula. President Lynne Pauldine had previously served as vice president of enrollment at a midwestern community college and continues to consult for a national enrollment management firm and teach online courses in strategic planning. She holds a doctorate in higher education administration and a bachelor's degree in communications. Early in her career, she taught in communication departments at both 2- and 4-year colleges. After taking the reins at HDCC, Pauldine initiated a campuswide program review that resulted in the elimination of 14 academic and vocational programs.

## Bifurcated Community College

Bifurcated Community College (BCC) consists of a main campus, two branch campuses, and four outreach centers in the western United States. It •

is one of four community colleges in a relatively large state; its service area encompasses 18,000 square miles. In order to increase full-time enrollment, one of the college's current goals, BCC has targeted outreach to area high schools and instituted bridge and dual-enrollment programs to introduce students to the college. BCC also serves as a cultural resource for the city in which it is located, hosting community theater events and lectures. Tensions exist at the college, with the branch campuses seeking more autonomy, which runs counter to the current push for centralization of functions and standard operating procedures across the campus.

BCC President Karen Fields followed a traditional path of leadership ascension within community colleges. She taught physics at a community college for nearly 20 years and occasionally held administrative leadership positions within the division. She then worked for 4 years as vice president of academic affairs at a college in the East before assuming her first presidency at BCC. One of Fields's initial goals when arriving on campus was to create a ladder curriculum in which students could easily move from a certificate to an associate degree and ultimately either earn a baccalaureate of technology from BCC or transfer to a university 4-year program.

### Strategic Community College

Strategic Community College (SCC) is a Hispanic-serving institution in the Southwest, where most students are the first in their family to attend college. The institution serves a 10,000-square-mile district spanning two counties and has 13 remote sites. The college also has a branch office out of which one of the state's 4-year public universities offers courses leading to certificates and select bachelor's and master's degrees. The college actively engages in strategic planning, annually updating its 5-year plan. Furthermore, administrators and faculty revisit the planning document on a regular basis, carrying printed copies to meetings and working toward attainment of specific performance outcomes.

Before taking over the presidency at SCC, Jon Hammond was president of a midwestern community college, which he led out of bankruptcy and successfully rebuilt. Hammond originally came to the community college sector via the public school system. He began his career as a middle and high school English teacher, eventually securing a full-time faculty position at a 2-year college. His path to the presidency was traditional, progressing from faculty to director to dean, then to vice president and finally to president. Hammond desired to increase academic standards at the college and to shore up administrative practices. He sought excellence for the college and envisioned the college holding a key role in community development.

## ✖ *Large and Growing Community College District*

Large and Growing Community College District (LGCCD) is composed of five individual college campuses in the southern United States, each with its own president (individual campuses and presidents are described shortly). At its founding, two colleges had charter status, giving them greater autonomy from state regulations in exchange for a commitment to meeting certain accountability standards. The district is currently expanding to meet community needs, yet faces significant fiscal restraints.

Chancellor Jack Pioneer oversaw the entire district from 1995 to 2007. Pioneer was previously president of a community college outside the district but in the same state. During his tenure, Pioneer expanded the district by establishing two new college campuses; the newest opened in fall 2003. He increased LGCCD's enrollment from less than 10,000 students in 1995 to 50,000 students in 2008. After his retirement in 2007, Pioneer was replaced by Robert Caplin. Caplin came to the district from out of state and brought with him more than 20 years of experience as a college president in six different states. One of the first acts of the new chancellor was to change the name of the district to help create an updated image that reflected the expansion to five campuses and to focus marketing efforts around a branding for the district that reflected a vision for the future.

### *Don't Make Waves Community College*

Don't Make Waves Community College (DMWCC), established in 1972, is one of the two charter colleges in LGCCD and enrolls 8,000 students. The challenge for the college was to coordinate curriculum with regional high schools to help connect high school preparation of graduates with college readiness. Additionally, a goal for the college was to smooth out problems created by previous midlevel administrators and to align the organizational structure within the college.

President Brenda Hales initially held a central office position and took over the presidency of DMWCC in 1999, retiring in 2008. Her ascension to the post did not involve a typical search process. Instead, Chancellor Pioneer instituted a position swap, installing Hales as president and moving the former president to a position in central office. Before her work at DMWCC, Hales oversaw curriculum development in the local K–12 school system. This position afforded her visibility throughout the state and allowed her to develop strong relationships within the community. At DMWCC, Hales saw herself as a mediator; she understood district operations and worked to establish methodical and equitable policies and processes at her own campus. The previous president tended to play favorites among groups of faculty and staff and around certain issues, so when Hales took over, she worked to establish a transparent process for decision making. The president who took over after Hales's retirement, Lisa Stewart, had been a long-serving member of the DMWCC team, but had left the district in 2005 to assume a presidency of her own out of state. Of note, Stewart was the lead administrator working with Hales on the curriculum alignment with the regional high schools.

### Rogue Community College

Rogue Community College (RCC) enrolls 8,000 students and is another of the five community colleges in the LGCCD. Students at RCC generally transferred into 4-year degree programs, and the college was viewed as a feeder school to several public universities in the region. More recent planning concerned a focus on developing more vocational programs to meet community needs. James Simon is the second president of RCC, which opened its doors in 1995. RCC's previous president had been known for his innovation, but his practices often ran counter to Chancellor Pioneer's plans for the district. The campus soon had a reputation for stretching boundaries and testing district rules. Although the innovation associated with the boundary testing was initially viewed positively, as the system matured the lack of adherence to district rules and regulations was tolerated less, and the president was encouraged to seek another position. The search committee for a replacement was looking for a team player, and Simon was hired to help steer RCC into districtwide compliance.

Simon's previous experience in a state higher education office in the eastern United States provided him with a macro view of the district and RCC's place within it. When I interviewed Simon in 2003, he had been at RCC for only a few months. He still serves as the president of RCC. To get a handle on campus culture, Simon initially met with all faculty and staff to understand how they perceived issues on campus. His intention was to develop a policy handbook to codify RCC practices and ensure alignment with overarching district policies.

*Me-Too Community College*

Me-Too Community College (MTCC), established in 1982, has more of a homogenous student body and grew rapidly after opening its doors. Corresponding growth of the campus infrastructure was haphazard and cobbled together as pressing space needs demanded. MTCC's culture conveys an attitude of trying to catch up. Community leaders had initially pushed for the college to be one of the district's charter colleges. However, charter status and acceptance into the district depended on collaboration with a nearby K–12 school system. The last-minute withdrawal by MTCC's K–12 partner meant that MTCC was excluded from the district at the time of its founding in 1972. Nonetheless, community leaders continued their quest for membership by supporting a special legislative bill that allowed an exemption from the district's initial membership requirements. As a result, MTCC was approved to join the district in 1982 and opened its doors 6 years later. Perhaps as a result of the college's late entry into the LGCCD, interviewees at MTCC noted a continuous lack of resources at the college and a need to fight for equity among the other colleges in the district.

Michael Garvey has been president of MTCC since January 2001. Garvey had previously served 14 years as president of another college in the state and had also filled several interim presidential positions at colleges in the region, including Tradition-Bound Community College (discussed next). Garvey came to MTCC as an interim president in fall 2000, at which time Chancellor Pioneer indicated that if things "worked out" during Garvey's stint as interim, he could stay on as president. Garvey was named president of MTCC a mere 3 months after taking over as interim. One of Garvey's key goals was to obtain financial resources for the college. He obtained significant increases in the operating budget and an additional $20 million dedicated to building construction on campus. In his first months on campus, Garvey engaged the campus community in a visioning process to eliminate what he referred to as the "hangdog attitude" he witnessed when arriving at MTCC.

*Tradition-Bound Community College*

Tradition-Bound Community College (TBCC) is the other charter college in the LGCCD system. It is the most urban of the district's five community colleges and enrolled 11,000 students in 2008. Before the opening of Cutting Edge Community College, TBCC maintained the largest student enrollment in the district. The history of the college demonstrates its desire to maintain campus-specific traditions. For example, the college has long provided a community center for the arts. Although TBCC's enrollment dipped when the district opened new colleges, its commitment to creating and maintaining distinguishing programs, as well as its physical proximity to the district's urban center, helped ensure a stable enrollment. TBCC is poised to play a larger role in the community as the urban area spreads out to the suburbs.

Shawn Williams, the only president of color in this study, led TBCC for many years but left the college in spring 2007 for another presidency in the Midwest. At that time, John Smith was named interim president and, after a failed presidential search, was promoted to president. Smith has a long history in the district. He was president of DMWCC from 1991 to 1999, then worked for LGCCD's central office until joining TBCC. Goals for the college were to provide educational opportunities to a growing urban minority population and to provide cultural opportunities for the community.

### Cutting Edge Community College

Cutting Edge Community College (CECC) is the newest college in the LGCCD system, although it had operated for several years as a branch campus of Me-Too Community College, enrolling 3,000 students at its center location. CECC was built around the concept of a learning college, with a focus on student-centered education. At the time of my interviews on campus in 2003, CECC had not yet opened its doors, and academic and extracurricular buildings were still under construction. The main administration office was partially completed and gave the impression of a fresh start.

President Jennifer Burke, who had spent 5 years as president of Me-Too Community College, had been charged with opening CECC and was determined to build a college based on best practices in place throughout the district and in the field. Learning from the challenges faced by Rogue Community College in its first few years, Chancellor Pioneer established a rule that at least 50% of CECC hires (in both faculty and staff ranks) must come from inside the district. The intention of this policy was to maintain district culture and not to create an institution with values or practices that would not mesh with those of LGCCD. Seeking an opportunity to be in on the ground floor of a new college, many faculty and staff from the four other colleges in the LGCCD and the district's central office were eager to transfer to CECC. The college officially opened its doors in fall 2003 and in fall 2008 was enrolling 15,000 students at its main campus and branch campus.

## Looking Forward

Community colleges are currently wrestling with challenges resulting from changes in leadership; an inherent need to respond to demands from the state, the local community, and campus constituents; and external pressures such as declines in funding, accreditation requirements, and public demands for accountability. These increasingly complex challenges create a need for skilled professionals to lead these vital institutions. This book aims to help higher education scholars and practitioners better understand and evaluate leadership at community colleges.

Readers may approach this volume in a number of ways. Those hoping to learn more about what it means to lead a community college will find that the book provides an overview of leadership and leadership development that is specific to the community college context. Readers interested in leadership theory in general will find the explication of a multidimensional model of community college leadership in chapter 7 particularly useful. As well, readers interested in specific aspects of community college leadership, such as the influence of gender or the ways in which leaders make meaning of their experiences, may choose to consult the chapters pertaining to those issues. Finally, community college faculty, administrators, and students may find the case studies presented in Appendix B useful in applying theory to practice or as a source for classroom exercises. The case studies are structured as learning tools that can be used in leadership development programs as examples for in-depth analysis. In particular, they provide aspiring leaders with opportunities to move beyond their own leadership experiences and role-play how they would handle different situations. See Appendix B for samples of the various case studies.

Chapter 2 provides a theoretical foundation for this book by reviewing philosophies of leadership and organizational change and presenting a set of propositions that undergird the multidimensional model of leadership proposed at the conclusion of the book. Because research shows that an individual's cognitive schema informs his or her leadership decisions (Harris, 1994; Neumann, 1995), chapter 3 describes how career pathways and leadership development experiences can shape an individual leader's schema and discusses the notion of ideals regarding learning to lead. Chapter 4 looks at the ways in which community college presidents frame and manage meaning on their campuses and calls particular attention to the role of communication in this process.

Chapter 5 revisits the American Association of Community Colleges' (2005) description of competencies necessary for community college leadership, analyzing how these competencies are enacted in different contexts. This chapter focuses specifically on the importance of cultural competency in leadership effectiveness. Because previous studies of community college leaders demonstrate a reliance on White male norms and expectations (Amey & Twombly, 1992; Eddy, 2009), chapter 6 addresses issues of gender and race in community college leadership. Finally, relying on empirical findings from site visits and interviews with community college presidents, chapter 7 highlights issues facing future community college presidents and proposes strategies to aid current and aspiring leaders. This final chapter presents the model for a multidimensional approach to leadership.

Throughout the book, excerpts from interviews with community college leaders illustrate how a multidimensional model of community college leadership can advance thinking about leadership and leadership development. The model is based on five propositions: (1) There is no single or universal model for leadership at community colleges; (2) leaders are multidimensional and multifaceted, relying on different skills and perspectives to address the complexity of their leadership challenges; (3) leaders are guided by their underlying cognitive schemas; (4) some central beliefs guiding leaders are less open than others to change; and (5) leadership development should be based on the tenets of adult learning theory, recognizing leaders as learners. Taken together, these propositions allow for a re-envisioning of community college leadership and ultimately a more nuanced idea regarding who tomorrow's community college leaders may be, how they can be developed and prepared for leadership roles, and how they will lead complex and challenging institutions.

# 2

# MULTIDIMENSIONAL
# LEADERSHIP

The significant problems we face cannot be
solved at the same level of thinking we were at
when we created them.

Albert Einstein

T his chapter begins with a discussion of leadership in the community
college context. This section reviews much of the community college leadership literature and argues that a multidimensional understanding of leadership is necessary if we are to truly support current
community college leaders and the challenges they face. Particular attention
is paid to leadership development and the intersection of gender, race, and
leadership because these issues are especially salient in today's community
colleges. A brief review of the evolution of leadership theories showcases how
leaders operated in different times and contexts. This background is critical
because many features of these theories are still espoused as useful today.
Juxtaposed to these historical ideals are the proposed propositions undergirding a multidimensional model that approaches leadership in a more dynamic
manner. The propositions are presented at the end of this chapter, whereas
the new model components are put forward in the remaining chapters, cul-
minating in a review of the model in the final chapter of the book. The
study of leaders in the field provided expanded ways to view leadership
beyond narrow bands of acceptable behavior, ultimately influencing the
flexibility proposed within the model.

## Leadership in the Community College Context

Compared with other institutions of higher education, community colleges
have a relatively short history: Even though the first junior college was

established in 1901, most of the institutions founded in the next few decades more closely resembled high school extensions than stand-alone colleges. Indeed, the modern-day community college—with its tripartite mission of academic preparation, vocational training, and community service—did not emerge until the 1960s. Twombly (1995) reviewed four distinct eras of community college leadership. From 1900 to 1930, community college presidents were described using the metaphor of the "great man." These leaders were portrayed as charismatic individuals who singularly provided the road map for creating new junior colleges. In the 1940s and 1950s, community college leaders sought independence from secondary schools and began to forge an identity of their own separate from public schools. Community college leaders during the 1960s and 1970s exhibited the strong, dominant leadership necessary to establish and secure a future for their fledgling institutions. Vaughan's (1986) seminal book, *The Community College Presidency*, provided a profile of community college leaders during this era. He described these pioneering presidents as sharing the qualities of integrity, judgment, courage, and concern for others. Over the next three decades, community college presidents had turned their attention to problems resulting from an increasing scarcity of resources. Many leaders borrowed models from the business world, emphasizing efficiency and strategic planning (Rowley & Sherman, 2001).

The millennium signaled a new era of community college leadership. Leaders are now cast as learners and are at the helms of institutions in transition (Alfred, Shults, Jaquette, & Strickland, 2009; Amey, 2005; Hockaday & Puyear, 2008). In particular, 2001 proved to be a significant year, as two American Association of Community Colleges (AACC) reports framed an urgent need for leadership development and planning. The first report, written by Shults (2001), introduced the idea that the community college was in a *leadership crisis* through its projection that 79% of sitting community college presidents—many of whom had helped found their institutions in the 1960s and 1970s—would retire by 2011. Shults contended that the community college was in a leadership crisis not simply because of the aging leadership ranks, but also because fewer people were pursuing advanced degrees in community college administration, and because those in the community college leadership pipeline faced several significant barriers in leadership ascension.

The Shults report spurred action by community college associations and researchers to better understand the scope and impact of this changing of the guard and to create programming that would address the needs of future community college leaders. Thus, later in 2001 AACC published a second report titled *Leadership 2020: Recruitment, Preparation, and Support.* This report addressed the leadership crisis directly by renewing AACC's mission statement and stating its commitment to preparing future leaders. In addition, AACC created a leadership task force to address the issue. The task force identified the recruitment, preparation, and support of community college presidents and upper-level managers as priorities and developed action plans for each. AACC also incorporated several workshops focused on presidential recruitment, development, and support into its annual conference in order to highlight the issue and to provide some initial leadership development training.

Furthermore, AACC held a series of four summits in which experts on community college leadership gathered to brainstorm the best way to train future leaders and encourage them to stay in the 2-year sector. Information from these summits was analyzed and summarized in a report titled *A Competency Framework for Community College Leaders,* published in 2004. Findings from this report were used to refine the necessary skills for community college presidents, and a year later, AACC published *Competencies for Community College Leaders* (2005), which outlined six competencies the association felt were imperative to community college presidents: organizational strategies, resource management skills, communication skills, a willingness to collaborate, advocacy skills, and professionalism. The *Competencies* report describes ways that community college leaders might acquire expertise in each competency, in effect offering potential leaders a template to help them assess which skills they have and how they might acquire or refine other competencies. Although the *Competencies* report was well received by community college leaders and scholars, a recent survey showed that leadership development and training programs were not yet addressing these skill areas (American Association of Community Colleges [AACC], 2008).

Shults's 2001 report focused AACC and other community college associations' attention on the leadership crisis, but university scholars had been examining community college leadership for some time. Like leadership theories in general, these examinations of community college leadership have evolved over time. By the late 1980s, researchers had begun to talk about community college leadership in times of transition. In particular, Vaughan (1989) moved beyond descriptions of individual presidential traits to acknowledge that women and minorities were taking on roles in community college leadership, and that founding presidents were giving way at many colleges to leaders who relied on their relationships with others to lead from a transformative perspective.

Roueche, Baker, and Rose (1989) also focused on the transformational roles of community college presidents. In the early 1990s, community colleges were facing steep declines in fiscal resources, a student body that included large and growing numbers of adults seeking vocational retraining, and an increased demand for development programming within communities. All of these factors indicated a need for a different kind of community college leader, one that would lead the institution through the myriad challenges it faced using a collaborative leadership approach that empowered campus members to aid in required changes. Recognizing the interdependence of organizational culture and leadership, Baker and Associates (1992) argued that these new community college leaders must work from a solid understanding of their campus culture and be adept at symbolic management of meaning among campus groups and stakeholders. Leaders need to frame the ongoing change to help define and create the meaning of the events for staff and community members. The framing messages may occur in a variety of formats, such as campus events, newsletters, awards and recognition, and college slogans.

In the late 1990s, conceptions of community college leadership that were based on top-down leadership models began shifting to learner- and community-based paradigms that scholars believed would better meet organizational demands (Myran, 1995). Specifically, the concept of the learning college (Boggs, 1993; O'Banion, 1997) gained traction among community college scholars and administrators. At the heart of the learning college paradigm is a call for shared leadership. As Gratton (1993) writes, shared leadership "means embracing organizational learning so leadership will be a responsibility shared by all members based on understanding, competence, and creativity" (p. 103). The learning college model calls for both leaders and followers to accept responsibility for student learning and success and to be active and accountable in college operations. In the years since the learning college idea emerged, several scholars have refined what it means to lead a learning college. In particular, Amey (2005) argued that college leaders must be lifelong learners but must also facilitate learning among others in the institution. She posited that contemporary community college leaders must be able to think in a complex way and use multiple frames of reference to understand a situation and aid others' understanding.

A focus on shared leadership led to greater attention regarding the development of a community college leadership pipeline. Several studies of presidential candidates relied on cognitive leadership theories that emphasized specific abilities. In particular, Bassoppo-Moyo and Townsend (1997) surveyed community college academic vice presidents and deans—often the most likely presidential candidates—to identify the skills necessary for presidential ascension. They argued that presidential candidates must possess contextual competence (i.e., the ability to lead within the circumstances of their current institution), as well as an understanding of the environment in which community colleges operate (e.g., diminished state funding, a diverse student body, multiple missions). Eddy's (2009) research focused on the importance of cultural competence for new community college leaders. In particular, I argue that college presidents must understand how their leadership preferences intersect with their cultural understanding of the institution and its constituents to determine the greatest needs on campus and assess how best to meet those needs.

Recently, some scholars have begun to use frameworks that emphasize the roles of subordinates and the importance of relationships between community college leaders and followers (Amey, 2005). These frameworks, as well as those based on shared leadership, call for new conceptualizations of what it means to be a community college president and leader. These new leaders must emphasize communication among campus constituents, restructure organizational reporting and responsibilities, and demand accountability from followers (Lewis, 1989).

## Leadership Development

Because community college presidents emerge via a variety of routes (Amey, VanDerLinden, & Brown, 2002), it is important to view leadership development holistically. Traditionally, community college leaders have risen through the academic ranks. However, a recent American Council on Education (ACE) report examining the faculty-to-leader pipeline at community colleges (King, 2008) showed a graying of the faculty. The ACE report also highlighted the increased reliance on part-time faculty (62% at some institutions), resulting in fewer full-time faculty who are willing or able to take on the midlevel administrative positions that lead to the presidency. We need to rethink the leadership career pipeline so that more faculty members are encouraged to think about seeking advancement and are exposed to the leadership development opportunities that would make advancement possible.

However, some evidence shows that the faculty-to-dean-to-president route may be becoming obsolete. Indeed, 38% of community college presidents have never been a faculty member, and 67% have been employed outside higher education for some portion of their careers (ACE, 2007). Thus, to fully understand the leadership development process, it is critical to understand that community college leaders are influenced by more than an academic culture and frequently emerge through on-the-job training or experiential learning opportunities within the colleges. Weisman and Vaughan (2007) found that 35% of community college presidents were hired from within their organization, and Amey and VanDerLinden (2002) found that 52% of chief academic officers (CAOs) were also promoted from within. (This career pathway is important because presidents most often come from CAO offices.) The reliance on promotion from within means that grow-your-own forms of leadership development are especially important at community colleges (Jeandron, 2006; Quinton, 2006).

Leadership development programs that focus on midlevel leaders are especially important in the community college given its reliance on promotion from within. However, Wallin (2006) found leadership development programs for midlevel leaders to be serendipitous and without clear focus. Indeed, as Garza Mitchell and Eddy (2008) found, many midlevel leaders come to their positions "accidentally" and without intentional career plans. The happenstance nature of promotion and advancement to midlevel administrative positions makes planning for leadership development and succession difficult.

Counterintuitively, planning leadership development for midlevel community college leaders is also complicated by the fact that many of them are generally satisfied with their position and not contemplating other positions, although some are open to career advancement. Because a high level of satisfaction with one's current positions is statistically linked to a decreased desire to seek advancement (Sawyer, 2008), the general satisfaction among midlevel leaders means that fewer people are willing to make the career adjustments necessary to ascend to the presidency. Barriers to career advancement include an unwillingness to move, lack of a terminal education degree, and a lack of opportunities within the person's home institution (Sawyer, 2008; VanDer-Linden, 2003, 2004). Furthermore, formal leadership development programs at community colleges are primarily geared toward those who identify themselves as presidential aspirants, rather than encompassing all those within the institution who may eventually rise up through the leadership ranks.

Four primary avenues for leadership development focus specifically on community colleges. First, the Chair's Academy, hosted by Maricopa Community College District, is often the only training that department chairs at smaller or resource-pressed institutions may receive. According to Hull and

Keim (2007), 24% of community college presidents had participated in the Chair's Academy, the highest level of participation in any community college leadership development program. Second, the AACC Presidents Academy and Future Leaders Institute (FLI) provides other development opportunities. The FLI program focuses on training for midlevel administrators, whereas the FLI/Advanced offering targets more senior-level administrators whose next step is a presidency. AACC has now graduated 580 FLI participants; 34 have been named to the presidency and 200 others have made significant career moves or are enrolled in doctoral programs (D. Wallin, September 2, 2009, personal communication).

The League for Innovation in the Community College also provides leadership development training—14% of presidents had participated in a league training session (Hull & Keim, 2007)—and doctoral programs with a focus on community college administration are the fourth formalized way of educating future leaders. Although these four leadership development avenues together provide training to a large percentage of community college leaders, 69% of the respondents in Hull and Keim's (2007) study felt that more development was needed. Aspiring leaders also participate in other venues for general college leadership training, such as the Harvard Executive Education Program or Bryn Mawr's Higher Education Resource Services Summer Institute. Unfortunately, budgetary constraints limit involvement for many campus constituents and future leaders. Because many incoming presidents come to their role without the benefit of any formal training, it is important to consider the ways in which incoming leaders come to understand what it means to lead a community college.

Although the four primary programs providing focused leadership development for community college presidents and presidential aspirants have begun to address the leadership crisis, they frequently come up short. Most of the leadership development opportunities provided through these programs focuses on skill acquisition, which, although important, is not adequate for preparing individuals for the larger demands of leading complex organizations. Future community college leaders need to know how to make tough, ethical choices regarding access, programming, faculty assignments, and resource decisions, all while supporting the culture and mission of their particular institution (Hellmich, 2007), yet few leadership development programs provide training for such scenarios given the nature of the short time they meet and the limited numbers able to participate. The lack of opportunity for participation in national programs given resource limitations or lack of sponsorship limits the impact of these programs in community colleges.

## Shared Leadership

A variety of approaches to leadership exists in practice. Today's leaders need to be nimble to address the multitude of challenges facing their institutions. Underpinning the type of leadership flexibility needed in today's colleges is a commitment to lifelong learning. What worked yesterday may not have the same impact on emerging issues. New conceptions of leadership "look at leadership as a process in which leaders are not seen as individuals in charge of followers, but as members of a community of practice" (Horner, 1997, p. 277). Although different authors use varying terms to describe this new conception of leadership (e.g., *shared leadership*, *distributed leadership*, *team leadership*, *webs of inclusion*), what they have in common is a shift away from thinking of leadership in purely hierarchical terms. Instead, they describe leadership more in terms of relationships and teams. This new model equally values the contributions of positional leaders and followers in decision making to address challenges and obtain successful outcomes. However, despite how attractive this expanded notion of leading may be in theory, moving from hierarchical to shared conceptions of leadership can be challenging in practice.

One model for shared leadership that has garnered attention at the K–12 level is *distributed leadership* (Gronn, 2000). Harris and Spillane (2008) define distributed leadership as having multiple leaders and leadership activities shared within and between organizations. In distributed leadership, responsibility for leading an organization is shared throughout the college. Instead of a focus on the president as a sole leader, distributed leadership models emphasize the interdependencies of relationships among campus constituents and acknowledge that roles may change over time. As Birnbaum (1992) noted, the differentiation between leader and follower thus becomes increasingly arbitrary.

The reliance on multiple leaders in distributed leadership models necessitates flat or lateral decision making. In practice, this may be especially difficult at community colleges, where entrenched reliance on hierarchical and bureaucratic operations (Levin, 1998) may prove to be resistant to more open and shared forms of leadership. In fact, the language of distributed leadership is problematic in and of itself because it is more appropriate to the K–12 sector where it originated. Before the notion of shared or distributed leadership can be fully embraced, it will be necessary to obtain precision in definitions and develop links to leadership development and change models that are more familiar to community college constituents.

Like distributed leadership, *expanded leadership* is "likely to be the result of a team effort or of participation at differing levels, rather than the capacity of a single individual" (Peterson, 1997, p. 154). Peterson's idea of expanded leadership is based on the concept of a team, which may assume that a captain exists. In team leadership, members of a leadership team take on various roles and functions in order to make decisions (Bensimon & Neumann, 1993). The root of the expanded or team leadership model is the old adage that *two heads are better than one*—the assumption that each team member has strengths that provide critical contributions to the larger whole. An advantage to expanded or team leadership is that in any given situation, a single leader may have a blind spot, which a team can help overcome.

In a sharp departure from traditional and hierarchical models of leadership, Helgesen (1995) conceptualizes leadership as a web in which there is structure but also an ever-evolving dynamic of change. For Helgesen, the leader at the center of the web works on building consensus and valuing different parts of the web, which are built on relationships developed by followers located throughout the organizational web. The dynamic nature of the web allows for change within a part of the system without disruption to the larger structure. Although the Learning College model (O'Banion, 1997) does not depend on a weblike model of leadership, it does support a model in which "presidents and senior administrative staff need to be comfortable with fluid organizational dynamics that promote continuous learning, rigorous analysis and creative responses at all levels of the organization" (Dever, 1997, p. 62). Central to learning organization success is the involvement and feedback from followers within the organization. As 21st-century community college leaders increasingly engage in more participatory forms of leadership, the way in which leaders are developed takes on heightened importance.

### Gender and Leadership

More women are community college presidents than ever before. In 1986, only 8% of community college presidents were female; this number has more than tripled in the past 20 years. However, women presidents have a way to go before reaching parity with men. In community colleges women make up 60% of the student body and 50% of the faculty ranks but only 29% of community college presidents (ACE, 2007; National Center for Education Statistics, 2007; Weisman & Vaughan, 2007). Furthermore, the impressive gains women have made over the past two decades show signs of slowing; between 2001 and 2006, women increased their representation among community college presidents by a mere 2%. As Acker (2006) notes, gender inequalities in organizations are apparent when there is "relative scarcity of women in most top level positions and the existence of large job categories filled almost entirely with low-wage women workers with little power and autonomy" (p. 111). These conditions certainly exist at community colleges, where women make up the majority (65%) of nonprofessional staff, including administrative support, clerical, and maintenance positions.

Research on female leaders highlights the fact that "in the United States women are increasingly praised for having excellent skills for leadership, and in fact, women, more than men, manifest leadership styles associated with effective performance as leaders" (Eagly, 2007, p. 1). Nonetheless, when subordinates are questioned, more prefer a male leader to a female (Eagly, 2007). In part, this paradox is because the community college is a gendered organization.

Acker (1990) posited that gendering in organizations occurs in at least five interacting processes: the construction of divisions along gender lines; the construction of symbols and images that explain, reinforce, or oppose those divisions; the interactions between women and men, women and women, and men and men that enact dominance and submission; the production of gendered components of individual identity; and the ongoing processes of creating and conceptualizing social structures. In a gendered organization, hierarchies and jobs are viewed as separate from the people who fill them; they have no occupants, no human bodies, and therefore no gender. According to Acker (1990), two of the fundamental components of gendered organizations are the disembodied worker and the job. The disembodied worker represents a man whose life centers on his full-time job while a woman takes care of his personal needs. Because the job is based on this separation of the private (female) and public (male) spheres and contains gender-based division of labor, it too is gendered. Thus, organizational hierarchies that are constructed on the underlying assumptions of the disembodied worker and the job rely on gendered processes and may contribute to the paradox just described. Furthermore, as Williams (2000) argues, when gendered assumptions permeate organizations, masculine attributes pervade work and organizational processes, and women are encouraged to behave like men in order to succeed.

According to Tedrow and Rhoads (1999), women react to gendered organizations by adapting, reconciling, or resisting. Those who opt to adapt assume the norms and expectations of the organization and work to fit in. Therefore, these women take male norms for granted and replicate them by becoming "ideal workers." Women who take the path of reconciliation instead try to work within the gender-normed system to make changes. DiCroce (1995) advocated this type of response, arguing that women would be able to influence the system only after they acquired leadership positions. The third cadre of women acts as active resistors, questioning the stereotypes and prescribed roles that community colleges attempt to assign to them. Unfortunately, these resistors are seldom rewarded with promotions, and many eventually opt out of systems that cannot support them (Tedrow & Rhoads, 1999). In the past, women have shouldered much of the blame for not fitting into gendered expectations for community college leaders. Rather than blame women for gender inequities in community colleges, however, it will be important to analyze gendered behaviors and processes and seek to better understand how women fit in the community college leadership ranks and how community colleges as institutions can discard a masculine paradigm of operations.

## Leaders of Color

As community colleges act as higher education gateway institutions, diversity—of students, faculty, and leaders—is especially important to consider. Although community colleges have more diverse presidential leadership ranks than most 4-year institutions, in part because of unique training opportunities that focus on aspiring leaders of color, the diversification of the leadership ranks has slowed in recent years. Indeed, in 2007 only 12% of community college presidents were leaders of color (ACE, 2007); this percentage has remained static for most of the last decade. Of the presidents highlighted in this book, only one is a person of color. To supplement this data, additional interviews were sought with minority presidents and chancellors to provide more information regarding issues they face.

The relatively small proportion of leaders of color serving in community colleges may exist partly because boards of trustees often act as gatekeepers to presidential positions (Glazer-Raymo, 1999). Hiring boards/committees and trustees most often hired leaders like themselves, which typically meant White men. However, as hiring committees and trustees become more diverse, community college leaders will probably follow suit. Furthermore, as Weisman and Vaughan (2007) have pointed out, a key to hiring more leaders of color in community colleges is encouraging more people of color to enter the leadership pipeline. The low percentage of faculty of color at community colleges, however, means that the largest population to enter the leadership pipeline is dominated by White men and women. Programs that specifically target the development of leaders of color (Ebbers, 1992; League for Innovation in the Community College, 2008) are starting to address this pressing need.

Half of community college leaders of color are women (Harvey & Anderson, 2005). These leaders must navigate issues of not only gender, but also color. The intersection of their identities adds additional complexity to their roles on campus. Green (2008) reflected on her role as a female leader of color at a large urban community college: "As an African-American woman, I faced double challenges based on race and gender—some questioned my ability to 'cut it' because I am a woman, my ability to 'cut it' because I am an African-American, and my ability to 'cut it' because I am a mother" (p. 813). Because female leaders of color navigate multiple borderlines of identity construction and face challenges based on both their gender and their race or ethnicity, we must consider the intersection of gender and color when thinking about community college leadership and leadership development.

## A Brief Overview of Leadership Philosophies

The word *leadership* implies change: taking an organization or some part of it in a new direction, solving problems, being creative, initiating new programs, building organizational structures, and improving quality (Davis, 2003). Several definitions and theories of leadership exist in the literature. As Rost (1991) notes, most traditional leadership scholars were concerned with the peripheries of leadership, such as traits, personality characteristics, and whether leaders are born or made. As well, many leadership scholars focused on identifying what leaders need to know in order to be influential in an organization. Less research has been "aimed at understanding the essential nature of what leadership is, and the processes whereby leaders and followers relate to one another to achieve a purpose" (Rost, 1991, p. 4). Leadership needs change over time in response to evolving contexts and demands and as our understanding of what works and is important develops.

Most of the early research on leadership was based on examples drawn from business rather than academics. Today colleges and universities still borrow heavily from these theories, making adjustments as necessary for the campus environment. Bensimon, Neumann, and Birnbaum (1989) reviewed leadership theories used by higher education practitioners over the years. Their topology of six distinct eras of leadership theory serves as a useful foundation for understanding the evolution of thinking about leadership.

## Trait Theories

Trait theories made up some of the first scholarly writings on leadership. Trait theories subscribed to an idea of the leader as a "hero" or "great man" who possessed a host of traits that made him effective (Heifetz, 1994). Trait theory explained leadership as a set of internal qualities with which a person was born (Bernard, 1938). Many of these traits were identified based on studies of men and therefore corresponded with characteristics generally ascribed to men, such as boldness, strength, vigor, and power. As well, these traits were invariably based on the values of their male authors (Amey & Twombly, 1992). Over time, leadership scholars came to understand that traits alone do not guarantee success as a leader, and trait theories gave way to theories of leadership as a social construction.

## Power and Influence Theories

How leaders influence others and the ways in which they exert their power to obtain outcomes serve as ways of understanding leadership. Leaders interact with others in a variety of ways, including getting others to act through compliance and transactions. Here, followers comply because they receive something in return. Once the reward is removed, however, the motivation for compliance disappears. Leaders may also get staff to follow by identifying with their underlying value system (Kelman, 1961). An alignment with internal values instead of outside agendas or relationships provides the foundation  for transformational leaders (Burns, 1978). Moreover, because their end goals are more likely to correlate with significant organizational change, transformational leaders are more likely to affect long-term shifts in followers' beliefs and behavior. As Leslie and Fretwell (1996) note, transformational leaders can be most effective in transforming institutions of higher education in periods of crisis, in situations rife with adversity, or on smaller campuses. Central to success in applying these theories of leadership are intentional change and mutual purposes. Changes are not always intentional, however, and furthermore, these theories of leadership assume that leaders and followers have the same goals in their roles within the college, which often is not the case.

## Behavioral Theories

Behavioral theories of leadership look at what successful leaders do, rather than how they appear to others. Two seminal leadership studies (Halpin & Winer, 1957; Katz & Kahn, 1952) used a behavioral approach to identify leaders' behaviors so that they could be taught to others. Like trait theories, behavioral leadership theories focus on a limited range of what it means to lead. Behavioral leadership theorists offer us a series of dichotomies or continua to describe leadership behavior; they focus on questions such as whether a leader is authoritarian or democratic or whether he or she values tasks and structure over actions more related to relationships. An effective leader by behavioral standards maintains a balance between dichotomous perspectives, drawing on certain behaviors or actions as the circumstances demand. Behavioral leadership theories, like trait theories, offer a narrow band of options and fit for leaders that fall short today with the rate of organizational change and institutional complexity.

## Contingency Theories

Contingency theories of leadership rest on the idea that a leader's actions depend on particular situations. Contingency theorists argue that leaders adapt their leadership style to match the events at hand (Fiedler, 1967). As Horner (1997) writes, the fundamental basis of this orientation is that the required leadership may be different for every situation. A difficulty with contingency theories is that leaders often have individual preferences about how to approach a given situation. Although certain leaders' preferences may be well aligned with the institution that they are leading in general, they may not be able to dramatically change their approach to deal with certain situations that may call for a different kind of leadership.

## Cultural and Symbolic Theories

Unlike contingency theories, cultural and symbolic theories of leadership rely less on how different situational variables bring about diverse leadership styles or approaches and more on how leaders interpret a situation and manage meaning for others (Smircich & Morgan, 1982; Weick, 1995). For cultural and symbolic leadership theorists, management of the culture of a college is the most important leadership skill. Tierney (1991) underscores that part of understanding culture includes a sense of use of time, space, and communication. Thus, part of the emphasis for leaders using a cultural lens is the creation of the organizational saga (Clark, 1972). Helping followers interpret and make meaning of a situation is the key to leadership success. The use of symbolism by leaders allows a portrayal of potential for campus members versus how the situation necessarily exists in reality (Thayer, 1988).

Deal and Kennedy (1982) use the metaphor of "tribes" to discuss different types of cultures present in organizations and how awareness of the particular culture by the leader is imperative to enabling change. How the leader tells the story and develops the saga can therefore shift the focus of the institution. However, "research does not suggest cultural leadership is used very often or particularly cultivated as a leadership strategy" (Amey, 2005, p. 701), making this an untested and underdeveloped area of leadership theory.

### Cognitive Theories

Cognitive theories of leadership differ from cultural theories because they include both individual leader cognition and the collective cognition of followers. On an individual level, leaders first develop their own understanding of a situation before helping to frame meaning for followers (Weick, 1995). Inherent in this process is the use of schemas or scripts that leaders use as shortcuts, "which then helps them assimilate environmental information and internal thoughts producing behavior" (Lord & Emrich, 2001, p. 554). Cognitive leadership theories evaluate leaders from followers' impressions rather than the leader's measurable accomplishments. Cognitive theories of leadership also attempt to link leaders and institutional outcomes (Birnbaum, 1992). Indeed, some scholars (e.g., Amey, 1992; Fairhurst & Sarr, 1996; Kuhnert & Lewis, 1987) suggest that the ways in which leaders make meaning for themselves affects how they make meaning for the organization. As a result, how leaders learn can become a critical lever for organizational change (Amey, 2005).

These more recent constructions of leadership recognize the complexity of higher education organizations and the need for administrative leaders to think in a nuanced manner, draw on an array of leadership tools and paradigms, and reflect on what they are learning (Amey, 2005). In addition, today's knowledge-based world requires leaders to frame issues from multiple perspectives and be willing to question organizational assumptions and past practices (Eddy, 2005; Senge, 1990). Indeed, Johnson (2008) argues, "what separates successful leaders from unsuccessful ones is their mental models or meaning structures, not their knowledge, information, training, or experience per se" (p. 85). Thus, the cognitive underpinnings of leadership take on heightened importance and contribute to advancing definitions of our understanding of leadership.

## Summary

The evolution of the way in which we understand and approach leadership is not complete. Despite new constructions of leadership (Kelley, 1998; Kezar, Carducci, & Contreras-McGavin, 2006; Spears & Lawrence, 2003), many people remain drawn to the idea of a *checklist* of specific traits that one must possess to be a successful leader. To fully embrace alternative definitions of leadership demands rethinking time-honored images of what it means to be a leader, as well as the traditional relationships between leaders and followers (Green, 1997). Furthermore, we must rely on a more nuanced understanding of leadership in order to shift from a theoretical discussion of leadership to one of application and to discuss how different leadership approaches affect practice in community colleges. The multidimensional leadership model proposed in this book aims to do just that; it highlights the ways in which key elements of leadership intersect and provides a visual model of how community college leaders exemplify different leadership characteristics in their day-to-day practice. The model begins to move us beyond the tendency to think about leadership as two-dimensional and instead encourages us to embrace the messiness involved in leading in a flexible, dynamic, and changing context.

## Multidimensional Leadership

The idea of multidimensional leadership differs from traditional leadership theories that rely heavily on two-dimensional tables or figures. A popular model developed by Blake and Mouton (1964), for instance, showcases a two-axis table with concern for people measured on one axis and concern for production on the other (see Figure 2.1). Individuals could see how they measured up on the model simply by locating the point formed by the intersection of the two axes' lines. This and other traditional models of leadership rely on two underlying assumptions: (1) that there is *a* (i.e., singular) way to lead, and (2) that a particular way of leading is better than all others. These models do not consider how a leader's individual characteristics may or may not align with the expectations of how one should lead and do not necessarily address a leader's underlying schema (i.e., the way he or she sees and understands the world).

Unlike traditional leadership models, a multidimensional model of leadership provides flexibility and a construction based on an individual's core

## FIGURE 2.1
**Blake and Mouton's (1964) Two-Dimensional Managerial Grid**

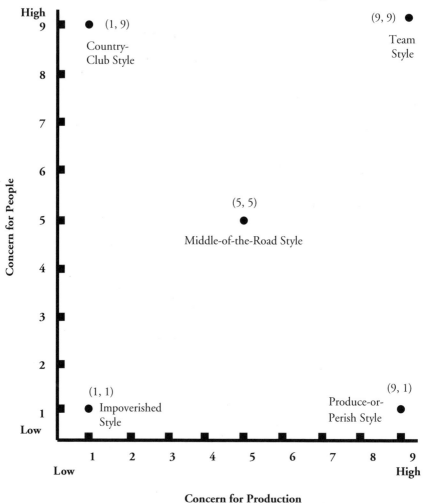

**Concern for Production**

experiences, beliefs, and capabilities. Furthermore, a multidimensional model recognizes that many of the leadership dimensions a leader possesses are part of a continuum and will change or evolve over time. The foundation for the multidimensional model of leadership presented in this book is built from five basic propositions: (1) There is no universal model for leadership,

(2) multidimensional leadership is necessary in complex organizations, (3) leaders rely on their underlying cognitive schema in making leadership decisions, (4) leaders often adhere to their core belief structure, and (5) leaders are learners.

### Proposition 1: There Is No Universal Model for Leadership

The multidimensional leadership model presented in this book begins with the understanding that there is no universal model for leading. This position does not necessarily undermine the leadership competencies outlined by AACC or other lists created by leadership theorists, but it does advocate that there is no right way to lead. This proposition broadens our definition of leadership and begins to move us beyond the hegemonic norms typical in trait theories. As Amey and Twombly (1992) point out, literature about community college leaders drew from studies about and by White men. It is important to begin thinking in more expansive ways about who gets to be a community college leader and how their approaches to leadership may differ from those of the White men who founded the colleges and began leading in a time when challenges were significantly different. Rethinking traditional leadership models allows us to better understand the complexities facing current and future leaders and opens up new ways of thinking about how those leaders may deal with problems and issues on their campuses.

### Proposition 2: Multidimensional Leadership Is Necessary in Complex Organizations

Since their conception, community colleges have become increasingly complex organizations. The demands of leading in today's context requires community college leaders to be flexible and adaptable (Heifetz, 1994), reacting in versatile ways to dynamic change and leading intended transformations. Leaders require a wide range of strengths and abilities. In the past, a stable context resulted in a certain amount of predictability, allowing leaders to reuse successful past strategies and techniques in new situations. The confluence of so much organizational change at once on multiple fronts (e.g., finance, governance, outreach, and student learning) requires an expanded skill and knowledge base and, more critically, the ability to adapt strategies to meet the new challenges. Leaders need to be adept at relationship building, use open communication, understand finance, employ team building, and be adroit at negotiations. Tough decisions are required of today's leaders, and thus they need decision-making skills. As well, leaders must pay attention to how they present changes to staff and stakeholders. The ways in which leaders opt to frame challenges to campus constituents depends on how the leaders first understand the complexity themselves. Complex organizations require leaders who can understand a given situation from a broad perspective and operate as campus facilitators in enacting change.

## Proposition 3: Leaders Rely on Their Underlying Cognitive Schema in Making Leadership Decisions

One of the critical elements of the multidimensional model is a leader's underlying schema. This schema, or understanding of how the world operates, guides "individual interpretations of the past and present and expectations for the future" (Harris, 1994, p. 310). Cognitive schemas, or mental maps (Senge, 1990), guide our thinking and provide shortcuts as we try to make sense of a large array of information. In some ways, schemas are like the Rorschach inkblot tests often used in psychology, in which a person is shown a shape or figure and asked to say what first comes to mind. In the case of leadership, if a situation (i.e., the inkblot) reminds a person of one he or she experienced or witnessed in the past, the person will be inclined to understand the current and new situation similarly. For example, when leaders are faced with a budget crisis, they tend to draw examples from their schema that worked in the past. Although mental maps help leaders understand a vast array of information, cognitive schema may also limit their responses to new situations because they interpret information through a distinct filter of previously held beliefs and experiences. As a result, leaders may misinterpret a situation or respond in a less effective way.

Mental maps are tough to change. According to Senge (1990), "mental models are deeply ingrained assumptions, generalizations, or even pictures or images that influence how we understand the world and how we take action" (p. 8). For most leaders, their views and perspectives on leadership are based on their experiences as followers. Given that leadership in educational settings is historically portrayed as bureaucratic and hierarchical (Birnbaum, 1992; Levin, 1998), new leaders often carry a mental model constructed on ideals of top-down leadership models. Once a leader breaks through his or her mental maps and views a situation differently, however, change can occur. The multidimensional leadership model is based on the premise that community college leaders rely heavily on their underlying cognitive schemas but also takes into account the fact that over time and with much reflection and new learning, leaders can shift their schemas so that they can more smoothly and appropriately respond to new and complex situations.

## Proposition 4: Leaders Often Adhere to Their Core Belief Structure

Cognitive schemas help leaders use shortcuts to quickly understand a situation based on their past experiences. Much of our underlying schemas, however, are built on our core belief structures, identity, and basic convictions. These core beliefs are central to the ways in which a leader leads because they shape the way he or she processes information and makes decisions. Indeed, Bensimon (1989) found that most community college leaders operated from a singular frame of reference that was heavily influenced by their core belief structures.

Leaders can augment their core belief structure by acquiring more information, but it can be difficult to change their basic assumptions about leading. As Argyris (1980) pointed out, most individuals are unaware of their underlying belief structures and the ways in which they guide behavior. Furthermore, sometimes leaders say that they would react to a particular situation in one way (i.e., they provide an espoused theory of action), but in reality they react in a different way entirely. Thus their actions, not their words, highlight their underlying core belief structure—their theory-in-use, as Argyris and Schön (1974) termed it. According to Argyris (1980), by engaging in reflection and questioning their underlying belief structures and assumptions, leaders can more closely align their espoused theory and theory-in-use.

## Proposition 5: Leaders Are Learners

Even though individuals use their underlying schemas and core beliefs to them help understand and respond to situations, they are also continuously learning new ways of leading. Indeed, the underlying assumption of the AACC competencies is that leaders are lifelong learners (AACC, 2005). As we know, when leaders question their actions and reflect on their leadership, they improve their understanding of their own actions, as well as the effects their actions have on others (Argyris, 1980, 1990; Schön, 1983). As a result, leaders can create a nexus for learning by connecting—in their own minds—their leadership actions and the outcomes of a given situation. According to Amey (2005), "by conceptualizing leadership as learning, one relinquishes the need for a specific career orientation, and can look at the ways in which leadership is developed and shared throughout the organization" (p. 690).

When leadership is viewed from a learning development perspective (Amey, 2005), the role of the leader shifts from the head of a hierarchical organization to a facilitator emphasizing teamwork (Bensimon & Neumann, 1993). Key to the leader-as-learner model is recognizing that leaders are adult learners. As Knowles (1970) pointed out, adult learners need to know why they are learning, require self-direction, and use their past experiences (and core beliefs) to understand new ideas and situations. Adult learners also understand that their social roles affect learning and are internally motivated to learn. The proposition that leaders are learners, combined with the four previous propositions, form the foundation for a multidimensional model of leadership and expand our ways of understanding leadership in the community college context.

## A Model for Multidimensional Leadership

Unlike two-dimensional leadership models in which a leader can locate his or her position by finding the intersection between two axes, with a multidimensional leadership model, each leader's model looks different from the next—the model is a personal and individual reflection of a particular leader's underlying schema, core beliefs, experiences, skills, and leadership style. Furthermore, multidimensional models of leadership are not static; as leaders experience new situations, learn, and adjust their leadership philosophies and actions, the model grows and becomes more complex. Nonetheless, multidimensional leadership models are all composed of similar elements, including a leader's underlying cognitive schema, core beliefs, communication skills, relationships, learning styles, decision-making approaches, gender-based understandings of leadership, ways of knowing and responding to an organization's culture and climate, and so forth.

The following chapters outline several key components of the multidimensional model. Each chapter includes a range of approaches that leaders may employ in a particular arena, such as communication. These approaches serve as the building blocks for the multidimensional model. Each component of the model possesses a continuum that underscores the range of ways leaders may respond that emphasizes the model's flexible and dynamic nature and the fact that there is not a singular way to lead. The chapters serve as building blocks for the ultimate presentation of the multidimensional model in chapter 7. Examples from the case studies provide illustrations regarding the range of ways leaders are successful and highlight how reflective practice aids in leadership development. Another central element of the model is the ability of leaders to change their leadership over time as they learn. This development process is illustrated by movement along the continuum of the particular attributes, which reiterates the response of leaders to working in changing systems.

## Conclusion

Community colleges are complex and multidimensional organizations. As such, they require complex and multidimensional leadership. Today's leaders must learn to facilitate cooperative work among campus constituents and must seek to develop their leadership dimensions to effectively respond to challenging new situations. Community college leaders must also engage in continuous reflection on their actions and the resulting organizational outcomes in order to strengthen aspects of their leadership that have worked well in the past and acquire new leadership competencies where necessary.

Our understanding of community college leadership must evolve from a two-dimensional conceptualization to one that encompasses many different dimensions. We need to understand that community college leaders come from different places, have unique experiences and beliefs, and approach challenging situations in diverse ways. All of these dimensions of leadership affect the ways that leaders lead, as well as the ways that they hone their leadership skills over time. The following chapters use data from the case studies and interviews to highlight various features of multidimensional leadership and to showcase how it works in practice. Specific examples from the case studies allow the reader to analyze the actions of the various leaders and their responses to different situations considering a dynamic perspective of leadership versus a static viewpoint. In particular, a multidimensional frame of reference allows the reader to move beyond zero-sum assessments of "good" or "bad" leadership and instead to understand community college leadership in all its complexity from a more holistic perspective.

# 3

# LEARNING TO LEAD

Leadership and learning are indispensable to
each other.

John Fitzgerald Kennedy

Individuals lead based on how they have learned to lead: through past
experiences and trial and error, from their own mistakes, and from mistakes they have observed in others. A leader's cognitive schema—a
ready-made map that allows him or her to decode incoming information
quickly based on past experiences—undergirds his or her leadership style
and processes. Schemas provide shortcuts that fill in missing information.
They also filter new information; anything that conflicts with a leader's
schema will either be ignored as an aberration, be cognitively recast (i.e.,
understood differently) to fit the schema, or—if the leader is adept at reflecting on his or her schema and making adjustments as necessary—generate a
new schema subcategory (Harris, 1994). Given the influence of a leader's
cognitive schema on his or her leadership, it is important to examine how
career pathways and leadership development programs can help inform a
leader's schema. Exploring different leadership styles and learning processes
also helps us understand how leaders approach relating with campus stakeholders and provides opportunities for leaders to reflect on the constructs
that guide their leadership decisions, change previously unexamined behaviors, and in the process expand their leadership skills.

This chapter begins by examining the leadership development opportunities that can be found in various formal and informal programs and situations. It then discusses the various learning styles exhibited by the presidents
in this study, focusing on the specific ways in which different leaders learn.
The chapter concludes with an examination of how reflecting on one's experience can transform simple leadership models into more complex multidimensional models that allow for greater flexibility and a wider range of ideas,

solutions, and tactics for leading contemporary community colleges. Throughout the chapter, the experiences of the nine presidents in this study and those of the supplemental minority presidents interviewed are shared as a way of contextualizing the information. The quotes and vignettes also provide current and aspiring community college leaders with examples of how other leaders have learned from their experiences and in turn improved their leadership on campus.

## Career Pathways

Several researchers have examined the pathways to the president's office in universities (Birnbaum & Umbach, 2001; McKenney & Cejda, 2001; Walton & McDade, 2001) and in community colleges (Amey, 2006; Amey & VanDerLinden, 2002; Vaughan, 1990). Many studies have identified a common leadership pathway beginning with a faculty position and ending with a presidency, although Amey, VanDerLinden, and Brown (2002) found that additional routes are emerging. As bureaucratic institutions, community colleges adhere to and reward an organizational hierarchy (Birnbaum, 1992). Thus, the route to upper-level positions, including the presidency, is most often marked by a series of promotions up the career ladder (department chair and/or a position on the faculty senate or union, then perhaps academic dean or vice president of academics). Indeed, 60% of community college presidents came to their current positions either from a previous presidency (26%) or from the chief academic officer position (34%; American Council on Education, 2007). These promotions often occur within the same college, especially in rural areas. Thus, a leader's previous experiences within a college take on heightened importance as a source of leadership development opportunities, as well as in our understanding of his or her cognitive schema.

Examining the experiences of faculty and administrators in community colleges can also help identify barriers that may discourage some candidates from pursuing leadership positions. Amey, VanDerLinden, and Brown (2002) investigated career pathways of 918 midlevel community college managers, and in 2003 VanDerLinden asked the same participants whether they had been promoted or had changed their position in the 3 years since the initial survey. Participants identified two key barriers to advancement: the lack of opportunities within their current institutions and unwillingness to relocate for a new position. This finding runs counter to research indicating that administrators in 4-year colleges and universities are willing to move for promotions (Sagaria, 1988) and underscores the need to create pathways for advancement within the community college.

The presidents in this study followed traditional career pathways before their current positions (see Table 3.1). In order to understand these pathways better, it is important to look at the timing of career moves, motivations for seeking the presidency, and the role of mentors.

## Career Planning and Timing

As is evident in Table 3.1, progressions up the career ladder for the presidents in this study often meant a physical move—to another college and often to another state. Some of these moves occurred within a large community college district, which meant a change in institution but not a physical move. Because moving to a new institution is often necessary if one is to achieve the presidency, career planning and timing is important. The female presidents in this study were most likely to note an issue of timing in making career moves, sometimes discussing having to time their moves to fit their spouses' careers and family needs.

Nationally, more than four out of five community college presidents are married, and all of the presidents in this study had a spouse. Two of the presidents, Lynne Pauldine of Hunkering Down Community College and Karen Fields of Bifurcated Community College, sought the presidency only after their husbands had retired from their academic careers. Pauldine simply stated, "Two-academic-career families are hard to find; my husband is a professor of mathematics and retired to come here with me. But, at the time, it was very difficult for me to think about moving on. He was someone who was very happy where he was." Pauldine used *career sequencing* in deciding to seek a presidency when she did. Career sequencing involves individuals deciding when and where to make a move on the career ladder relative to timing of child-rearing responsibilities and spousal career considerations. This is often referred to as the "mommy track."

Likewise, Fields noted that she had delayed a move into administration because of her family. She stated, "It was clear to me at the point my son was 3 or 4 years old that I could not take an administrative position and protect what was important to me, which was the stability of my marriage, my son's growing up in a stable environment, so I left the associate dean's position, took a sabbatical, got back into teaching." It was not until her son was out of college that Fields sought a deanship and made her subsequent

# TABLE 3.1
## Career Pathways of Community College Presidents

| President, Current College | Step 1 | Step 2 | Step 3 | Step 4 | Step 5 | Step 6 | Step 7 |
|---|---|---|---|---|---|---|---|
| Jennifer Burke, *Cutting Edge CC* | Faculty, *College A* | Dean, *College A* | Chief Academic Officer, *College B* | President, *Me-Too CC* | President, *Cutting Edge CC* | | |
| Karen Fields, *Bifurcated CC** | Faculty, *College A* | Department Chair, *College A* | Dean, *College A* | Chief Academic Officer, *College B* | President, *Bifurcated CC* | | |
| Michael Garvey, *Me-Too CC* | Faculty, *College A* | Director, State CC Agency | Dean, *College B* | President, *College A* | Consultant, Interim President at 5 campuses | President, *Me-Too CC* | |
| Brenda Hales, *Don't Make Waves CC* | High School Teacher | Faculty, *College A* | Director, Business Education Teacher Certification, *[State] Education Agency* | Director of Continuing Education, *CC District B* | VP Instruction, *College C in District B* | Vice Chancellor, Student Development, *Large & Growing CC District* | President, *Don't Make Waves CC* |
| Jon Hammond, *Strategic CC* | High School Teacher | Faculty, *College A* | Dean, *College A* | Vice President Administrative Services, *College A* | President, *College B* | President, *Strategic CC* | |
| Chris Jones, *Technology CC* | Auto Design Firm | Technical Faculty, *College A (four-year institution)* | Dean, *College A* | President, *College B* | President, *Technology CC* | | |
| Lynne Pauldine, *Hunkering Down CC* | Adjunct Faculty, *College A,* Enrollment Management Consultant | VP Enrollment Management, *College A* | President, *Hunkering Down CC* | | | | |
| James Simon, *Rogue CC* | Adjunct Faculty, *College A* | Faculty, *College B* | Consultant and Director, State Agency | Dean, *College C* | Provost, *College C* | President, *Rogue CC* | President, *College E* |
| Shawn Williams, *Tradition-Bound CC* | Director International Education, *College A* | Faculty, *College B* | Dean, *College C* | VP Instruction, Acting VP Finance, *College D* | Dean, Technical Education, *College E* | President, *Tradition-Bound CC* | President, *College G* |

*Karen Fields made several moves back to the faculty from administrative positions within College A. For simplicity's sake, these moves are not shown.

moves to vice president and ultimately president. The latter move into a presidency occurred only after her husband retired from his own academic career as a university professor.

President James Simon was the only male president who acknowledged considering his wife's career in his career planning. He stated, "My wife is a college librarian. She wanted to find work. I knew we had to be in a place where she could do that." For him, this meant not seeking presidential positions in rural areas. As it happened, Rogue Community College was located in his home state. As he related, "Coming back home to [State] was a plus. I would have gone other places, but don't tell my mother that. She's convinced I came back here to see her." Clearly, family played a part in Simon's career decision making.

Decisions about when to seek the presidency are often based on personal circumstances, as well as how well the opening "fits." Pauldine summed up the sentiments of several of the participants when she related the following about her own presidential search: "I guess I kept thinking what harm would it do to apply for this position here and what harm would it do to pursue the next step. It was kind of like, well, I'd take one step and see if that felt okay and then take the next step." This step-by-step assessment of job "fit" is common among community college presidents, although the nine participants in this study related various motivations for seeking the presidency.

### Motivations

Individuals are motivated to seek the presidency for a variety of reasons. For some of the presidents in this study, it was merely the next step along the career pathway, for others it was a nudge by a trusted mentor, and for some it was self-awareness that they could do the job. Overall, there was a lack of intentionality in planning to achieve the corner office. Just as Garza Mitchell and Eddy (2008) found that most department chairs and deans arrived at their leadership positions accidentally, the presidents in this study did not always have the presidency in mind as they progressed along their career pathways. Rather, restlessness or dissatisfaction within a current position was a frequent impetus to seeking a more challenging role. This was the case for President Pauldine, as well as for President Fields, who noted, "Now I would have been happy to have been an academic dean or an academic vice president for a long time. But when you are into a position like that, you recognize that you are one of the two types of people: Either you can take direction and you like the detail work, the curriculum detail work, or you find yourself watching your boss and thinking he's making mistakes that I wouldn't make. Which is terribly unfair to a president, and when a vice president starts thinking that way, she has a duty to apply for presidencies of her own and leave the poor people alone that she's working for."

The presidents also found motivation to seek the corner office as they acquired more experience and developed greater abilities to meet a diverse set of challenges. Some recognized this shift in themselves, and others had a mentor who encouraged them to seek a higher position and reinforced that they were up for the challenge. One of the additional presidents of color interviewed stated, "Probably my strongest inspiration for everything I do, I want women, I want women of color to know that they can do it too." Recognizing the role model status obtained by occupying the corner office provides a means to showcase for others not traditionally occupying the office, namely, women and leaders of color, that leadership can be an option for them. Role models and mentors played a central role in opening doors for the presidents in this study.

### Mentors

Mentoring provided essential leverage in helping several of the presidents obtain their positions. Jack Pioneer, former chancellor of the Large and Growing Community College District, illustrates the power of a mentor because he appointed three of the five presidents in his district without engaging in external searches. He promoted Jennifer Burke from president of Me-Too Community College to the newly created Cutting Edge Community College presidency. Pioneer also appointed President Garvey at Me-Too Community College and Brenda Hales as president of Don't Make Waves Community College, moving the previous president to central administration.

Michael Garvey had served as interim president of two of the colleges within the Large and Growing Community College District before being named president of Me-Too Community College by Pioneer. Garvey reflected, "The chancellor and I had been friends for the better part of 20 years. [When I arrived as interim] he said, 'If you'd like this, why don't we just make a deal that you stay for a while? If they like you.' [laugh] After 3 months of being interim here, he got enough feedback, [and] he said, 'Why don't we just make you permanent?'" The organizational structure of the Large and Growing Community College District gave Pioneer particular control over presidential positions at individual campuses, and thus he had great influence over the career pathways of the presidents. The unique nature of this form of mentoring within the district is not commonly found but underscores the role an influential mentor may have on a president's career. These actions also highlight how some individuals may not be included for consideration of top-level positions if they are not on the chancellor's radar.

Pioneer was not the only influential mentor cited in this study. Several presidents mentioned other mentors who helped in networking or encouraged them to strive for the next level. One of President Shawn Williams's first supervisors encouraged him to enter the administrative ranks and then provided numerous opportunities for him to hone his skills and to broaden his network. However, not all presidents have had favorable mentoring experiences (or mentoring experiences at all). President Karen Fields described how the lack of a mentor led to some of her initial missteps as a new president: "I didn't look closely enough at the problems the college had, and I think that's a mistake that people might make in their first presidency, particularly if they don't have a lot of mentoring, and I didn't. And women, I think, and maybe it's changing, but I just have a sense that some of my male colleagues have stronger mentoring arrangements than I did. And nobody was saying to me that that college is in trouble; are you ready for what you're going to have to do there?" In Fields's experience, the lack of a mentor meant that she was forced to navigate a rocky career pathway. As a result, she intentionally works to mentor others at her college and help prepare them for advanced leadership positions.

Tellingly, observing bad leadership also served as a learning opportunity. One of the presidents of color interviewed stated, "I tell people, when you are picking your mentors, look at people you don't want to be like; you can learn so much from them on what not to do. As I was growing my skills, there was this one leader who was horrible. How she treated people and by the way she used her so-called powers as an executive leader was such a turnoff. I would never treat people like that. I don't want to be treated like that. I tell people, look at that person and how you feel in their presence and how you feel as their employee and save that and put that in your mentor pocket and you can learn a lot about that. I have never treated others like she treated me." This president of color actively mentors others but also recognizes that her mere presence and actions provide an example of leadership to others, and as a result she treats staff as she would like to be treated. Another president of color added, "For minority professionals, in my experience, advancement occurs from very deliberate help from others; it does not just happen." He added, "I felt that people offered me opportunities and led me in good directions. I think they sincerely wanted me as a minority to be able to get into positions that would be important to the profession."

As an up-and-coming leader, this president of color received direct support to help him navigate the career pathway, in particular by making opportunities available to gain skills and providing support in his application for his ultimately successful presidential position. In turn, he now mentors others to give the same type of opportunities to groom for leadership.

Noting the importance of a mentor, several of the presidents discussed their mentorship of others. President Jon Hammond stated, "I've had great success mentoring women presidents starting with a GED and moving clear up to presidents of colleges." Often the presidents mentored others by providing informal support within the leadership cabinet, or by tapping individuals who had the potential to contribute to the college to participate in leadership support groups. President Williams stated that he worked with potential leaders on an informal basis, looking over their resumes, talking about leadership issues, and replicating practices his own mentor did for him.

Just as many of their own mentors had brought them to a new college when they accepted a leadership position, some of the presidents in this study hired individuals from their previous campuses after they achieved the presidency. As President Garvey noted, "I brought in my colleague from [my last college] to head up the educational program, and the leadership he gave to the faculty allowed several to grow into these new roles as faculty leaders, as instructional leaders. They learned about collaborative leadership and those sorts of things which I had seen in [my position as dean and president], and he was modeling those behaviors."

Garvey concluded, "In fact, I can think of two or three people who have come out of that environment and have become presidents, deans, and vice presidents now. Not because of anything I did but simply because of the changes that we effected that allowed people to grow and develop." Providing an environment to learn about leadership and to practice skills was critical not only to the presidents in the study, but also to those they mentored.

Pathways to the presidency are thus affected greatly by issues related to career planning and timing, by a variety of motivations, and by mentors and supervisors who take active roles in advising individuals on their careers. As the following vignette illustrates, the presidents in this study reached their positions via a variety of routes, some attributable to mentors, some to initiative, and some to chance. Exploring these pathways—in the process coming to a greater understanding of the constructs that make up these presidents' cognitive schemas—helps us contextualize their leadership decisions and actions. The vignette presented here (as well as those that follow in this and subsequent chapters) can also provide an opportunity for future leaders to reflect on their own experiences and career pathways. Current leaders may see situations that are similar to their own in these vignettes and thus be able to think of their own challenges differently or in expanded ways.

## Vignette 1: Mentors Versus Initiative Versus Chance

Community college presidents come to their positions in a variety of ways. For Jennifer Burke, the top position at Me-Too Community College was simply the logical next step. She commented, "People come to the presidency from such different walks; my trek was through the academic world, through the community college, just having every kind of job that you can possibly have in a college and then, well, what else is there?" Burke's path to the presidency at Cutting Edge Community College was a little different, however. "I was already serving the Cutting Edge area as president of Me-Too Community College, and it just so happened I was going to be chairman of the Chamber of Commerce at Cutting Edge City that year as well." Because the district was changing and growing so quickly, the chancellor of the community college district, Jack Pioneer, had extensive and unusual power to appoint presidents, and Burke was soon made president of Cutting Edge. She discussed her ascension to this position and the role her mentor played in the move in the following way: "It just made things easier, it made us be able to be on fast track to get the college open within 3 years . . . rather than spending a year doing a presidential search. . . . Not a normal situation, really, that you can just appoint a president, you know; normally you would have a national search and so forth." Thus, Burke obtained her first presidency at Me-Too Community College by progressing up the next rung of the career ladder, but her position at Cutting Edge can be attributed to the role of a mentor and serendipitous chance.

Unlike President Burke, Lynne Pauldine's pathway to the presidency at Hunkering Down Community College (HDCC) came from a personal epiphany about her skills and ability. Roughly a year before taking over her current position, Pauldine was doing some consulting work at another college in the Midwest. At one point during her consultancy, the president of the college asked her if she would speak to his board of trustees regarding their program enrollment assessment. Pauldine thought, "Wow, I could so be doing this job! You know he thinks I could be doing this job obviously, so that kind of was an eye-opener for me." When the presidency opened up at HDCC, she applied and got the position. Pauldine's sense of agency and self-efficacy was aided by an outsider's observations of her leadership abilities.

President Shawn Williams's pathway to the presidency can be attributed largely to an active mentor, a supervisor from his first position as a director of international education. When Williams's mentor moved out of state to take a vice presidential position, she asked him to accompany her and become the dean of natural and social science. In reflecting on his mentor, Williams stated, "I remember back in '89 when I was at [College B] my former boss called me about becoming a dean. And that was within my first year and I said no. I wasn't interested. So 9 months later she called again and said the position is still available. I said, 'No, I'm enjoying what I'm doing and everything.' She said 'Shawn, I think you have the potential to be a president one day, so start thinking about that. She was the one who prompted me the first time."

Like many community college instructors, Williams enjoyed his faculty position and did not consider entering the administration until his mentor planted a seed and was persistent in encouraging him to seek a promotion. For example, when Williams's mentor accepted her first presidency, she asked Williams to come in as vice president of instruction. During his time in this position, his mentor sponsored a visit to the Executive Leadership Institute and suggested he take on the acting position of VP of business and finance. As Williams noted, "As she said at that time and as I know, it was going to be useful in my future in my application. Usually you describe your experiences in budgeting and financial activities." He summed up, "Throughout the three places that I worked for her, she gave me opportunities to prepare me for this role.

## Leadership Development

Community college leadership development occurs in a variety of ways, some formal, some informal. Formal programming may involve attending leadership training programs, enrolling in a doctoral leadership program, or participating in short workshops to hone specific skills, such as dealing with difficult employees or improving negotiating skills. Professional associations such as the American Association of Community Colleges (AACC) and the League for Innovation in the Community College (the League) offer programs and conferences that focus on leadership skill acquisition. In these formal trainings, leaders new to their positions are often paired with a mentor, usually a seasoned community college president. Frequently, the initial move from the faculty ranks to an administrative position constitutes a major role shift—this is often referred to as *moving to the dark side*. To aid new presidents in their transition to the office, many state community college associations and coordinating boards also provide formalized leadership training; in some cases, this programming is the only formal training that a leader receives before becoming president.

Unlike formal leadership training, informal development is not structured and may occur by reading on one's own, through on-the-job learning, or via observation. All leaders are involved in informal learning, although how often and deeply they critically reflect on what they see and experience may affect how much learning occurs. Reflection on their leadership development, whether formal or informal, is key to a leader's learning and effectiveness on campus. The nine presidents and the additional minority interviewees in this study participated in both formal and informal leadership development; the following pages explore their experiences.

### *Formal Leadership Development*

As noted, AACC's annual conference and associated preconference workshops for new presidents and presidential aspirants are popular avenues for formal leadership development, although leaders often must wait until they have taken over the presidency before they can attend presidential training workshops, leaving them to fend for themselves through their early days in the job. Those attending the preconference sessions geared toward aspiring leaders must have the foresight to participate, which assumes they are already thinking about seeking a presidency. Typical preconference workshops have titles like *The New CEO Institute: Hit the Ground Leading* and include topics such as working with the board of trustees, identifying the culture of the institution, effectively using technology, and learning from the experiences of more seasoned presidents. The sessions also incorporate a number of networking opportunities for new presidents. One of the additional presidents of color interviewed for this research noted that she opted to attend the AACC workshop to see whether a college presidency was for her, and ultimately her attendance cinched her decision to pursue a presidency.

Despite the historic popularity of AACC's annual training, the recent economic downturn affected attendance. As President James Simon noted, "Given the budget cuts, I didn't feel very good about continuing my own professional development when I was cutting staff training, so I'm not going to the AACC new president training. They make a big deal out of it, but I told them I'm just not going to be there." Simon did not put priority on attending and wanted to symbolically show that his office was tightening its fiscal belt along with the rest of campus. President Shawn Williams, on the other hand, did attend the training and found value in the networking opportunities it provided. For Williams, the training reinforced the importance of mentoring in his own learning process, as well as the role of relationships in his underlying cognitive schema. He reaffirmed his desire to be intentional in his mentorship of others within the community college.

In addition to the annual conference and workshops, AACC also sponsors a 5-day summer institute, called the Presidents Academy Summer Institute, which is open to all chief executive officers (CEOs) from member institutions and pairs new leaders with seasoned mentors. A corresponding 5-day leadership institute is also open to midlevel leaders. The Future Leaders Institute (FLI) covers similar topics as the Presidents Academy, such as team building, negotiating skills, conflict management, ethics, leading change, and community partnerships. Additionally, the FLI includes an assessment of leadership styles and a reflection on ethics and approaches to organizational change. Many of the FLI sessions focus on issues central to relationship building and working with diverse groups of people. Presidents Burke and Hales both participated in AACC trainings, and subsequently continued their involvement both within the AACC and on their state board for community colleges. Key to their decision to attend was the ability to network with other leaders, to share the challenges they were facing on their campus, and to learn from others. Hales noted, "It's interesting; you're going to see a lot of people here that have never been anywhere else. They don't realize that these same issues arise in other places. I serve on a number of national boards, I'm a [accreditation board] leader, have chaired committees—I've just chaired one a couple of months ago. When you do that you get perspectives." Knowing that one is not alone in the challenges facing one's campus and finding camaraderie among other leaders facing issues generates a unique learning opportunity.

Similar to AACC's Future Leaders Institute, the League hosts the annual Executive Leadership Institute (ELI), which focuses on preparing senior-level administrators for advancement to the presidency. Key elements within this program include a review of the application process and tips for interviewing. An assessment is provided to help participants determine the best fit between their leadership style, type of institution, and presidential role. The ELI also reviews important aspects of the presidency, including working with the board, fund-raising, legal and ethical concerns, planning for strategic change, reviewing national trends, and determining one's leadership preferences—both as an internal leader and an external representative of the college. As with the AACC workshops for aspiring presidents, the ELI focuses on skills that help an individual attain the presidency, as well as tools that can help aspiring presidents determine whether an institution is a good fit for them.

The League boasts that 43% of its ELI participants since 1988 have obtained a presidential position. Indeed, both Presidents Simon and Williams attended the ELI. As Simon noted, it "helped with some networking and also kind of clarified my thinking on what I really wanted to do and where I wanted to be." He added that the training helped him clarify that he did not want to work at a rural community college. President Williams benefited from the ELI in another way: He used the network he built at the training to inquire about the open presidential position at Tradition-Bound Community College.

The League, in partnership with the American Association of Women in Community Colleges and the Maricopa Community Colleges, also sponsors the National Institute for Leadership Development (NILD) for female leaders. This program has prepared more than 4,000 women for leadership positions in community colleges (League for Innovation in the Community College, 2007), but none of the women in this study reported attending the NILD. One of the female presidents of color interviewed noted, "I didn't know about this at the time and did not participate. Additionally, each of the various trainings is expensive and I had a limited budget." Aspiring presidents are picking and choosing their training opportunities given limited funding.

The Chair Academy, run by the Maricopa Community Colleges, is often the first formal training that administrators engage in as first-line administrators. For some, this training is their first exposure to a systemic study of leadership. Students attending the Chair Academy can earn up to nine graduate credits that they can then apply to a degree program, allowing them to augment their graduate work with a concentration in leadership studies. The opportunity to earn credits is also helpful in motivating community college leaders to begin a graduate program.

The Chair Academies are hosted at various locations across the United States and, to a limited extent, internationally to provide access to leadership development opportunities for individuals from small or rural colleges, as well as those with limited resources. Because becoming a department chair is often the first step in a career path toward the presidency, training at this level can reach a broad and diverse group of potential leaders. However, none of the presidents in this study noted participating in a Chair Academy, although some sent staff.

Formal leadership development also occurs in doctoral programs. Increasingly, the doctorate is a must for candidates seeking top-level positions at community colleges; 78% of current community college presidents have a Ph.D. (most often in education) or an Ed.D. in educational leadership. Amey (2006) reviewed six university-based education leadership programs; all allowed administrators to pursue their degree while working full time. A central element for the success of these programs was a small and dedicated faculty core, many of whom had careers in community college administration themselves.

All of the presidents in this study had a doctorate; eight had a doctorate focused on educational leadership or higher education administration. President Karen Fields was the exception; she held a doctorate in theoretical physics. Two of the presidents graduated from the community college leadership program at the University of Texas–Austin; others were in more general programs without a specific focus on community colleges. When President Jon Hammond was a vice president, he decided that one of his goals was to read more on leadership, and thus he opted to take some graduate courses. As he related, "I was getting into administration late in life. . . . I enrolled in nine credits and thought this is going to be hard, and pretty soon within 26 months I had a doctorate. I had done research and really enjoyed it." Because of his experiences in graduate school, Hammond encouraged his mentees to obtain a doctorate and helped support them during their programs. All the participants realized that a doctorate was a necessary ticket for consideration for pursuit of upper-level positions. Some eschewed the notion of thinking too theoretically about leadership but noted how the academic learning about leadership expanded their thinking about how to approach issues in practice.

The additional leaders of color interviewed also had doctorates. One had a degree in policy and research and came to her presidency after 18 years in the state's systemwide office. She had received one of 12 fellowships funded from the Office of Women and Minority Affairs at her doctoral institution to focus on training in the field of higher education. Another of the minority presidents had a doctorate in school psychology and spent 20 years in the K–12 system before transitioning to the community college setting. The final additional president of color interviewed had her doctorate in higher education administration. She noted that she worked to get her degree when she had aspirations to become a dean. She had served on a regional accreditation team and observed, "I was the only one on the list that didn't have a doctorate. It seemed as if each time I'd go out, I'd be the only one without the Ph.D. and felt like people were asking, 'Why are you here?'" Clearly, the presidents knew that the doctorate was the requisite credential they needed for advancement.

### *Informal Leadership Development*

Informal leadership development occurred for the nine presidents in this study and the additional presidents interviewed via observation, by working through tough situations in a variety of positions, through their own reading, and through advice from mentors. As noted earlier, President Fields was the only president to hold a doctorate in a field outside education. Indeed, Fields's background in a hard science meant that she relied more on her experiences than her doctoral study to inform her practice of leadership and develop her cognitive schema. She reflected on her rough start at Bifurcated Community College, stating, "After this experience, I would do something I never thought that I would do. If I ever became a president again I would ask for written letters of resignation from all the senior staff. I've always felt that that was an inhumane and cruel and uncivilized way to move into a new job. Having had the experience I did here, I don't feel that way anymore." Fields learned from her experiences and altered her approach to leadership as a result, creating a new mental map of how to begin a presidency at a new college.

President Pauldine also learned much through informal leadership development experiences. As a consultant, she had the opportunity to visit more than 50 different community colleges. As she noted, "This kind of gave me a chance to do some professional development and to enhance my skills and really, in terms of being a president, prepared me in a lot of ways that working as an administrator at a single campus could not have." Visiting different campuses provided Pauldine with various perspectives on college operations and governance, giving her a variety of options for leading her own campus.

President Simon's break from higher education provided an opportunity for learning. He reflected, "When I think about the things that were important—there's no question that that 10-year break was really, really important. If I had been on a linear path from faculty member to some sort of an administrator or president, I would have approached this job in a very different way. Especially true, the consulting work I was doing—all of the people who were my clients were heads of large organizations. You could see how they thought; you could see everything they did and you were their adviser. You could see the good things and the bad things and the sick organizations and the healthy organizations. That was very helpful." Having a chance to see how leaders outside academe worked provided Simon with a chance to look differently at the issues he faced as a college president. In particular, while Simon was director of a state agency, there were several budget cuts. Simon stated that he learned a lot from his mentor during this time—in particular regarding the need to provide employees with as much information as possible. When Simon returned to higher education, his leadership was directly influenced by the cognitive schema he had developed at his previous agency, and he pointedly drew from his past experiences in making decisions and sharing information with his staff.

Informal leadership development was also important for those whose careers within the community college were more traditional. As President Hammond stated, "I've been a vice president of student services, a vice president of administrative services, an interim vice president for instructional services, a planning officer, a personnel officer, so I know this business. This is what I've done my entire life." Similarly, President Garvey served in a variety of positions, one of which was on the National Council of State Directors of Community Colleges. He reflected on this experience: "We met three times a year and rubbed elbows with people who did that kind of work in every state. That was an eye-opening experience because we got to see the whole range of governing structures and funding structures and different issues in different states." For Hammond and Garvey, informal leadership development occurred through everyday experiences in different roles and through relationships with peers.

The presidents also developed their leadership skills through reading leadership literature and by attending conferences. President Fields commented on how she looked at transformational change differently on her campus as a result of hearing higher education scholar Alexander Astin speak at a conference. Likewise, President Pauldine commented on a conversation she had with Arthur Levine, the former president of Teachers College, just before taking over her presidency. She reflected that he advised her to rest because she would need a lot of energy when arriving on campus. He also encouraged her to spend a significant amount of time getting to know the campus and finding out what was on the minds of faculty, administrators, and students. As a result, Pauldine noted, "From August until the end of December I listened; I made the rounds." Pauldine took to heart the advice she received through an informal development opportunity and incorporated it into her leadership style and cognitive schema.

## Learning Styles

Just as multiple opportunities for leadership development are available to community college presidents and presidential aspirants, leaders rely on different styles to incorporate new learning into their underlying schemas. As Kolb (1998) writes, "most of us develop learning styles that emphasize some learning abilities over others" (p. 131). As adult learners, community college leaders have preferred learning orientations. Kolb's Learning Style Inventory (LSI), which identifies four types of learning styles, as shown in Figure 3.1, is useful in understanding how the nine presidents in this study incorporated what they learned from formal and informal situations into their leadership on campus.

Each quadrant in Kolb's LSI identifies a different learning style. *Accommodators*, *divergers*, *assimilators*, and *convergers* each have distinct learning preferences and incorporate new information in different ways. *Accommodators* often prefer to learn through active investigation. For example, President Chris Jones had experimented with a ThinkPad system on his previous campus, and when he took over as president of Technology Community College, he implemented a similar program. Here, he successfully applied what he had learned from a previous experiment to a new context.

*Divergers*, on the other hand, prefer to learn by reflecting on concrete experiences. President Burke falls into the diverger category. As she related,

# FIGURE 3.1
## Kolb's (1998) Dominant Learning Styles

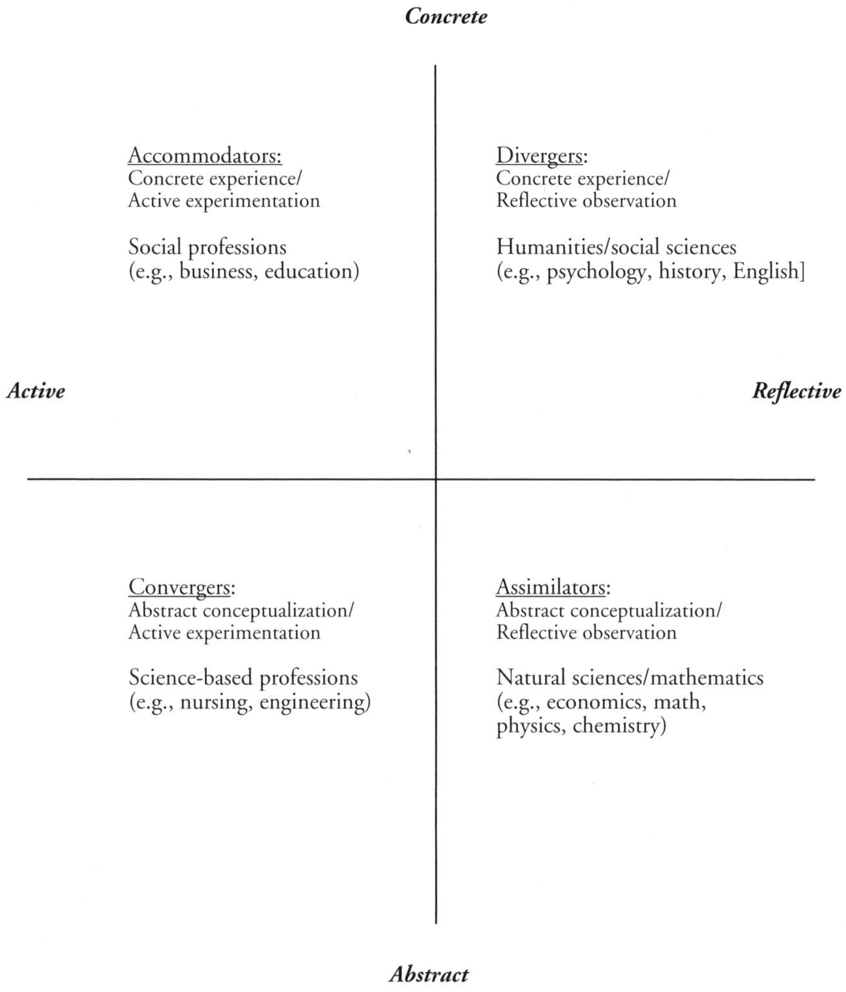

*Concrete*

*Active*

*Reflective*

Accommodators:
Concrete experience/
Active experimentation

Social professions
(e.g., business, education)

Divergers:
Concrete experience/
Reflective observation

Humanities/social sciences
(e.g., psychology, history, English]

Convergers:
Abstract conceptualization/
Active experimentation

Science-based professions
(e.g., nursing, engineering)

Assimilators:
Abstract conceptualization/
Reflective observation

Natural sciences/mathematics
(e.g., economics, math,
physics, chemistry)

*Abstract*

"I've had some experiences where there were institutions that did not want to change—that was a painful lesson, but it was a really good experience that was pretty valuable for me. Not comfortable, but boy, you can learn a lot from being in an institution where change is just really rejected as a value." Through reflecting on the concrete experiences that came out of trying to change a resistant institution, Burke learned much about leadership in different environments and can now apply that knowledge to other situations. Presidents Simon and Hales are also divergers; their willingness to reflect on past experiences and apply that knowledge to new contexts can be seen clearly in the following vignette.

---

### Vignette 2: The Value of Learning From Experience

As noted earlier, President Simon's professional experiences outside higher education were extremely influential in how he chose to communicate with his staff and make decisions on campus. Soon after assuming the presidency at Rogue Community College, he met individually with everyone on campus to learn more about them and the institution. As he stated, "It's very important for me to get to know everybody. That was something I learned how to do as a consultant. You know, you go in and interview lots of people to find out how the organization works." The importance of building relationships that Simon learned in his position outside academics underscored for him the need to engage campus members immediately on arrival on campus. Additionally, in order for Simon to rein in the rogue nature of the campus, he needed to know more about operations and the culture in order to enact changes.

Because community college presidents, like all adult learners, link new learning to past experiences, having a variety and depth of experiences allows for enhanced learning opportunities. In reflecting on the resources she uses to make decisions, President Hales stated, "A lot of it is experience, experience in a multicollege environment both [at another college in the state] and now here, almost 30 years' worth. . . . I serve on a number of national boards, I'm a SAC leader, have chaired committees. When you do that you get perspectives. I think between that, between my colleagues from the other campuses and certainly the chancellor and just reading, et cetera, there are just things that you know we could do sometimes that we're not doing." By reflecting on her diverse experiences, Hales identified a broad array of ways to approach problems and to see that issues facing her campus were not unique. Her previous experiences created an expanded database of information to call on when she needed to make new decisions.

Unlike divergers, who reflect on concrete experiences, *assimilators* prefer to reflect on abstract conceptualizations. The new understanding of community college leadership that President Fields experienced as a result of listening to Alexander Astin speak at a conference provides an excellent example of how an assimilator learns. As Fields noted, Astin's speech helped crystallize for her the change processes underway on her campus. She mused that his speech "sticks with me because it was so profoundly descriptive of the scene I'm in." Fields thus used an abstract conceptualization—Astin's model of transformational change—to reflect on her own situation and applied her new understanding of a theoretical framework to improve her leadership.

*Convergers* make up the fourth quadrant in Kolb's LSI. Convergers take abstract conceptualizations and test them through active experimentation. This learning style is most often used in the natural sciences, in which researchers test theoretical models through controlled experiments. Not surprisingly, this type of learning is less evident on college campuses because they are social environments with real-world consequences if an experiment does not work or works only for a select group of people. Therefore, none of the presidents in this study engaged in this type of learning.

What all four of Kolb's learning styles have in common is a willingness to reflect on an experience or an idea and to apply that learning through active experimentation or well-thought-out modifications to existing processes. It is through reflection that a leader can build on his or her existing cognitive schema. However, there are times when a leader's schema can be altered, leading to dramatic changes in how one leads. Mezirow (1997) describes transformational learning as a process of critical reflection through which one changes his or her frame of reference. This most often occurs through reading, listening to a presentation, or influential experiences. These shifts in thinking result from the "aha" moments of life.

All nine of the case study presidents described instances that were critical to their learning—for example, President Burke's failure to change a resistant institution, and the different perspectives President Hammond gained from holding a wide variety of campus positions. Most of these experiences led to modifications of the leaders' cognitive schemas, but President Fields described an instance in which she experienced a fundamental shift in perspective. She recalled, "I can remember the night I met with the president [of my college] and I was interim dean of academic affairs at this point and I was going to apply for the permanent position. . . . I don't even remember what got us started, but there was something that he wanted to do that I had a strong disagreement about and I told him in my firm way . . . and he called me a bitch. I remember walking out of there and thinking, 'I can't work for this man, and what's more, I probably can't work for anyone; I've got to be my own boss.' " This singular instance led Fields to acknowledge that she needed to strike out on her own and seek a leadership position at another campus.

As the preceding paragraphs demonstrate, through reflection, community college leaders can build on and even fundamentally shift their underlying cognitive schema, which in turn contributes to their ability to respond effectively to different situations and lead their campuses through trying times. Regardless of their learning style, adults are self-directed learners, and thus learning occurs through both formal and informal leadership development opportunities. Therefore, aspiring leaders should consider engaging in opportunities that can help expand their worldview and expose them to ideas and experiences that may expand or change their existing frames of reference. In addition to being open to the informal learning opportunities that occur on campus every day, aspiring leaders can volunteer for campus projects, take on new responsibilities within their department or administrative structure, and join regional and state professional associations. Formal educational opportunities can also provide opportunities for leadership development, especially when they are accompanied by critical reflection.

## Leadership Development From a Multidimensional Perspective

As adult learners, leaders rely on their experiences as learning opportunities. Each leader's core schema provides a starting point to which new learning and experiences are added. By "hooking" new information to their underlying schema, leaders develop a greater level of complexity in their leadership. This complexity is represented by a wider and more developed expanse of skills to draw on in leading. More-experienced leaders who have critically reflected on their experiences develop more intricate world perspectives than their counterparts who do not take the time to question their experiences and draw lessons from events. Community college leaders who do not actively reflect on their experiences and learning opportunities retain more static and underdeveloped approaches to leading and are unlikely to experience long-term success given the external pressures facing the institutions today.

Mezirow's (1997) typology of the four processes of learning is useful in understanding how new knowledge and experiences are incorporated into a leader's multidimensional leadership model. The first process of learning allows for expansion of current perspectives. With respect to the multidimensional model, this would involve the development or expansion of an area of leadership or movement on the continuum from novice to expert. For example, President Burke learned a "painful lesson" when her change initiative at a previous college was rejected. At her new college, Burke's approach to leadership regarding change did not involve failure. She held a limited view of how to effect change on a college campus based on her previous experiences. After her initial attempt failed, Burke reflected on her experience; when she moved to Cutting Edge Community College, her approach to change now reflected more experiences and understanding that it is necessary for a leader to provide for open communication and feedback loops to make the steps in a change process more transparent. This experience, and her reflection on it, would also have expanded the elements in Burke's leadership model representing flexibility, communication, and so forth, making her leadership more multidimensional and complex.

The second learning process in Mezirow's typology relates to the creation of new points of view; in the multidimensional model this would mean the addition of new facets and perspectives, representing more tools in a leadership toolbox. In President Fields's experience, a new element would have been added to her multidimensional leadership model after her rocky start at Bifurcated Community College. After reflecting on that experience, Fields learned that in the future, before taking over a presidential position, she would need to ask a lot more questions of the board of trustees to find out more about the difficulties facing the college and to identify the administrators that might stand in the way of change. This new knowledge provides an additional element in Fields's multidimensional model versus the mere expansion or growth in expertise. Ultimately, given more experience, Fields may also move from one point to another regarding her personal development from novice to expert.

Mezirow's third learning process involves a transformation in point of view. In the multidimensional leadership model, this would involve a change in leadership instead of an additional way of looking at situations or the mere gaining of experience. Let's imagine that early in President Simon's career, he developed a perspective that represented how a leader might go about slashing a college budget that might be represented by a limited range of options regarding resource management. During his 10 years working outside higher education, Simon learned about budget cuts from nonacademic leaders, and by the time he accepted the presidency at Rogue Community College, he had completely transformed the way he would approach funding reductions on campus. As he commented, "I learned a lot about a budget crisis and how to do that and how to come out the other end and survive, which is good because there seems to be kind of a recurring path of cuts." Simon learned that if he shared information about funding reductions with the people in his unit, they were more focused and less distracted by rumors. This experience transformed the way in which he communicated with his staff at Rogue as well as the level of transparency he had with them. As he stated, "Nobody's afraid of me. [laugh] I mean, I'm about as approachable as they come." In essence, Simon's experiences outside academe transformed elements in his own leadership model that now reflect his more open communication style and flexibility as he leads on campus.

The fourth learning process in Mezirow's typology involves an epochal change to an underlying schema. An epochal change to the way one organizes his or her understanding of the world is rare and often associated with an unparalleled experience of such profound significance that an individual's worldview shifts. This type of learning is uncommon; rather, an individual's underlying leadership schema or sense of self is less malleable.

Critical reflection of one's underlying assumptions and experiences is key to developing a more complex approach to leadership (as well as a more complex multidimensional model). For example, when President Burke was tapped to lead Cutting Edge Community College, a brand-new institution, she had the opportunity to create new norms and expectations on campus. As she related, "The vision came out of the ability to build a college from scratch in the 21st century, taking best practices of everything we all wish we could do but can't because there's always limitations either by organizations or by people you have employed, or by habit, or by physical plant. And really then to take full advantage of the opportunity to take the blank page and actually build a learning college. . . . We're really building a college around learning engagement . . . to try to get a different outcome." Burke reflected on her previous experiences as a faculty member, dean, administrator, and president, and questioned everything, even the most basic assumptions about the way a campus should be run. She stated, "It all leads back into that end result of a higher emphasis on active collaborative learning. All of what that means in terms of organization and physical plant." Thus Burke's critical reflection not only helped her clarify her goals for the new college, but also led to a reliance on consensus building and collaborative decision making at Cutting Edge, which in turn instilled critical reflection as a component of all campus decision making.

Similarly, President Garvey's reflections on the autocratic leadership of a college where he was a faculty member led him to seek an administrative role, believing that "there's got to be a better way to run an institution." Furthermore, Garvey's reflections on an internship that was part of his doctoral program led to expansion of his leadership capabilities: "The beauty of an internship is that you're there as a semi-, quasi-employee but you really are an observer to see how they model and see if that sort of style and approach could be effective in achieving the institution's mission." Critically reflecting on his internship experience allowed Garvey to observe institutional actions and outcomes and learn from them without being responsible for the results. When he became a leader at his own college, he drew on these experiences—allowing his multidimensional model of leadership to expand and become more complex.

Leaders must be conscious of the learning process if they are to intentionally expand their leadership skills and capabilities. As this growth occurs, whether through formal or informal learning opportunities, the elements in leaders' multidimensional leadership models multiply and expand, providing them with a broader set of solutions, ideas, and tactics that can help them successfully lead their institutions.

# 4

# COMMUNICATING AND FRAMING INFORMATION ON CAMPUS

Leadership is a language game, one that many
do not know they are playing.

Gail Fairhurst and Robert Sarr (1996, p. xi)

ollege leaders are judged by what they say and do on campus. Campus constituents come to their own conclusions about what is going on based on how presidents communicate their vision and plans. Leaders, then, have the ability to frame information, as well as how constituents make meaning of that information, on their campuses (Eddy, 2003; Fairhurst & Sarr, 1996; Neumann, 1995). When leaders frame information for others, they offer their own interpretations above others, much like how a picture frame focuses one's attention on a particular view or aspect of a picture or painting. College presidents communicate and frame information to campus constituents in a variety of ways. For example, President Jones from Technology Community College used a framing technique that focused campus members' attention on the positive aspects of his agenda in order to initiate a new laptop program on campus. As he shared, "Now part of the change is that I didn't dwell on, at no point did I dwell on the negatives or even really talk about them much: the lack of funding, the sort of depressed state, the physical condition of the campus." Instead, Jones painted a picture of TCC that highlighted forward movement, accomplished through the use of technology in student and campus operations. In his public talks and informal conversations, Jones did not make any references to the college's depressed economic situation or declining physical plant. Rather, he painted a rosy picture of campus life, one that would become even rosier with more technology integration. He even hosted the beginning-of-the-year meeting in the college's new automotive facility, which communicated to faculty and staff that new buildings were being built, that the vocational aspect of the campus was integral to the college's identity, and that technology was integrated throughout campus programming—including the vocational programs.

In choosing how to frame issues on campus, presidents must be mindful of how the message may be interpreted by various stakeholders. President Pauldine of Hunkering Down Community College thought that she had been communicating with faculty and staff fairly well. Yet during an accreditation visit, she was asked to communicate better. As she related, "One of the things that came up in the oral summary report was that they'd like to see us improve communication. And I just kind of smiled. Because I think that's probably something you say everywhere, and I turned to somebody and I said, 'Just tell me what I could do that I'm not doing.'" Still, when she stopped to think about it, there were tensions on campus between long-serving faculty and newer faculty. HDCC was in the midst of some significant mission-related changes, including instituting baccalaureate programs and moving away from the prior focus on technical and agricultural education. Different faculty members probably interpreted Pauldine's message to mean that these changes, as well as a challenging fiscal climate, meant that faculty would have to do more with less in their own way. Indeed, she described the newer faculty as the "lifeblood of the college," adding that "I think some of the senior faculty become very cynical and just go to class and do their thing. And this mission has evolved." Because Pauldine did not think through how her message would be interpreted differently by the two groups of faculty, she may have exacerbated some of the internal divisions, which in turn detracted from her larger message regarding change.

Presidents do not communicate in a vacuum. Both leaders and followers play a role, with leaders providing one way of interpreting a piece of information and followers then interpreting this reality either in the suggested manner or in their own way (Fairhurst, 2001). Leaders and followers both make meaning of what they hear and see through interactions with each other on campus (Berger & Luckmann, 1966). But when leaders frame information in different ways, it results in different interpretations by followers (Kelman, 1961). Before leaders can frame information for others, however, they must first make sense of it for themselves. This chapter explores how leaders communicate and frame information on campus. In particular, it begins by discussing communicating as sensemaking, then draws from the experiences of the nine community college presidents to examine how leaders frame messages, the role of the messenger, and ways in which leaders work to get their messages across. The chapter concludes with an analysis of how communicating and framing contributes to multidimensional leadership.

## Communicating as Sensemaking

Times of uncertainty and change provide ripe opportunities for leaders to help campus members make sense of new events and to connect new information with past experiences (Senge, 1990; Weick, 1995). As Weick (1995) points out, "sensemaking begins with the sensemaker" (p. 18). Thus, before college presidents can help others understand and interpret events and information, they must first make sense of the situation for themselves. In sensemaking, leaders draw on their own personal ways of interpreting and creating knowledge, as well as past experiences and interactions with campus members.

Weick's (1995) sensemaking model, which contains seven properties, is useful in understanding how one moves through the process of sensemaking. Table 4.1 presents elements of Weick's framework and the ways in which leaders can use these stages to create meaning for campus members. The first property relates to the ways in which individuals make sense of a situation in a personal way. In other words, when presented with new information, leaders begin to make sense of it by drawing on their underlying schemas and mental maps of how the world works.

The table outlining Weick's sensemaking model lists his seven properties and then provides a categorization of these properties into three key components: the areas that support leaders' underlying schema, the elements that contribute to feedback loops, and finally the framing of the story. The third column of the table shows actions leaders can take at each step to develop, expand, and diversify their approach, ultimately helping to create their own multidimensional leadership.

Weick's second property deals with the retrospective nature of sensemaking. Here people use their past experiences to understand how to make sense of a new occurrence. President Hammond noted, "I've been a vice president of student services, a vice president of administrative services, an interim vice president of instructional services, a planning officer, a personnel officer. So I know this business. This is what I've done all my life." Thus, when Hammond tries to make sense of an issue facing his college, he first draws on his previous experiences.

**TABLE 4.1**
**Making Sense on Campus**

| Themes | Weick's (1995) Sensemaking Properties | Developing Multidimensional Leaders |
|---|---|---|
| **Underlying Schema** | Identity construction | • Disciplinary background<br>• Underlying schema<br>• Career pathway<br>• Role definition<br>• Personal and professional influences |
| | Retrospective | • Critical reflection<br>• Mentoring guidance<br>• Perspectives on leadership<br>• Reflection of previous actions<br>• Evaluation of leadership outcomes |
| **Feedback Loops** | Enactment | • Creation of scripted patterns<br>• Actions creating routines<br>• Conscious actions by individuals<br>• Social construction of reality<br>• Flexibility |
| | Social interaction | • Communication styles<br>• Multiple types of communication<br>• Use of formal and informal venues for communicating<br>• Spreading the message through messengers |
| | Ongoing sensemaking | • Creation of new meaning<br>• Adjustments using feedback<br>• Awareness of external influences<br>• Use of leadership circle<br>• Guidance from past<br>• Help from mentors |
| **Framing the Story** | Extracted cues | • Influence of experiences<br>• Changing schemas<br>• Ability to reframe cues for others<br>• Use of feedback to see new understanding of cues |
| | Plausible versus accurate | • Framing of possibilities<br>• Adjustments based on feedback loops<br>• Communication venues<br>• Joint creation of culture and reality<br>• Formulation of expectations |

Enactment is the third property in Weick's (1995) schematic and a pivotal junction in the sensemaking process because it is the stage when leaders, having made sense of a situation for themselves, begin to frame information and communicate it to others on campus. How the college president opts to share information and interact with campus members can affect how people on campus attach meaning to events. Periodically, President Jones sent out what he referred to as his "Presidential Ramblings," occasional e-mail messages with updates on campus initiatives that were sent to the entire campus. President Pauldine, on the other hand, communicated her set of eight strategic steps for her college's future by formally presenting her "Program of Work" and accompanying agenda to campus constituents. Although Jones and Pauldine communicated information to staff and faculty in different ways—one more participatory, one more autocratic—they did so in a way that helped their constituents make sense of it. Followers also play a role in the enactment process, although their impact is supported or constrained by the campus culture for participation.

The fourth element of Weick's sensemaking model deals with the ways in which individuals begin to make sense of information presented by their leader. This process occurs largely through social interactions; as individuals try to understand what is going on, they talk with one another, send e-mails, or write position papers. Social interactions such as these were especially critical at the newly opened Cutting Edge Community College, where President Burke actively promoted a culture that supported student learning. In order to help faculty and staff understand the importance of the new one-stop student services center, Burke initiated a training program in which "everyone does financial aid, everyone does registration, everybody does everything." The training program underscored the college's emphasis on collaboration and student support and provided opportunities for staff to get to know one another and to learn more about job functions that are typically out of their defined area of expertise.

As a result of the training program, a great amount of ongoing staff interaction exists at CECC, allowing staff members to make sense out of how their work—and the work of others—influences and reinforces a culture of student learning. Social interactions thus provide opportunities for people to begin to understand situations and process information. The critical element in this stage is how social conversations and interactions help reinforce the message; here actions result in the type of meaning understood by staff. The fact that dedicated meetings occur to discuss ways to improve student success and that funding is devoted to leading these efforts underscores the message that student learning is central.

The fifth property in Weick's model concerns the ongoing nature of sensemaking. The process of trying to make sense of a situation never has a definite beginning or end. Rather, a continuous filtering and processing of information leads to greater understanding. As well, one's understanding of a situation may shift as new information emerges. Community college presidents receive information from a wide variety of sources. All of the presidents in this study had a leadership cabinet of some sort, although the exact composition of members varied. These inner circles had a strong influence on the information the presidents received. Sometimes leaders decide that they are getting too much information—or too detailed information—from those reporting to them and act to reduce the number of followers who influence their decisions on a daily basis. For example, President Fields decreased the number of her direct reports from 12 to 3 when she arrived at Bifurcated Community College.

The nature of symbols and outside information informs individual schemas and provides the basis for the sixth property of Weick's (1995) model. Extracted cues serve as a point of reference to help with sensemaking and to identify points of change and, with experience, guide interpretations (Harris, 1994). "Extracted cues are the simple, familiar structures that are seeds from which people develop a larger sense of what may be occurring" (Weick, 1995, p. 50). For example, when President Hammond arrived on campus, his first action was to create a long-term strategic plan. To help others understand the critical importance of planning for the college, he created a red-covered book for the plan that campus leaders followed and reported on at cabinet meetings. This tangible cue helped focus attention on a new direction. Additionally, to underscore the tie-in of the strategic plan to the mission of the college, Hammond recrafted the mission statement in open meetings on campus and had it placed on the back of all signage on the college grounds and on all college business cards. Leaders can help with campus sensemaking by making use of the cues that staff see and hear on campus.

The final property of sensemaking in Weick's model pertains to the notion that situations are interpreted as being plausible as opposed to being accurate. Plausibility is grounded in expected, credible outcomes. For instance, when a leader anticipates the outcomes of a particular situation, the details of the actual reality are overshadowed by the expected reality. In other words, leaders often focus on the plausible outcomes of a situation instead of the accurate outcomes because they rely too much on their underlying schemas and find it difficult to question or modify their mental maps in order to make sense of the situation in a more accurate manner. In focusing on the forward progress of his college in discussions about the new technology integration, President Jones overlooked to some extent the reality of the college's difficult fiscal setting and declining infrastructure. The danger inherent here occurs if leaders pose plausible scenarios over reality or have deluded perspectives of reality and use this stage to mislead stakeholders.

As leaders become adept at making sense of a new situation for themselves and then communicating that understanding to others, they begin to serve as "sense-*givers*" (Thayer, 1988, p. 250, italics in the original). The following vignette illustrates how the presidents in the Large and Growing Community College District framed changes in organizational structure on their campuses in different ways.

## Vignette 3: Sensemaking on Campus

In the Large and Growing Community College District, a systemwide change was implemented in 2002. All associate deans' positions were eliminated; some were promoted to dean, some were let go, and some administrative assistants were asked to assume more responsibilities for paperwork formerly done by the associate deans. The espoused reason for this change was to allow the deans to provide more leadership rather than merely functioning as administrative paper-movers. Rumors on the campuses, however, pointed to a need to "clean house." Each of the five colleges in the district was affected by this organizational change, but each president helped his or her campus make sense of the changes in different ways.

### Cutting Edge Community College

President Burke was fortunate in being able to design the organizational structure at Cutting Edge Community College from the beginning; thus there was not a long-standing history of a particular structure, and she did not need to fire any associate deans. However, she was required to follow the academic structure laid out by the central office, which precluded her from trying something completely new. As she stated, "In formulating our organizational structure, we really wanted to get away from an academic structure. That's where being in a district limited us." However, Burke retained some flexibility by hiring three individuals to oversee academic responsibilities: a vice president of student learning, a vice president for student success, and a dean of the branch campus. She added, "All three share academic CEO/CAO responsibilities, which makes it harder to work in a way, but it also forces collaboration and forces a collegewide view on decisions that normally are made by one academic officer." Despite the limitations of the district-imposed structure, Burke created academic manager positions that were aligned with her vision of a learning college and, more important, communicated the *meaning* of those positions and the reporting structure to campus constituents. It is clear to staff that a premium is placed on student learning because the positions include a vice president for student learning, a vice president for student success, and a dedicated academic dean for the branch campus. All three share chief academic officer responsibilities rather than this job function being vested with one vice president for instruction.

## Don't Make Waves Community College

Unlike Cutting Edge, Don't Make Waves Community College was initially resistant to the plans for reorganization because they required President Hales to eliminate one deanship. This meant that departments had to be reorganized to fit into three reporting streams versus four. Hales held some open meetings on campus about how to deal with this, but campus members felt that the four-dean structure was appropriate and would offer no input for a change. Ultimately, Hales and her vice president decided on a new departmental reporting structure. She noted that unlike other colleges that were using this opportunity to "get rid of probably some dead wood that was there," DMWCC had some good associate deans who were ultimately hired as deans. She was honest and open with campus constituents in relating the new dean structure, telling faculty, "This will be a year of transition!" She also acknowledged the fact that "turf wars" were occurring and that she was working on creating policies to define new work functions. Thus, Hales helped her faculty and staff make meaning of the organizational changes on campus through honest and open communication and by trying to establish order and routine. Her commitment to transparent communication resulted in increased levels of trust on campus.

## Me-Too Community College

The reorganization at Me-Too Community College was complicated by a corresponding cut in the budget. As President Garvey stated, "People are feeling squeezed! Some people are feeling squeezed not only by the budget constraints but by having to adjust to a new academic organization. . . . For them it is like a calf staring at a new gate." Staff at MTCC did not know how to make sense of the new changes. To help abate these feelings, Garvey brought in an outside consultant to work with the entire campus on change processes. His approach was to try to help campus members make sense of the rapid pace of change by giving them tools to work through the changes and to provide opportunities for them to better understand their feelings about the changes. Garvey was a storyteller when talking to campus members, conjuring up parables to illustrate the organizational changes and how the campus would face them. He wanted to provide support to his faculty and staff, but at the same time he knew he needed to be clear on his own priorities, which were to obtain more resources for his campus. He described this process as encouraging change when you "put the hay down where the goats can get it." His good-old-boy approach fit his campus culture and enabled him to get his message across so that faculty and staff could make sense of it.

## Rogue Community College

President Simon arrived on the campus of Rogue Community College just after the reorganization took place, and thus he got the benefit of the change without being blamed for the termination of the associate deans. Indeed, he was pleased with the organizational changes, especially because the new deans were more tolerant of letting faculty speak about issues and were less likely to cut off dialogue than the previous administrators. This type of communicating on campus fit Simon's style. He stated, "Most of my involvement is with the people who report to me and to the other deans and directors and making sure that the things I think are important are the things that they think are important." He added that as long as his values are aligned with those of his deans, he is confident that the midlevel leaders can get the job done. Because Simon was not responsible for the organizational changes, he did not need to focus his sensemaking on the new structure. Rather, he focused his attention (and that of his faculty and staff) on the changes he wanted to accomplish on campus.

### Tradition-Bound Community College

President Williams did not work as hard as the other presidents in this study to help his campus constituents make sense of the organizational changes. But because the changes in reporting structure were dramatic at Tradition-Bound Community College, there was much apprehension on campus. Although Williams brought in a speaker to discuss the changes on campus, he himself did not focus on the change process, preferring to concentrate on the new strategic plan. Perhaps as a result, faculty on campus had mixed feelings about the changes. One long-serving faculty member noted that the restructuring was a top-down decision with little faculty input. Although the faculty member ultimately supported the decision, he added, "It was a good blueprint, but the execution wasn't thought through, no one thought through the execution. . . . Plans don't work that way, and I believe that as a result, we haven't really changed." Because Williams did not spend time helping the campus make sense of the reorganization, he may have reduced the ultimate impact of the organizational change.

## Framing the Message

Leaders play the central role in framing meaning on their campuses (Eddy, 2003). "The actions and utterances of leaders frame and shape the context of action in such a way that the members of that context are able to use the meaning thus created as a point of reference for their own action and understanding of the situation" (Smircich & Morgan, 1982, p. 261). When a college president understands his or her role in framing messages, he or she can use information to advance the college mission. Framing is a powerful tool and one that should always be used for the benefit of the campus and its constituents. It should never be used, however, for self-serving or unethical purposes.

A variety of tools exist for framing information, including rituals or traditions, stories, jargons, and metaphors. In particular, creating an *institutional saga* (Clark, 1972) can help constituents reflect on the culture of the college and interpret new information in a way that is consistent with its mission and goals. How leaders communicate and frame information is linked to their underlying schema and their approach to leadership (Fairhurst, 2001). For instance, some leaders act in *transactional* ways with their followers. In this case, they promise followers certain actions or items in return for their support. Other leaders have a more *transformational* leadership style, in which leadership actions stem from an ongoing dialogue between leaders and followers. Leadership approaches and communication styles are closely linked, and presidents' leadership preferences affect the ways in which they frame new information to campus constituents. The following vignette illustrates how two presidents framed information on campus in different ways, one transactional and one transformational.

## Vignette 4: Communicating via Transaction or Transformation

Transactional leaders view leadership as a series of transactions between themselves and campus members, whereas transformational leaders conceptualize leadership as creating a shared sense of ownership on campus. Each of these leadership styles influences the ways in which leaders frame new information and help campus members make sense of it. President Pauldine of Hunkering Down Community College is more of a transactional leader and thus relied on an established hierarchy and a set of steps to achieve the overarching campus mission. These steps were incremental and occurred in a linear fashion. The way in which she communicated followed a similar pattern. Pauldine commented, "The one thing I don't particu-

larly care for that has been a tradition here is what has been classi-
fied as the forum. And that is, historically the president has stood up
in the front of the room and people have asked questions. And it's
not that I have anything to hide. People will tell you I'm pretty open,
but I feel uncomfortable because I have no idea of what the focus is
or what the discussion is. I just kind of feel tense about it and so my
own personal feeling would be I don't have any problem with holding
these open meetings, but I would like them to be more structured."
Instead of the open forum, Pauldine instituted focused dialogues on
topics she wanted to review with the campus. This shift in forum
structure allowed her to intentionally frame the issues she felt were
most important and immediate to guide campus conversations. This
format has worked for Pauldine; one faculty member noted, "It just
seems to me there's more communication about what's going on on
campus than there was in the past."

President Jones of Technology Community College had a different approach to leadership and communication. He relied on creating a vision for the campus with input of faculty and staff and using
that vision as the focal point for change. As he shared, "Just because
I had the vision, I couldn't implement it. I needed to do something
before that, I needed to develop a consensus—*consensus* is the
wrong term. I needed to develop strong support from a group of faculty and staff . . . so there was universal ownership, much more universal ownership than the direction I wanted to go." By asking faculty
and staff to take ownership of the plan and have a stake in the process, Jones transformed his initial vision into a campus vision. He
used the "bully pulpit" and power of his position to communicate the
plans and its ideals, but his approach to communication is informal.
When addressing the entire campus, he does not have a prepared
speech. Rather he goes into the session with a short list of bullet
points to cover. He gathers feedback from campus members and
stakeholders through informal conversations and is a fixture at community events and campus sporting contests.

Jones's vision kept the campus focused on what they *could be*
rather than what they currently are. This transformational leadership
style is refreshing to many campus constituents and even helps
Jones attract new faculty and staff. As the director of public relations

at the college related, "I was a reporter and I came to campus to interview President Jones about his philosophy because I had heard that some really dynamic things were happening down at this college in the middle of nowhere." When the position in public relations came open, she applied for and got the job.

When framing information to campus constituents, leaders must be aware of the existing campus culture as well as the prevailing attitudes and experiences of faculty, staff, and students. Eavesdropping on campus conversations provides presidents with useful perspectives and helps them take the pulse of the campus. Leaders can do this during informal conversations, by attending meetings, and through e-mail exchanges. By interacting with all campus members—including students—leaders can learn about the context in which they are working, which in turn should influence the way that they frame and communicate information to others. For example, if a president's previous college expected all campus members to attend a welcome-back-to-school speech each fall, he or she will probably expect the same to occur at the new institution. However, the culture of the new college may not support this type of attendance or participation. A president who wants all campus stakeholders to attend his or her "State of the College Address" cannot simply assume that people will attend; he or she must actively work to change the culture, perhaps by clearly explaining what he or she plans on discussing, what opportunities there will be to ask questions, and what campus constituents can expect to come out of the gathering.

Leaders use a variety of framing tools to get their message across. President Burke at Cutting Edge Community College related how her campus created its institutional story. She said, "We have a formal orientation process that's really fun. It involves the ducks—our mascot is the ducks because they paddle like crazy under the water but they're calm on the outside, and that's our customer-service philosophy. Everybody, full or part time, police officer to custodian, goes to the customer-service training. That's the first thing they do—that helps builds our culture a little bit." Although in this instance a metaphor helped Burke frame information about the new customer-service training to her faculty and staff, leaders must be careful not to incorporate complex metaphors or institutional sagas that do not have shared meaning for constituents. The leader needs to use care to ensure that the intended message and the meaning actually understood are the same.

Symbols and stories can also help frame and communicate a message (Bolman & Deal, 2008; Frost & Morgan, 1983). Indeed, leaders can use symbols to draw attention to specific versions of a campus story they are creating. President Hammond of Strategic Community College used several logos and symbols to sell his new mission statement. These images were added to all of the signs on campus and incorporated into college business cards. He also had the 5-year strategic plan bound with a red cover to signify its importance. Campus leaders frequently relied on their little red book in campus meetings and monthly progress updates—it was a living document and was integral to how Hammond framed change and priorities on campus. Similarly, President Jones created a logo for Technology Community College that emphasized the campus's entrepreneurial students and dedication to technology and student learning. The fact that multiple campus members recited the meaning of the logo almost verbatim underscores how effective it was as a symbol for Jones's (and thus the college's) vision for the future.

The preceding examples clearly show that the ways in which a leader frames information greatly affect how faculty and staff respond, and in turn influence campus operations. Community college presidents have several opportunities to directly communicate information to campus constituents, but because they are not omnipresent, they must often rely on a messenger to communicate their views and ideas.

## Role of the Messenger

More recent conceptions of leadership envision it operating at many levels throughout the college (Alfred, Shults, Jaquette, & Strickland, 2009; Peterson, 1997). As community colleges have become more complex, it has become impossible for a college president to be everywhere and do everything. Increased demands from external stakeholders and a greater need for fund-raising mean that presidents must split their focus between external and internal constituents. As a result, they must rely on others in the college's leadership circle to play a role in framing information and communicating it to faculty, staff, and students.

Just because a leader relies on messengers to help spread messages does not mean that the way in which one chooses to frame the information is less important or impactful. Indeed, if a variety of messengers or emissaries are enlisted to spread a particular message in a consistent and oft-repeated manner, chances are greater that members of the community will be on the same page. College cultures are based on shared stories, rituals, and understandings; leaders who understand the culture of their institution can simultaneously reinforce it and use it to share information with constituents.

Lunenburg and Ornstein (2007) have identified five basic ways in which information is disseminated within an organization: through chains, Y-networks, circles, wheels, and stars. In *chain networks*, presidents pass information to their vice presidents, who in turn tell the deans, who ultimately inform the faculty. This type of communication is highly structured and is often found in the military and other hierarchical organizations. *Y-networks* are similar in that information is shared in one direction only, but there may be more than one source of information in Y-network communication.

*Circle networks* are also autocratic, as the leader controls the information that is passed around the circle. In this communication pattern, individuals interact with a limited number of people—those located on either side of them in the circle (in community colleges, this may mean that a president communicates mainly with his or her vice presidents and/or the leaders of the academic senate). The director of outreach at Bifurcated Community College described the circular communication route at her college by noting, "The president has kind of closed herself off, to be honest. Instead of having a large president's council like we had with about 15 people—all the deans, some of the directors, and the VPs—she went to a strict 'I talk to three people' model, and I don't think it has benefited her in terms of communication." At BCC, President Fields is located at the top of her circular communication network and uses the messengers closest to her to pass along information. In turn, she receives information only from this same limited circle.

In *wheel networks*, the leader is positioned in the center of a wheel and passes information to the campus community along the spokes (e.g., a president may use the vice president of academic affairs to communicate with his or her deans and faculty or may rely on the vice president of student services to pass information to counselors and financial aid officers). President Simon described the wheel communication model when he stated, "A lot of communication goes down, not directly from me; it goes through other people. When we have our meetings, these president council meetings, every week I'm sure I'm told a lot of stuff from the meetings that gets transferred down."

What differentiates the wheel model from a chain network or Y-network is that people located at the other end of a spoke can access the leader without having to go through another layer of the hierarchy. Additionally, those at the outer level of the wheel have access to one another. By incorporating additional avenues for communication at many levels, the wheel can be effective in reinforcing stories and perspectives that the leader wants to highlight. For instance, several different staff members at Technology Community College shared the same vision for their campus. As President Jones said, "In a very flippant way our goal is to graduate students who not only have a very valuable degree, but walk across the stage with a degree in one hand, the laptop loaded with software—it's theirs—in the other, and their own business waiting for them when they walk off the stage." This same story was related by the vice president of academic affairs: "We occasionally used the notion that a student who would graduate had a diploma in their hand and that business plan under their arm, but at the same time would have a laptop under their arm as well. So you would have [these] three overlapping globes of academic programs, entrepreneurial initiatives, and applied business practices, all of which is encompassed in this sort of infusion or environment of technology." And the dean of enrollment management echoed, "The president has students in mind. He envisions a student at graduation that has a diploma in one hand, a business plan in the other hand, and a laptop under their arm." Clearly, Jones's vision for a campus that has integrated technology with entrepreneurialism and student learning is reinforced by messengers in the leadership cabinet who shared this vision with other campus members.

*Star* or *open networks* are the final communication pattern in Lunenburg and Ornstein's (2007) typology. At colleges that communicate via star networks, an individual has open communication lines not only to others at the same level (those located to each side of them in the network), but also with those who work in different parts of the college or who operate at different levels (those who may be located on the other side of the diagram). Communication to these latter individuals is represented by the intersecting lines of the star. In star networks, emissaries are located at all points of the organization and can communicate freely across the institution. Ties to the community are also included in this type of communication network. One faculty member at Hunkering Down Community College noted a conversation she overheard at the local discount store. She said, "I was just doing Christmas shopping and I heard some older people there in the aisle and I heard them talking about the college. . . . And it was interesting because they were [changes voice to sound raspy], 'Oh things have really changed over there,' and they said, 'They're getting 4-year degree programs now and they're not a 2-year college anymore and things are so different!'" The changes in the college had become obvious to the community because college constituents had served as conduits for that information. In this case, because President

Pauldine's vision for the future of HDCC was clearly transmitted within the college, it was also cohesive when it was conveyed outside the campus.

President Hammond of Strategic Community College intentionally used his campus colleagues to convey messages to the greater community. As he said, "You have to communicate. People have to feel positive. The internal community has to feel positive. . . . The communication radiates out. So, if I've got 400 employees and they talk to 10 people a month about the college, then that's 4,000 contacts. Multiply that by people who talk to key influencers, it's probably 8,000 to 10,000 people." When campus communication is open and the leader has clearly framed a message, everyone on campus can serve as a messenger.

Star networks provide leaders with the greatest amount of feedback because, instead of receiving information from a small number of individuals, they can gather varied viewpoints from multiple campus members. As President Hammond noted, "There's a filter there when you are around the president. You have to get out of that layer of insulation." Getting out of isolated streams of communication provides opportunities for presidents to engage in feedback loops with campus constituents, which can challenge assumptions and allow for change. It is important for leaders to move beyond a circle of "yes" associates to allow for critical reflection on their leadership and their decisions. As an example, President Williams at Tradition-Bound Community College actively solicits feedback from faculty and staff. As he related, "I encourage people to contact me—e-mail, mail, voice mail, or any way that they need to reach me." Allowing for a variety of ways to provide feedback to campus leaders can result in a greater amount of feedback because individuals who may not participate in formal feedback sessions can communicate with leaders in their preferred format.

## Getting the Message Across

As this chapter has described, college presidents must first make sense of new information themselves, then they must frame their message, and finally they must use messengers to help disseminate that information to the rest of the community. In the dissemination stage, college leaders and their messengers can use four distinct methods for getting a message across: *talking the frame, walking the frame, writing the frame,* and *symbolizing the frame.* Different leaders may be more comfortable with some of these communication methods over others, depending on their leadership preferences. Key to effectively framing and communicating information is the alignment of message to messenger; there is no *right* way to communicate or lead. Trying to assume a communication style that conflicts with an individual's leadership style could be less than effective (consider how a structured leader may flounder in a campus town hall meeting in which questioning is random, or how a shoot-from-the-hip communicator would feel if required to stick to a scripted speech). Leaders must understand their communication strengths and rely on messengers or emissaries to communicate a message in ways that they cannot. For example, a president may be comfortable walking the frame and talking the frame but may not be an effective writer; in this instance, she may rely on a vice president for written communications with the campus community. The following sections highlight the variety of ways in which the presidents in this study used the four communication methods to get their message across to campus constituents and to help them make sense of that information.

## Talking the Frame

Campus members often learn about new change initiatives during open campus forums or in small-group discussions. These meetings may occur at the beginning of the year or during regularly scheduled times and provide excellent opportunities for college leaders or their messengers to *talk the frame* (i.e., verbally discuss the information in a way that is consistent with the leader's frame). Talking the frame can also occur in ad hoc meetings pertaining to specific campus needs, events, or challenges.

In talking the frame, campus leaders can speak in a more formal, scripted format or in a more freestyle manner, depending on the leader's preferences and the particular way in which he or she has chosen to frame the message. For example, President Pauldine described talking the frame during a typical large-group session on her campus. Her approach during the fall of her first year on campus had been to listen to campus members and to scan the college environment in order to uncover current issues, possibilities, and threats. She noted, "In January at the opening of the spring semester, I presented my Program of Work; it has eight goals. I did it in a generic way and I said, "These are the areas that I'm going to be paying attention to over the next 18 months.'" This session was formal in orientation, with a PowerPoint program outlining each of the eight steps. Pauldine supplemented her verbal presentation with written information. Nonetheless, campus members could not readily recall the name of the strategic initiative, sometimes referring to it as *The President's Plan* or saying, "What'd she call it? Thing of Work?" The plan itself did not conjure up a feeling of solidarity or ownership among campus members. Although Pauldine talked the frame, the formalized way in which she did so may have prevented some campus members from seeing their own contributions to the plan and did not allow enough dialogue to create shared meaning.

President Hammond talked the frame in a different way, relying on small-group meetings to frame messages. A faculty member at Strategic Community College shared, "We have the Vision Shared Meeting every Monday, and then every other week we have Learning Services Council and that includes all of instruction, chairs, deans, vice presidents, directors of our off-campus sites, and support office representatives." Another faculty member underscored the importance of talking about the campus vision by stating, "Often what seems to be the safest way is a meeting with all people because you can be assured they get the same type of message." Thus, by talking about Hammond's message at many different meetings, the college community arrived at a shared understanding of the actions that needed to be taken.

## Walking the Frame

Another method of conveying a particular message is to *walk the frame*. Campus leaders and their emissaries can do this by acting in ways that are consistent with the leader's message and through leading by example. Walking the frame occurs in informal, casual conversations with college presidents and others carrying the message, both on campus and off campus, with the ultimate outcome of getting the framing message out in the trenches. For President Simon at Rogue Community College, open communication among all levels of campus constituents was an important goal and one he worked hard to convey to faculty and staff. He felt that creating personal connections with campus members was a critical part of his job; being approachable was a critical leadership attribute. In order to walk this frame, Simon said, "I set up private meetings with everybody who works here. So all the employees get to visit with me—I don't really have an agenda. They can talk about their work, they can talk about their families, whatever they want to do. Each meeting is about 15, 20, 30 minutes. It's very important for me to get to know everybody." These meetings helped Simon effectively walk the frame he wanted to convey: that open communication is important and necessary on campus.

Being available and present to campus members sends a strong message from the president. Presidents who are perceived as less accessible may not be considered by campus members as understanding the real needs of campus stakeholders and hence have less of a connection when trying to frame events.

President Williams believed in the importance of establishing relationships. According to a faculty member, "If I had to describe Shawn, I would say he uses his personality, his personal relationships with people. He believes in getting out and being visible. He's an extremely dynamic speaker and that energy comes through when he's addressing the faculty." Similar recounting was noted by faculty and administrators at Technology Community College about President Jones. Staff commented how common it was to see him "out and about" on the campus and at events. These chance encounters underscore the connection the president has with the campus and provide a leader with yet another opportunity to build relationships and influence campus opinions. The random interactions the president encounters on campus are more or less accepted by staff depending on established relationships and past experiences. For instance, faculty may think a president is coming to "check up on them" if walking about campus and interacting with staff are infrequent or correspond with other events, such as accreditation visits, negotiations, or rumors of staff reductions.

## Writing the Frame

Yet another method for communicating a message to campus constituents involves *writing the frame*. Presidents and their messengers can use written policies, reports, strategic plans, memos, meeting notes, web postings, or e-mails to inform college members of current events and provide new information about campus decisions and requirements. Formal ways of writing the frame include written policies, reports, and strategic plans. Leaders who are more comfortable in structured or hierarchical environments may prefer to write the frame using these more formal forms of communication.

Other leaders may prefer to communicate with the campus community through more informal venues, including e-mails, blogs, wikis, and web sites. As President Jones shared, "I try to send periodic e-mails; I call them Presidential Ramblings. I just ramble about the things that are going on." This informal format aligns well with his more fluid communication preferences. President Pauldine also sends out campus e-mails, but hers tend to be more formal and underscore points she wants to reiterate about the campus strategic plan. President Hammond may be an unusual leader because he effectively writes the frame in both formal and informal ways. In addition to his little red book that formally describes the college's strategic plan and the college vision pamphlet, he also writes news articles for the local paper and scripts for the college television station.

Because getting large groups together can be difficult on community college campuses, memos can be an effective means of getting messages out to faculty and staff. Indeed, some people prefer to receive information in a written format so that they can review new initiatives at their own speed and have time to repeatedly read the material. Sending out detailed plans in this manner and keeping policies and plans posted on the college web site can help communicate a leader's message to campus members. However, making information available does not ensure that staff actually read the material (recall the staff at Hunkering Down Community College who could not recall the name of Pauldine's strategic initiative).

Enlisting other campus constituents to help write the frame can help cement a president's vision for the future and drive home a particular message. One faculty member at the newly established Cutting Edge Community College discussed how written communication had benefited the campus, particularly its understanding of learning communities. She stated, "There is more in writing about the problematic initiatives and startups so that there's not this wishy-washy perception of what a learning community is. We're doing white papers—they're faculty driven for the most part—well, some are faculty driven; some are administrative driven only because they were here beforehand and they spent a lot of time up front, I think, really thinking about what they want the district to be." At Cutting Edge, both faculty and administrators were engaged in writing about the new campus's goals and challenges, which ultimately helped them come together with a unified vision of the institution and its mission.

Writing the frame may be an especially effective method of communicating on campus when a leader is less skilled in talking the frame. As an example, the director of public relations at Bifurcated Community College discussed President Fields, saying, "She's very shy, and so many times I've tried to encourage her to take doughnuts to staff meetings and just try to get to know people. I think that it has been somewhat unfortunate because people haven't gotten to see what a wonderful person she is, because she hasn't had the personality to go and sit in on staff meetings, and by the other side of it hasn't been able to have regular conversations with a lot of people, or hasn't chosen to have." Fields knows where her strengths lie. As she stated, "Well, I write, obviously, and that seems to work for this group. There is an essay on the web site on the President's Page on workforce education, so that's a mechanism I use." Although Fields relies on her communication strengths, focusing on writing the frame, she may benefit from using messengers to talk and walk the frame for her, as relying on one form of getting messages out at the expense of others can result in an inability to reach some campus members who prefer to learn about issues in particular ways.

### Symbolizing the Frame

Finally, leaders can communicate information to their constituents by *symbolizing the frame*. By using particular symbols, either literal or metaphorical, presidents can provide faculty and staff with a particular lens for understanding the president's vision, an interpretation of the campus mission, or ideas for organizational change. Some presidents used symbolism intentionally and were comfortable doing so, but others missed opportunities to get their messages across because they did not engage in symbolizing the frame.

President Hammond was adept at using symbolism and sought out occasions such as his weekly television show on the college station to highlight campus events. Similarly, President Jones called attention to issues he wanted to highlight (in particular the restoration or renovation of campus facilities) by hosting meetings and forums in new campus buildings. As one campus member noted, "The reason [that morale is so high] is that we have so much going on in terms of new buildings. We opened four new buildings, and that in itself gets you all charged up." By holding meetings in strategic locations, Jones leveraged the completion of new facilities in order to symbolize forward movement of the college.

Campus stories are a central component of symbolizing the frame. Stories told by the president or campus members to one another are a means of passing along information on campus. As well, when new presidents can clearly communicate an understanding of long-standing college stories or sagas, they are more likely to be judged positively by campus constituents. This was particularly true when a new president communicated to faculty and staff that, unlike the previous leader, she would not operate in an autocratic way. For instance, at Hunkering Down Community College, one of the previous presidents would sit in his office with the blinds drawn, personifying a recluse who was not connected to the campus. Because President Pauldine understood how the former president's actions had affected faculty and staff, she acted in a different way, effectively conveying the message that a new era of leadership had arrived.

Clark (1972) wrote about the importance of the institutional saga on college campuses. The stories recounted by leaders help define campus culture and in turn help presidents frame their messages. At Cutting Edge Community College, President Burke continually underscored the ideal of equity among students and staff in the learning process. In order to symbolize the frame, she "decided that there would be no reserved parking because we believe that students are as important as faculty and administrators." Although this act symbolized to students that they are at the center of the college, some faculty felt that their status had been devalued. This example illustrates the necessity of using more than one method of getting a message across. Symbolizing the frame worked for the students, but Burke and her administrators also needed to communicate with faculty about how they arrived at this decision so that the faculty did not feel less valued. Perhaps if the administration had more clearly framed the decision for staff, talking explicitly about how unreserved parking benefits a culture of student-centered learning, they would not have received push-back. Clearly, talking the frame, walking the frame, writing the frame, and symbolizing the frame are all important ways to get a message across to campus constituents. One method may be more appropriate than another at any given time, and sometimes a leader and his or her messengers should use more than one method (or even all four) to ensure that faculty and staff understand new information from the perspective that the leader feels would most benefit the campus. The following section takes what we have learned about communicating and framing information on campus and applies it to this book's conception of multidimensional leadership.

## Communicating as an Element of Multidimensional Leadership

Communicating with the campus community—in particular, conveying certain messages and visions for the future—is essential for a community college leader and is an important element of multidimensional leadership. As we think about how communication and framing relate to the multidimensional model of leadership proposed in this book, it is helpful to explore the three major ways in which the presidents framed and communicated information on their campuses: visionary framing, step-by-step framing, and connective framing. Each of these methods can be represented in the multidimensional model by what is highlighted when communicating on campus and the links to a leader's approach to leading. These shifts convey changes regarding both expertise in relating to others and depth of experience. Likewise, individuals may shift their location along the continuum of communication from closed communication to more open communication. For instance, through experience and feedback, a leader may shift from an autocratic, hierarchical mode of communication to an inclusive and multifaceted mode that captures campus feedback and makes adjustments. As with other aspects of leadership, as individuals learn more about themselves and, through experience, what works on campus, they can begin to shift their mental maps of how they communicate. Here you see development from novice communicator to expert.

### Visionary Framing

Some leaders focus campus members' attention on the college's future and possibilities rather than the current state of the campus. Visionary framing relates to the final property of Weick's (1995) sensemaking model—namely, framing information in terms of plausible (as opposed to accurate or current) outcomes. Framing information in a visionary way requires college leaders to operate on the cusp of uncertainty (Morgan, 2006) but may be especially useful in turbulent and uncertain times because it allows followers to focus on the college's possibilities rather than its realities. Framing a vision requires extensive verbal, nonverbal, and written communication, but communicating through symbolism can be especially effective.

President Hammond was successful in framing and communicating his vision for Strategic Community College largely because he was an adept symbolic framer. This helped faculty and staff relate to him and his goals, which translated into greater support for his vision. As one faculty member stated, "My second semester I started listening to what the president was saying, to his vision, and I thought, 'Wow, I can really identify with this person. We have the same values about education and where he sees the college wanting to go.' I got excited—this is someone who is not just taking a job; he's got a vision and direction as to where he wants to go with the college!" Hammond was especially successful in framing his vision for the college because he asked for input and listened closely to others' advice. Another faculty member touched on this point, adding, "President Hammond talks to different people according to where their expertise is and then makes the best decision he feels is appropriate to direct us in the right way." Even though Hammond had developed his own vision for the college, he ensured buy-in from campus members, his leadership team, and external stakeholders by allowing them to have a voice in the process.

President Jones also successfully framed his ideas for change at Technology Community College, in particular his ideas for a technologically integrated, student-centered campus. As one long-serving faculty member stated, "He's probably the closest to a visionary I've seen in many years, the first one that I've seen on this campus in 22 years. He's visionary. He has ideas. Some of his ideas include putting a telephone in every student's hand, and those kind of things were well received."

As Jones's vision for TCC started to become a reality, he found it even easier to frame and communicate his ideas and receive acceptance from campus constituents. As he shared, "You know we were ranked nationally as the most wired campus. The first time that happened, I think people were in a state of shock. Now we just got it again, and that's something they never envisioned. It's a national ranking by an outside organization and it's phenomenal. Being written up in the *Chronicle of Higher Education*, being recognized as being very technical. The campus believes that now. They believe we are the most technical campus around. The third and fourth phase of our plan goes into effect next year, and they just sort of look at me and shake their heads. This concept of understanding the application of technology and it being integrated throughout the classroom activities and student life on this campus is pervasive. They understand that. That's been accomplished." Although campus constituents at TCC were initially skeptical about the integration of technology, the outside recognition and the continued messages from Jones about how technology was the future helped the faculty claim his vision as their own. His visionary framing focused their attention on the future, and at the same time he worked behind the scenes to put together the structures necessary to support the vision.

In a multidimensional leadership model, visionary framing is represented by a fluidity in processing information for campus members. Communication is adaptable and flexible. The leader has the flexibility to create the message needed for the varied stakeholder preferences. Corresponding to this adaptability is a location on the communication continuum that allows for the greatest level of campus input. The greater the opportunities for interactions with stakeholders, the more opportunity the leader has to create a vision of the future. Increased feedback loops also provide leaders with a chance to frame their visionary message based on the current campus mind-set.

## Step-by-Step Framing

Not all leaders are adept at framing information in a way that is visionary. Indeed, although most community college presidents have ideas about what they would like their college to look like in the future, many find it easier to focus their own attention (and that of campus constituents) on the immediate next steps to accomplishing the longer-range goals. Although this framing method can be effective in moving the college along, leaders sometimes forget to remind campus members of the final destination—the reasons why they are doing what they are doing. Nonetheless, framing information in a step-by-step manner can still lead to successful campus ventures.

President Pauldine at Hunkering Down Community College provides an excellent example of a leader who frames and communicates information in a step-by-step manner. She inherited a campus with serious issues, including low enrollment, revenue losses in auxiliary services, debt from a failed venture, and overspending of scholarships relative to foundation income. By communicating the immediate next steps to fixing these problems, Pauldine succeeded in remedying three of the four issues she faced within 2 years. However, although her leadership staff knew of this progress, the overall campus did not. Moreover, even as Pauldine spoke frequently about her eight-step Program of Work, some campus members did not make the connections between their contributions during breakout sessions and small-group meetings and campus progress toward its goals. Ultimately, although Pauldine moved her campus forward, campus constituents lost focus on her overall vision for the future.

Focusing on immediate needs and celebrating short-term successes can be enormously helpful in systematically moving a college campus toward a president's vision. However, campus leaders must continually work to help faculty and staff make sense of that forward progress and remind them how each step contributes to the overall vision. In the multidimensional model, this step-by-step framing can be portrayed by less flexibility in communication. As individual leaders gain experience and their models become more complex, forms and approaches to communication expand, allowing for better matches of the president's message and the interpretation of the message. Each successful incremental step to improve communication may also shift an individual along the communication continuum, resulting in increases in the ways in which he or she communicates on campus and creating a more open communication forum on campus.

## Connective Framing

Leaders who frame information in a connective manner create a reality in which the campus learns and grows together (Fairhurst, 2001). These leaders work closely with campus members to create and communicate a vision for the institution. Connective framers often rely on connected ways of knowing (Belenky, Clinchy, Goldberger, & Tarule, 1997) and emphasize understanding, empathy, acceptance, and collaboration. Often connective framers are transformational leaders who prioritize dialogue. Connective framers work collaboratively with constituents across campus and frame issues from multiple perspectives so that campus members can see not only the next steps but also the future direction of the college. Sensemaking is therefore central to connective framing.

According to Birnbaum (1988), framing information in a connective way "means providing forums for interaction in which the 'negotiations' that determine reality can be carried out, making more explicit the assumptions behind present rules and ongoing processes so that they can be accepted or challenged, and giving prominence to certain activities that can serve as attention cues for others in the institution" (p. 78). Connective framing provides opportunities for dialogue and allows leaders and followers to together determine what assumptions they bring to the table and discuss how these help or hinder the forward movement of the college.

President Burke is an example of a connective framer. Because Cutting Edge Community College was a new college, there were many opportunities to build the college into an institution that valued and prioritized student learning. As President Burke reflected, "The vision came out of the ability to build a college from scratch in the 21st century, taking best practice of everything we all wish we could do but can't because there's always limitations either by organizations or by people you have employed, or by habit, or by physical plant." The organizing team spent a great deal of time talking about how they wanted to make the college operate in a different way from "traditional" colleges. The leadership team sought to intentionally capture the recommendations of all the initial task force teams so that a diversity of voices were heard as the college was being created.

So that CECC maintained some consistency with the larger institutional history and saga of the district, Chancellor Pioneer required Burke to hire 50% of her staff from within the district. Thus, Burke saw her job as being "to keep the collaborative process on track and make sure we get the outcome, we communicate the outcomes, and that we involve the people." Consensus building was at the center of Burke's connective framing process.

Another element at the core of connective framing is making information abundant across all levels of the campus. Transparency in communication and in decision making allows individual campus members to feel part of the process. President Simon described the changes he implemented at Rogue Community College and the connective ways in which he worked to build a jointly created culture. He stated, "These people don't really know how to make group decisions. They know how to make decisions in their own particular area and they know how to carry out decisions that have been given to them, but they have never been part of a decision-making process in any real way and they're not used to making decisions as a group. We had to take a 3% cut to this year's budget. They brought those decisions to the table. Before it was a game of conceal and hope they don't find you and when they do, you give it up. Now, they had to do the opposite. They had to go round and round the table until we reached that amount of money. People were starting to collaborate with each other; they would say, 'Well, I can give up something here' and 'You shouldn't have to do that, that's too important.' Everybody felt really good about that meeting." By framing the budget cuts in a connective manner, Simon helped the campus come to a consensus on how and where to make the cuts.

In a multidimensional model, connective framing is evident through communication adaptability, resulting in changes based on feedback. Here adaptability and flexibility are different from that in visionary framing. Instead of a focus on reporting the leaders' vision to best match the campus stakeholders, campus members are intricately tied to the formation of the framing message and can readily identify their contributions. Only through joint creation of plans using dialogue is a final approach formed. Within the communication function in multidimensional leadership, it is not only the president's perspective that helps guide forms of communication, but also the reliance on campus dialogue and input. Leaders operating from a connective perspective use the star model of communicating, adjusting actions based on these interactions because connective leaders don't simply rely on their own thoughts and orientations, but rather take into consideration a wide array of perspectives. Thus their leadership occurs in many ways through the facilitation of dialogue on campus. Therefore, connective leaders must be skilled in communicating in multiple formats (walking the frame, talking the frame, etc.).

Regardless of the mode of communication, framing meaning for campus members is a central component of multidimensional leadership. Communication acts as the linchpin to other actions on campus, reinforcing planning efforts, decisions, and actions. How leaders communicate is based on their own preferences, but adeptness at multiple forms of getting the message to campus members ensures that more stakeholders hear the message and make sense out of campus priorities. Leaders have great power in managing meaning on campus and can use the various communication venues to their advantage in moving their campuses forward.

# 5

# LEADERSHIP COMPETENCIES

Leaders are more powerful role models when
they learn than when they teach.

Rosabeth Moss Kantor

When viewed from a multidimensional perspective, successful
community college leadership requires a variety of competencies—some skill based, some personality based, and others
learned through years on the job. Leadership takes place in the context of a
larger organizational structure, making an understanding of the theoretical
underpinnings of the organization critical to interpreting how the various
competencies are enacted. This chapter discusses several competencies shown
to be integral to successful community college leadership, whereas discussion
of organizational theory is found in Appendix A. In particular, the chapter
explores the voices and experiences of the nine primary presidents in this
study (as well as the additional presidents of color) as they pertain to each of
the six competencies identified by the American Association of Community
Colleges (AACC). The chapter then discusses the role of cultural competency in community college leadership and concludes with an analysis of
how specific competencies—cultural competency in particular—contribute
to multidimensional leadership.

## AACC's List of Six Competencies

In 2005, AACC created a set of six competencies central to community college
leadership as part of its Leading Forward initiative, which addressed pending
turnovers in leadership. The intent of this list was to give up-and-coming
leaders a template of the skills and attributes that current leaders and scholars
found important in high-level positions. Even though the listing is finite,

AACC's intention was not to be limiting, but rather to provide a starting point for leadership development. The Leading Forward initiative recognized that learning is a lifelong endeavor, and thus a lifelong learning philosophy underlies the entire competency framework. Each of the six competencies is broadly defined and begins to move beyond mere leadership traits, although one must remember that at its core, this list of competencies is just that: a list. Approaching the competencies as a checklist of skills to acquire or master runs the risk of minimizing the dynamic nature of leadership required to lead in complex times. Nonetheless, AACC's list of competencies can be useful to prospective community college leaders and those interested in leadership development. The following sections illustrate the ways in which the presidents in this study enacted the six competencies on their campuses.

## *Organizational Strategy*

Skills in organizational strategy are critical to community college operations as these institutions become more complex. AACC defines a leader competent in organizational strategy as one who "strategically improves the quality of the institution, protects the long-term health of the organization, promotes the success of all students, and sustains the community college mission, based on knowledge of the organization, its environment, and future trends" (American Association of Community Colleges [AACC], 2005, p. 3). This competency is primarily concerned with management issues associated with operations, human resources, and strategy, which when done well can lead to the creation of a positive culture and work environment.

Organizational structure was often one of the initial areas addressed by the presidents when they first arrived on campus. The Large and Growing Community College District implemented a districtwide change in the reporting structure for deans that filtered down to each of the five individual campuses, whereas President Fields (BCC) and President Pauldine (HDCC) both shifted their reporting structures to rely on a stricter hierarchy. President Jones (TCC) and President Hammond (SCC) were not concerned with the organizational reporting structure and instead focused their energy on strategic planning.

Typical strategic planning on campus involves developing a long-range planning document with a finite number of goals. These goals can be presented to the campus community at large and reinforced in periodic campus updates. Because the planning documents are a critical linchpin to campus activity, leaders must consider both how they are created and how they are put in motion. Central to the development of strategic planning at Technology Community College was the co-creation of the plans. President Jones reflected, "Our strategic planning sessions were interactive, more of a dialogue and smaller groups in the summer and in the beginning and end of summer. Those were more effective to try to sort out the problems and to sift through all of the stuff so that the more generally agreed-upon ideas surfaced. Then it was my job to put that into context: read it and study it, reorganize it, and then be able to communicate it succinctly and directly, one-on-one, and in presentations. 'This is the strategic plan. You've been involved in it. This is where I want to go. I want you to go there with me. I can't go there by myself and I'm asking you to support this and to buy into this. And I want your feedback on this stuff. My interpretation of all the information we shared.' And then it would come back in an e-mail, but that was the presentation. Then we translated that into an operational plan." Key to the competency of organizational strategy is the connection between strategy and outcomes. Jones was clear on his role as the leader in the process of filtering campus members' ideas and contextualizing them with other college plans. He communicated that this was not merely a plan he invented, but rather what the campus said they wanted.

The creation of Cutting Edge Community College involved an organizational strategy that allowed for the incorporation of new ideas and concepts, while still retaining close ties to the culture of the Large and Growing Community College District. President Burke reflected that the physical campus "was built from our desire to create a different set of skills to prepare students for a changing world. It all leads back into that end result of having a higher emphasis on active collaborative learning and then all of what that means in terms of organization and physical plant." The focus on strategy and ties to the mission called on Burke's organizational strategy competency. The president posed questions such as, "If we think students are going to need the ability to change rapidly to adjust to new jobs and careers and to have all those kinds of skills, then what kind of a learning environment do we have to have? If we want that kind of a learning environment, then what kind of an organizational structure do we have to have?" The answers to these questions helped shape the structure and strategies employed at the college.

Clearly, planning and organizational strategy is a cornerstone of the work for all the presidents in this study. However, how they chose to develop and implement the strategic plans varied. For the most part, campuswide involvement was used to identify future directions and to establish goals. Implementation of the plans occurred through constant reference to the goals and the progress being made, through meeting the strategic objectives, and through more subtle references to planning documents. In all cases, organizational planning was affected by both the existing culture of the college and the background of the president.

## Resource Management

Closely tied to organizational strategy is the way in which resources are managed. The fiscal health of a college underpins the opportunities it can provide to students, community members, and staff. AACC outlined this competency as follows: "An effective community college leader equitably and ethically sustains people, processes, and information as well as physical and financial assets to fulfill the mission, vision, and goals of the community college" (AACC, 2005, p. 3). Noteworthy in this competency is the intersection of resource management with ethical leadership, implying that ethical leadership applies not only to resource issues, but also to other forms of decision making (Hellmich, 2007; Kezar, Carducci, & Contreras-McGavin, 2006). Included within this competency is the ability to manage administrative services and personnel efficiently and the ability to ensure optimal funding allocations to match strategic priorities. Ensuring clear accountability in record keeping is also central to this competency. Additionally, this competency covers the critical need for community college leaders to seek alternative funding sources, given the continued decrease in state funding for the institutions. Recent job postings for community college presidents emphasize the need for fund-raising and development expertise (Leist, 2007).

Links between planning efforts and acquiring or maintaining the resources required to fulfill them were evident in interviews with the presidents in this study. All of the presidents referred to the challenges of fulfilling their expanding missions at the same time that state support was decreasing. How the leaders addressed these resource dilemmas, however, differed. At Technology Community College, President Jones felt the impact of a strained budget but framed the situation positively. He did not point out the dire straits when communicating with campus members; instead his message focused on the future. He took an entrepreneurial approach to resource development. Jones stated, "They can't believe we're building barns and building buildings and so forth without any money: 'How are you doing this?' Well, I'm paying for it out of the milk check. Or I'm paying for it out of the revenue for the horses or I'm paying for it out of the revenue from the automotive program. 'Well, how can you do that?' Well, it's a business

LEADERSHIP COMPETENCIES     *95*

plan. We borrowed money against anticipated revenue." His approach was business oriented. He borrowed money to start businesses on campus versus waiting for state funding. He stated his focus as follows: "I've got to raise more funds outside of traditional means, and really finding ways to improve the economic development of this region. Growing business right here." Jones emphasized the need to develop the region and its economy because the college and community were so intractably linked. This type of creative systems approach to resource management was paying off at Technology Community College.

Less funding at Rogue Community College meant that college leaders needed to reconsider operations and past practices and become creative in coming up with alternative solutions. As President Simon reflected, "Focusing on dealing with the budget crises in such a way that everybody is kind of focusing on a bigger picture, not just the 'oh poor me, they took my money away and I can't travel' but the fact that we have an important job to do and the college needs us, we're going to serve our students and so forth." Rogue Community College focused on the college's mission of serving and educating students despite a reduction in financial resources. The college also prioritized the college's ethical obligation to the community, but doing so meant making hard decisions about how to allocate resources and what missions to prioritize at any given time.

All community college leaders must deal with resource constraints, and skills in this competency area are often used every day. As President Pauldine noted, "We haven't had a tuition increase in 6 years, and it's when the political climate is accepting of the tuition increases that you get a big whopping raise and then you have to live with that for an indeterminate period of time. So in terms of meeting inflation costs or growing, it's very difficult without extensive external resources. And [for] a campus of this size and in this location with this mission, that is a big challenge." Living within a budget often means that the campus must limit its plans for growth if it is to meet built-in cost increases for staffing and operations. How each president communicated and framed these issues on campus affected campus reactions. President Garvey noted, "My role is to probably help people here understand that even though we've got to tighten our belt and we're having to do these undesirable things, it's going to be okay. . . . You know, if we stay the course then probably it will be okay on the other side. Well, I think that's the same thing we're facing here, is to reassure people that even though we have to make some changes, we'll rebound and get back on course."

Reassuring campus constituents that things will be all right communicated a focus and commitment to sustaining the college mission.

## *Communication*

Communication within a college and with external stakeholders is a central competency for community college leaders (the topic of communication was comprehensively reviewed in chapter 4 of this book). According to AACC (2005), "An effective community college leader uses clear listening, speaking, and writing skills to engage in honest, open dialogue at all levels of the college and its surrounding community, to promote the success of all students, and to sustain the community college mission" (p. 6). A college president—who must often take the role of chief communicator—must listen to campus feedback and clearly articulate the college's vision and strategies to fulfill it. Key to effective campus communication is the use not only of typical verbal communication routes, but also of nonverbal methods of communicating on campus (such as the use of logos, taking away reserved parking for faculty, and location of campus meetings).

Communicating with campus stakeholders begins during the interview process. Interactions with the search committee, with faculty and staff in campus forums, and with students all set the stage for expectations when the new leader arrives on campus. President Williams related how he engaged with some students during his campus tour: "I stopped the students and started talking to them. I guess the chancellor noticed that I was able to strike up a conversation with total strangers who are students here. That must have been something positive." Some conversations can serve as clues about the campus culture and dynamics. President Fields recounted conversations that occurred during her interview: "But there are issues that, frankly, people would say things like, uh, 'How did the meeting go with the [branch] faculty?' This from a board member during my interview. I'd say, 'Oh, fine.' And I can remember this regent saying, 'Oh, that's great. That's a relief.' What's he saying?" In retrospect, Fields understood the board member's message more clearly as she came to realize the divide on her campus between the main campus and the branch campuses. The message sent during the interview was subtle but proved to be the basis of a key issue she faced when arriving on campus.

Effective communication on campus also requires taking a systems perspective. As previously noted, the presidents in this study employed a variety of communication styles, including talking with individuals and groups, writing strategic plans and receiving feedback, and communicating by non-verbal symbols. Often, they employed more than one communication strategy at a time. President Williams stated, "Sometimes you have to put four, five, six pieces together. You talk to different people and then you put it all together." In particular, seeking out divergent voices and ideas can help create a fuller picture of campus life. The presidents in this study were drawn to a particular form of communicating, but when they used multiple forms to reach people, they were more successful in getting their message across.

## Collaboration

Increasingly, colleges are called on to partner with others to achieve mutual goals. Collaboration, however, also includes working within the college in a collegial and complementary fashion. AACC (2005) defines an effective community college collaborator as one who "develops and maintains responsive, cooperative, mutually beneficial, and ethical internal and external relationships that nurture diversity, promote the success of all students, and sustain the community college mission" (p. 6). The abilities to include all constituents and create win-win partnerships are important attributes for community college leaders. Often overlooked in discussions about collaboration, however, are power differentials between partnering groups that may undermine cooperative efforts. Leaders need to be adept at negotiating between parties and developing trusting relationships that foster collaborations. Internally, the key stakeholders are students, faculty, and staff. Externally, partners may include community leaders, other colleges, and public school systems. State policy makers are increasingly turning toward P–16 educational systems to encourage collaboration among schools, colleges, and universities.

President Fields faced challenges related to internal collaboration when she started on campus. She stated, "All these deans had carved off their little fiefdoms. And they were all fighting with one another and their staff were fighting with one another. So there was no collegelike cohesion." In October of her first year, the first draft of her college's self-study was completed. She reflected, "It's not that long, but it's a zinger. Allegations of nepotism, misleading advertising, schedules that are not reliable, cancellation of elective courses needed for graduation because of low enrollment. . . . This is the first inclination I've had or intimation that I've had that anything is seriously wrong." Shortly after the report was released, Fields attended a faculty senate meeting. She stated, "I had a pretty frank conversation with that senate, and I wanted to know why it is that everyone here seems to be fighting with everybody else. . . . One of the senators . . . said to me, 'You need to think about this as abuse, formerly abused children. We have a lot suspicion and a lot of hostility toward administration.' Wow! So that was quite a story." Before internal collaboration could occur, Fields needed to facilitate a great deal of fence mending among the faculty and between faculty and administrators.

The presidents also engaged in external collaborations. President Pauldine recounted a new program in Hunkering Down Community College's nursing department: "They did a partnership at [a company] in [a nearby city], which is affiliated with [a major city] University. Very innovative partnership where the tuition is scholarship and [the company] guarantees employment for them. I mean just some really innovative stuff." The ability to partner with 4-year universities and companies provides increased opportunities for revenue enhancement and ensures access for a broader range of students. Hunkering Down Community College is also involved in another academic collaboration. "We're doing a very unusual partnership with [another] community college in hospitality. It's a model for the state. We actually shared paying a faculty member, and we're offering baccalaureate courses on their campus." This partnership with another community college resulted in benefits to the larger community.

In the end, the success of a collaboration is highly dependent on the actions of college constituents. President Hammond noted, "The process of being visionary and leading—it's very difficult for that to occur unless you've got people in the organization who are competent managers within the organization." Group efforts help move a vision forward. Hammond added, "Learning systems must facilitate change. There had been more change in the last 10 years in community colleges. We're assessing more information. Fiscal resources must be leveraged if you're going to survive. The staff must work as a team. . . . It's a learning consortium here." Hammond viewed collaboration through a lens of learning, complete with feedback loops to help guide change.

### Community College Advocacy

Community colleges have a unique location in the higher education system that often subjects them to greater budget cuts and higher expectations. Therefore, leaders are often called on to be advocates for their colleges. In recognition of this, AACC (2005) defines an effective community college leader as one who "understands, commits to, and advocates for the mission, vision, and goals of the community college" (p. 6). Promoting the open-access mission of the college and its focus on teaching and learning are central to community college advocacy. Leaders advocate by attending community events and participating in state and national policy forums. Depending on the state's structure, community college leaders may operate independently or within a coordinating board. Leaders who keep the needs of their college at the forefront of policy discussions are more successful in garnering financial and other forms of support.

Of all the colleges in this study, advocacy was most prevalent in the founding of Cutting Edge Community College. To begin, the area where the college is located was not included in the Large and Growing Community College District's service area (it was not in *any* district's area!). Thus, students from that community always had to pay out-of-district tuition. In 2000, voters in the area launched a petition drive to choose a community college district, and the resulting referendum resulted in the community affiliating themselves with the Large and Growing Community College District. President Burke recounted, "[The referendum] passed 75 to 25. We had strong community support. Three months later, the community passed in our district, the whole district, all 11 school districts [and] passed [a] $197 million bond issue, $90 million [of] which was designated to build Cutting Edge Community College." Advocacy paid off with the funding to construct the new college and to include the area in the Large and Growing Community College District, resulting in students now paying in-district tuition.

President Jones was intentional in advocating the mission and vision of Technical Community College within the surrounding community. He noted, "The college typically views itself as being apart from the region, and I'm trying to build the image within the minds of our faculty and staff that we are the region. And without us, it will not change. Therefore we have to lead change in this region. And that principally will come through economic development. Jobs. Businesses. Let's grow businesses. It's going to be difficult to attract them here." By advocating the college's mission for community development, Jones secured local support for his initiatives.

Advocacy is inexorably linked with several of the other AACC competencies, including communication and organizational strategy. Indeed, community college presidents often find it hard to step out of the advocacy role; a leader often serves as a constant representative of his or her college. This role came as a surprise to President Pauldine. She mused, "Well, on a personal note, that means there's no anonymity for me in the community. And that was something that was kind of a surprise to me. Something that I had not been prepared for in any way. It's not that I need to be anonymous, but you run out in your jeans and sweatshirt to get something for dinner and somebody talks to you about an issue on campus. Or I'm trying to learn to play golf . . . because of the golf course on campus. But, you know, I'll go down to the golf course to have a lesson and four or five people buttonhole me about this problem or that problem and so it's a small fishbowl! And that wasn't something I had really thought about all that much." Clearly, all conversations a president has with internal or external constituents, even those that occur in a grocery store or on the golf course, provide opportunities to advocate for the college and its mission.

## Professionalism

The ways in which community college leaders serve as role models for others and how they represent their colleges—in other words, their professionalism—is key to their leadership effectiveness. This responsibility is more complex for leaders of color and women because they also represent their race, gender, or ethnicity. Female or non-White leaders often take an active role in mentoring others and sharing tips on what worked for them as they navigated the community college leadership hierarchy. As AACC (2005) states, "An effective community college leader works ethically to set high standards for self and others, continuously improve self and surroundings, demonstrate accountability to and for the institution, and ensure the long-term viability of the college and community" (p. 6). Key to a community college leader's professionalism is transformational leadership, an ability to assess one's own performance and identify areas of self-improvement, and an acknowledgment of the need for work-life integration and balance. Leaders are also expected to give back to the profession by participating in professional development programs and taking on leadership roles within community college associations.

Several of the presidents interviewed for this book instituted mentoring programs on their colleges. President Hammond noted his role as a mentor based on his wide range of experiences. He offered, "People basically know that Dr. Hammond knows this business." He added, "You need to let people know the expectations if you're going to work successfully within this team." By modeling his expectations of others, he helped others develop and expand their own leadership skill sets. Similarly, President Williams reflected, "My hope is that I'm modeling a certain behavior. That people can learn from me whether it's through a formal or informal mentoring system."

All of the leaders noted a responsibility for fostering development of the next generation of community college leaders. Some did this more formally, like President Hammond, whereas others did this more informally. An additional interview with a female minority president addressed the role of mentoring in preparation for entering the corner office. She advised, "Develop a confidence that you can do it. I think White males are raised that way. I think it is a kind of entitlement. I've never been in a position to feel or think I can achieve just because it's an entitlement; I've had to work for everything." This same president added, "I want women of color to know that they can do it too. They've got to develop those survival skills. Being there [in the president's office] is important to me. I hesitate to retire because who is going to replace me? Who is going to replace me as the placeholder? I am the only African American female president in [the state]. As soon as I retire I will be replaced by someone who will not look like me. Who will carry the torch? In every position I've had, I was a placeholder—I was a torch." For this president, mentoring others who can represent women and leaders of color in top offices was a key element of her professionalism.

When asked what resources they drew on in their leadership, many of the leaders interviewed for this book referred to their professional networks. President Burke noted that the networks she developed through AACC trainings and conferences supported her ongoing learning and professionalism. President Hales reflected on how important it is to gain a wider perspective of organizational operations. Hales increased her professionalism by continuously getting off campus to see other operations and networking with a broad range of individuals. Similarly, President Pauldine spent time consulting at colleges across the country on recruitment and retention. She noted, "This kind of gave me a chance to do some professional development and to enhance my skills and really, in terms of being a president, prepared me in a lot of ways that working as an administrator at a single campus could not have." Pauldine's experience outside her own campus provided essential opportunities for professional development; other leaders learned by serving on accreditation teams or national committees or by keeping up broad networks across the country.

## Cultural Competency

In addition to the six competencies identified by AACC, several scholars have suggested that cultural competency is also essential for presidents and other leaders of community colleges (Amey, 1992, 2005; Eddy, 2009; Kezar et al., 2006). Here, cultural competency is defined as the ability to understand an organization's culture—what is valued, how traditions influence operations, and how symbolism is used to reinforce actions (Rhoads & Tierney, 1992). If new leaders are to ultimately put their own stamp on the culture of a college, they must first scan their college setting to understand what is valued and operate in a way that respects those values.

Even though the AACC competencies do not have a separate category for the role of culture per se, references to the role of culture are embedded within some of the illustrations of the six competencies. The examples highlight a focus on culture from three different perspectives. First, culture is an entity to assess and respond to with organizational strategies. Second, culture is something to embrace with respect to diversity and location within a global society. Finally, culture reflects and respects the history of the college. Traditionally, the culture of 2-year colleges is built on the mission of access, student-centeredness, and the ability to offer second chances to individuals. More recently, Levin (2005) argues that a business culture within community colleges takes precedent, focusing on efficiency over student learning and development. The increased attention on the role of community colleges in the educational pipeline and as an important lever for economic recovery underscores the business culture. The intersection of these competing notions of culture affects how leaders understand and develop cultural competency.

Throughout interviews with the presidents in this study, it was clear that a sense of initial "fit" between leader and college affected their perceived cultural capital years later. President Pauldine reflected, "You know, I had a good job, and I guess I'm a great believer in the goodness of fit between a presidency and a campus. I think it'll be interesting to see what other people think, but I guess I think they would say that the best way to characterize my candidacy was I was a really good fit for this campus." Campus members agreed. One vice president noted, "She's [a] very engaging, very energetic, knowledgeable person; to me [she] was exactly what we needed here. We needed someone who was a go-getter." Implied in statements that the president is a good fit is the sense that she "gets" the culture of the institution and can work within it.

Pauldine also discussed another opportunity where she did not feel a sense of connection with the campus culture. She stated, "I had been encouraged to apply at one college in [the state], and actually the president was retiring and he called and asked me to come up and consider it. And I drove up; I took a day of vacation and I drove there. And I just couldn't see myself in that environment at all. It just, it just didn't feel like a good fit. I don't know how else to describe it. I came back kind of discouraged and said, 'You know, maybe I don't really want to be a president, maybe I don't really want to do this!' [laugh]" In this instance, Pauldine did not feel aligned with the culture at this particular college and, as a result, did not feel prepared to take the leadership reins.

President Jones also compared offers before deciding to come to Technology Community College. He commented, "I had two other offers on the table at the time, and this was not the most financially attractive, in fact by a long shot, but it felt very good. The Ag component, my background—I was raised on a farm; I was heavily involved in that. I'm really into technology and computer applications and the like. I came here prepared to do a lot of that. I was up front about that. And, also I'm real keen on the whole concept of a diverse campus. And this campus has this mixture, this unbelievable mixture of students of color." Jones was up front about his desire to infuse a technical orientation to campus operations and academics. Indeed, he began framing his goals for the college even before arriving. One director recounted an instance from Jones's interview. He said, "I can remember even before [Jones] came, sitting in on a videoconference with him, and he asked the director of the computing center what type of coaxial cable she was rigging the dorms with, and she happened to mention something, and he goes, 'Well, you might want to try something else.' And I turned to the business officer and said, 'We're in trouble. We don't know anything about computers.' Jones seemed to know about everything. He knew financial aid. He knew computers. He knew the works. We were very impressed with the depth of his knowledge. And we haven't been disappointed yet." For his part, Jones felt that the campus was "ripe for change," that the context fit his personal background, and that it provided him with a chance to put his own stamp and vision on a campus culture that was willing to embrace his ideas.

The vice president of administration at Technology Community College commented on the cultural competency and fit that Jones brought to his candidacy. He stated, "It was that we were a technical campus and we got a guy who's a technical sort of a person. He's beyond that. He's the sort of guy who could give you a discourse on the history of the industrial revolution, tell you how it's changed society and give you a great speech about it for 2 hours. And then take a pair of wrenches out of his pocket and rebuild the internal combustion engine. And I've seen him do it; I know he can do it with outboard motors, for example. So he runs the entire gamut of theory and practice. So he's a fit. If you can't go along with him, there's something wrong with you. That's my own opinion. He's a lot of fun. We're having fun." The wide range of skills Jones brought to his position, as well as his background in technical and agricultural fields, allowed him to achieve changes on campus that might not have been possible if he had had less cultural competency.

Unlike Jones, President Fields had a rockier start at Bifurcated Community College. Even though she felt that the campus's location was personally satisfying, in her interview process she had missed signals about the culture of the institution. It was only in retrospect that she understood that a board member's comments clearly indicated a troubled campus. Fields was blunt in her assessment of cultural fit: "I like this community, but I didn't look closely enough at some of the problems the institution had. And I think that's a mistake that maybe that people might make in their first presidency." Change slowly occurred within the culture at BCC, however, partly in response to Fields's strategic plan and progress reports. Fields recounted, "I can remember one of my business faculty saying, and she's not someone who's always agreed with me, but she was saying, 'My feeling about this college has always been, we're like a family that never sits down and has dinner together. We're always doing other things. And so we never talk to one another, we're never together. And my feeling about transformation is suddenly somebody's saying, "We're going to eat a meal together, and we're going to talk."'" And that was her analogy. And I thought that captures it. That really does." Fields's efforts to build a more cohesive campus culture paid off but took time to implement. She added, "I mean, if a college could be said to be like a dysfunctional family, ya know, the kid who always marries the wrong person? He gets one divorce after another. This college is like that." Fields's ability to build cultural competence within her institution—despite the rough induction—was critical to her success in making changes in the college.

Presidents must also think about cultural fit within the greater community. One of the additional interviews conducted with a minority president highlighted how racism and sexism are still alive in the United States. She noted, "We were refused housing when we first moved here. We landed [in the state] and in 24 hours had a blatant housing discrimination case." The president's family were told they could not rent an apartment because of the color of their skin. In this case, a prominent college leader who was hired to lead an institution whose mission is to develop the community found herself in a region that did not welcome people like her. She needed to quickly develop and display a level of cultural competency that would allow her not only to navigate the internal campus climate, but also to deal with personal affronts in the community. She noted the need to "have thick skin" to manage. Helping to pave the way for other women of color was a strong motivator for this president and aided her in developing the competencies required to lead in a culture that was not always supportive of—and often demeaning to—her race.

As discussed in chapter 3, leaders have an underlying schema that influences how they see the world. Leaders come to know their college by viewing it through their past experiences. For instance, when President Jones first came to Technology Community College, he brought a focus on technology as a central part of his vision. Thus, the laptop programs initiated at TCC were similar to those Jones had started at his previous college. Similarly, President Hammond brought to Strategic Community College a lifelong learning model that he had used at his previous institution, and President Fields started an academic ladder program at Bifurcated Community College that she had developed while working as a vice president of academic affairs.

However, an important aspect of cultural competency is also the ability to respect campus traditions, which are often a central component of the college's culture. Pauldine noted the symbolic value of traditions at Hunkering Down Community College: "I think a lack of community is a concern for me here, and I'm trying to see what we can do about that in terms of traditions. One of the traditions that was new to me was [that] we get into academic garb for convocation, and it's a more formal tradition than the campuses I had been on previously, and I like it. I think that it's very nice. When I see everyone in their academic regalia it is really aesthetically pleasing, it's visually impressive, but it's also an emotional attachment, to the institution and to the academy overall. And I liked that. I thought that was a tradition that I wouldn't have expected that I liked a lot." Pauldine understood that she could use this campus tradition as a focal point to help build community on campus. Additionally, she reinstituted a holiday party to build on this sense of community. Because the college is financially strapped, the vice president of administration suggested that they should charge admission to this event to cover food costs. Pauldine was emphatic in her response: "No! We're not going to charge. This is going to be a celebration, a party that we get together and have a good time because we're here and because we're a community."

Because many community colleges are part of larger district cultures, leaders often must figure out how to work within the culture of their own college as well as that of the larger system. The following vignette explores how presidents in the Large and Growing Community College District used their cultural competencies to effectively navigate college- and district-level cultures.

## Vignette 5: Cultural Competency in a Large District

Within the Large and Growing Community College District, each of the five campuses has its own unique culture. As President Williams reflected, "Each college has its own character. We do things that further the character, the history, the traditions in each institution." Yet each campus is embedded within the larger district culture, which felt to all involved like an organization on the move. At the time the interviews for this study occurred, the district was growing and adding enrollments and was building the new campus for Cutting Edge Community College. There was also a strong sense of centralization as the entire district shifted its organizational reporting structure. Underscoring the strength of the central office was the fact that Chancellor Pioneer appointed three of the five community college presidents without a national search process, despite faculty outcry. The following sections illustrate how each college president used his or her cultural competency to navigate between district- and college-level cultures.

### Cutting Edge Community College

The culture being created at CECC was that of an institution focused on student learning. President Burke's ability to influence the creation of the campus culture was unique. As she noted, "One thing that we . . . spent a lot of time on initially was what could we do as an organization to build an organization that was capable of change. . . . We want to better prepare our students for a changing world and . . . that meant we had to model that." Burke was conscious that a leader could not merely state that a particular culture would exist on campus. Rather, she knew that it would take a conscious effort to mold these practices. To that end, Burke established team meetings, researched best practices of learning colleges, and modeled collaborative work by setting up startup committees. She brought her past leadership experiences to bear in creating this new college and relied on her ability to scan the environment for issues before they derailed the ideal of collaboration she was striving to create within the organization.

## Don't Make Waves Community College

President Hales recognized that one of the first issues she had to overcome on campus was disgruntlement on the part of campus members over the lack of input into her selection as their leader. She noted, "Everybody wanted to have some say-so regarding who their president was, and they didn't get any. There had to be a period of time [to adjust]; there was not much trust here. . . . They didn't know who I was—this district person who has come here. They don't know I had been in another college system and done jobs like this before and so forth, but it's fine now. It took a while to build that level of trust." Hales entered the presidency understanding that she needed to build trust among campus constituents, especially those who were not involved in her selection. She added, "Well, I had some advantage having worked in the district already, and I was on the campus a lot for meetings and I pretty much knew what the culture was. It was one of the reasons I was real interested in coming here." This level of advance awareness of a campus culture is rare among community college presidents, and it meant that Hales's adjustment period was quicker. Her leadership approach was to follow the lead of the district office decisions and apply them to the college effectively. Because Hales had a different perspective on the rationale behind district-level decisions, she was predisposed to falling in line with district requests.

## Tradition-Bound Community College

Because Tradition-Bound Community College was one of the original colleges in the Large and Growing Community College District, campus traditions were important to its culture. When President Williams arrived, he recalled stating, "I don't think there is anything major that we want to change here." He opted to retain a strategic plan that was created before his arrival because he believed in observing operations before advocating any changes. One of Williams's faculty members added, "He's slow to change, very conservative about change, and that's probably a good thing at a college like ours that is as old as we are. He treads lightly on that line [and] is probably wise."

Recently, this faculty member was charged with heading up the new strategic planning committee. He added that the lines of communication between the district and the college are often convoluted. He recounted, "The faculty feel that there's a great deal of duplicity at the district level, that the chancellor's office says things they don't mean and gives mixed messages. . . . I think the district sends out mixed messages to the faculty and to the staff through e-mails, and meetings with deans, and department chairs and faculty, so horrid rumor starts. 'Well, we went to a meeting and heard this; I went to a meeting and heard that.' Faculty senate presidents, I think, are right to have a lot of input, but I think the chancellor's office needs to have a clean-cut, clear line of communication to people and allow the president's office to convey those messages because Dr. Williams has been in a situation where he has had to convey messages to us about the budget, and then have to retract those messages because the district made other decisions." Clearly, President Williams's position required not only a cultural understanding of campus dynamics, but an understanding of larger district operations as well.

## Rogue Community College

The reputation of Rogue Community College preceded the arrival of President Simon. Simon recognized this: "This was the rogue campus before I came. That's why I'm here and that person's not. That adds a certain dimension to your job if you know you were hired because someone didn't want that kind of problem to exist anymore. And that really wasn't hard for me because I came from a system that was very easy for me to understand—running a campus that had five large community colleges, and I had the biggest campus then. You really you can't be any stronger than the system as a whole. If you don't have a strong system, it becomes a drag on you. So that's what I told [the search committee]. And they wanted to hear that anyway. I'm very supportive of the role of the district. They do things for me that I don't want to have to do."

Simon reflected on how the previous president of RCC tested the district's boundaries by making campus-centric decisions. The previous president was encouraged to look for another position, which signaled a tightening of the district reins. Simon commented, "Everybody else at a different campus probably now understands there's a limit of how far you can test the district like that." Simon's past experience as a president of a college within a large district system provided him with the cultural competency necessary to lead Rogue Community College. He understood the political dynamics of working (and surviving) in such an organizational structure and focused on the issues over which he had control—namely, curriculum and recruitment efforts and increasing the number of vocational programs.

## Me-Too Community College

President Garvey started at Me-Too Community College in an interim position. He had already filled a similar role at Tradition-Bound Community College and had a 20-year professional relationship with the chancellor of LGCCD. Thus, the chancellor felt he could tap Garvey for the presidency at MTCC and count on his direction. Garvey entered as the interim president with the understanding that if "they like you," the position would become permanent. The fact that Garvey was not automatically named president provided him with an opportunity to bond with campus members and allowed them to feel that they had buy-in to the final decision.

Garvey's previous experience as an interim president in the district provided him with a wealth of knowledge on which to draw. He used this cultural competency to quickly assess the need for increased resources and to communicate to the campus at large that he understood their issues and was willing to fight for resources. Garvey stated, "We had to work hard; the provost and I have had to work harder the last 3 years to get that [negative attitude] turned around. Not to only to get people to quit saying and thinking that [we're the poor third cousin], but to demonstrate that we can get resources in here to help." By investing in the college's physical plant and hiring new faculty members, Garvey began to shift the college culture to one that is more positive. Garvey's cultural competency and leveraging of his long-standing friendship with the chancellor helped him enact change at MTCC.

Minority leaders reported that there is often another facet to cultural competence: the sense of difference they brought to the position by the virtue of the color of their skin. One additional president of color shared, "The most significant issue is combating, throughout a life's journey, always having to be twice as good, always trying to be better, more perfect. Always aware that people either say it or think it that you have your job because you are a minority and they got you there to fill a quota . . . always having to fight the affirmative action mind-set." Minority leaders must often fight perceptions that they lack the ability or possess the requisite skills required to lead a college. Another leader of color noted that obtaining her Ph.D. was key to her credibility with others. As more and more leaders of color enter the presidency and other leadership positions at community colleges, they are slowly changing the culture. Nonetheless, until the generally accepted definition of a community college leader is broadened to include minorities and other people with different perspectives, leaders of color are likely to be judged against higher standards.

Because cultural competency is filtered through past experiences, it may be more complex when the leader is female or a racial or ethnic minority because these leaders must break through campus perceptions based on their gender or the color of their skin. One campus director described her female president as follows: "Oh, she's a really good president. I think that she really is genuinely driven by her vision. She's comparative to many men presidents that I have known." Clearly, White male presidents are still the ubiquitous standard on community college campuses across the country. Cultural competence and a sense of "fit" within the campus and community are essential for any college leader, but women and leaders of color must use finesse and heightened levels of cultural competency to effectively lead their campuses.

## A Holistic Perspective of Leadership Competencies

Analyzing cultural competency and the AACC leadership competencies clearly shows that many of them are linked. For instance, communication plays a pivotal role in collaborations and in community college advocacy. Likewise, resource management is a building block for the implementation of organizational strategy. Cultural competency permeates all of the competencies but is enacted in different manners in each. Considering the competencies in clusters provides a different way of looking at leadership skill acquisition and moves beyond the type of thinking that leads one to assume that the competencies make up a mere list of items to learn and master. Thus, this chapter proposes four competency clusters: inclusivity, framing meaning, minding the bottom line, and systems thinking. Each of these leadership clusters contributes to one's multidimensional leadership model.

## *Inclusivity*

The cluster of inclusivity starts with communication and collaboration but moves beyond these competencies because some leaders' collaborative efforts tend to break down to mere transactional practices. When leaders think of exchanges with others as inclusive, however, the power dynamic changes, and a culture of shared values and trust is assumed.

President Williams described his collaborations on campus often. In one example, he offered, "I see my leadership style in ways similar to a team—a team like baseball in that I play multiple roles in that. I'm the team manager. I play that role. I'm also the coach. So I'll take people aside and be a mentor. At times I'm a player; I play the game with them meaning we are all there, we are doing that. I'm also a cheerleader. When things are going well I don't need to wave a flag to point out that I'm the president, no, no, but I'm cheering—'Keep doing that!' I'm also a scout. I go out and I check out what is happening there. You notice in all of this I didn't mention the team owner. I'm not a team owner. It's ours. We are all in this together. And we have various roles. For some our roles may be fixed, but mine varies dependent upon the period of time that we are in."

In this example, Williams relied on his inclusivity competency not only by seeking collaborative opportunities with campus members, but also by building a culture based on mutual value for all stakeholders and by working hard to instill this type of collaboration into the college culture. He relied on open and frequent communication, attended campus events, engaged in informal hallway conversations, and valued the planning effort already underway at the college. By acting in an inclusive manner, Williams allowed all the various stakeholders to attach similar meaning and value to the desired campus changes.

The opportunity to build a campus from scratch provided President Burke with a unique opportunity to craft an organization from a "blank page." The president noted that for the "executive team, almost all the decisions so far were done in a collaborative way so we really [reached] consensus on those as we developed it." The college's focus on a learning organization reinforced the ideal of inclusivity. The vice president for student success noted, "My job as administrator is to make sure that collaboration, that oneness that we're working for a cause here, is maintained. That we do work as a big team. We certainly have our individual operations that we have to do to manage, but [we can] never lose the focus of what our overall purpose is. That's what I hope is happening. That's what I hope our culture will still be 2 years [after] we get there finally." Embedded into the assumptions undergirding campus operations at Cutting Edge Community College is the ideal that it operates with all stakeholders in mind and works collaboratively.

A faculty member concurred with Burke's desire to reach consensual decisions. She added, "We have 'imagine luncheons,' which are vision luncheons where the president updates us and she praises particular initiatives, individuals, pins new faculty and employees who have come on. She e-mails or she responds so quickly to her e-mail [so we] have that access to her, and [she] is completely open to meeting with faculty. She does an excellent job [of] creating this inclusivity, this feeling of inclusivity at all levels—with the community, with the employees, and with students. And to me it's been really remarkable." For organizational learning to occur, and for this level of campus connection to be sustained, college leaders must pay constant attention to communication and to feedback loops. The attention Burke pays this level of detail ensures effective communication on campus as well as an overall sense of inclusivity.

### Framing Meaning

Traditional forms of communication ensure that information is exchanged but do not necessarily infuse meaning into the message. Effectively framing the meaning of a given message requires leaders to understand how the message should be framed and to interpret that meaning to campus members. In this case, framing meaning requires linking communication to organizational strategy, collaboration, and advocacy. To a certain extent, the need to frame meaning is based on an individual campus's needs and culture. Three of the presidents interviewed for this study used the framing meaning cluster of competencies to address issues on their campuses.

When President Fields arrived at Bifurcated Community College, she was forced to deal with a dysfunctional campus in which deans had created fiefdoms, there was a lack of faculty trust, and ethical issues had arisen in a campus accreditation self-study. Fields needed to work to break the negative cycles inherent in the campus climate and instill a sense of community. She used a number of mechanisms to do this. First, she reorganized the administrative structure by recasting job responsibilities and reporting mechanisms. This action symbolized that she represented a change from business as usual. Second, she worked with trusted campus members. She recounted, "I trust most of my faculty, but for advice, there are a few people who have been here 30 to 35 years who care about the college, who understand the problem." She added, "It was a little cadre of very sincere, devoted faculty who cared about the institution and [wanted] to see a change [who attended my strategic planning sessions]." Fields collaborated with this group of faculty to create a new, positive climate of change at the college. Finally, she addressed issues of ethical responsibility on campus, including the predictability of course scheduling, more frequent use of campus facilities, and greater communication with the faculty senate to close loopholes that could lead to problems in the future. Fields framed a new campus culture of cooperation and ethical decision making on campus with these decisions and changes.

Like Fields, President Hales also worked to frame a new meaning on her campus. The main issue Hales faced was rebuilding trust among faculty. As noted in vignette 5, she had been appointed to her position without a formal search. To help re-create a sense of collaborative spirit on campus, Hales instituted a number of opportunities for campus interaction. Not only did she meet individually with all faculty members, but she hosted small gatherings to get to know the campus members better and to provide them with a chance to get to know her and her intentions for the college. In doing so, Hales began to frame meaning in a different way and, as a result, slowly started changing the campus culture. Hales expanded, "The major things I heard were from the people that had been the pets, so to speak, of the former president. They were all lined up to find out how I'm going to treat them. Then those who felt like they never were the pets are lining up because they want to be my pet. You have this jockeying for position going on for 6 months or so with everybody."

Hales did not want to continue the culture of favoritism. She said, "I'm much more for fairness and equity because I think in the long run it pays off. That was the major issue I had, [was] letting people see I was going to be fair and equitable, but I wasn't playing favorites. Many people really appreciate that; they understand it." Hales had to work to create a new meaning for the culture on campus—one that was based on trust and fairness.

The need to frame a more positive environment on campus was also important to President Simon. He inherited a campus known as the rebel of the district; his task was to bring the institution into line with the district. Thus, Simon worked on framing meaning among campus members that they were a part of a larger system, but that the individual college culture was still important. In particular, Simon focused on ensuring holistic learning for students and creating a better balance between transfer programs and work-force development initiatives. Simons was described as "gentle but firm" in his approach, a stark contrast to his predecessor, who was a "million-ideas-a-day kind of person and if he had something in mind that he wanted to see happen, he would say, 'This is what I want us to do.'" Simon was successful in framing his vision of the college because he relied extensively on collabora-tion and dialogue with campus members to move initiatives forward. His outspoken advocacy for more vocationally oriented programs also helped frame meaning on campus and in the community.

## Minding the Bottom Line

Leaders of colleges that have extreme resource constraints must rely on com-petencies that help them pay attention to the financial bottom line. Even though resource management is a critical element of this competency cluster, leaders must also link organizational planning to financial support and must convey this connection to stakeholders in a manner that shows the rationale behind these decisions. Furthermore, the way that collaborations are devel-oped and maintained, and the way the various stakeholders understand the situation, can also affect the resources available.

The fact that Me-Too Community College felt like the "poor third cousin" of the Large and Growing Community College District was rooted in the lack of resources it had at its disposal relative to the other campuses. According to one of the college's founding faculty, "And again, we just didn't know why MTCC was understaffed for faculty; we're talking full-time faculty and staff, compared to the other campuses. We have more enrollment and less full-time faculty. We have more enrollment and less staff than the other campuses. Why, when we were understaffed and we had the increasing enrollment, were we the ones that got the short end of the stick?"

When President Garvey arrived on campus, he understood that increas-ing the campus's resource base was a priority. And indeed, he was successful in securing more resources and hiring additional full-time faculty. Garvey reflected, "I've been in several different kinds of settings, from the largest urban systems, multicampus or multicollege, to a president of a large single-campus institution, to even one of the very smallest colleges in the state, and in different regions of the state." He drew on these experiences to leverage arguments for additional resources for his campus.

The main problem Garvey encountered was the need to acquire more financial resources. Tightly coupled with this, however, was a need to develop a strategic vision for the college. Garvey engaged the campus in focus group sessions to create a long-range strategic plan, which itself focused on how additional resources could help the campus achieve its goals. Next, he clearly communicated the strategic plan to campus constituents, framing it as a way for the college to finally get the resources it deserved in order to move forward. As Garvey noted, "And [the creation of organizational strategy has] done a lot to dampen down that hangdog attitude that I saw when I came here. 'Cause we've got significant increases in our operating budget. We've gotten significant increases in our number of full-time faculty and staff." The payoff to Garvey's planning efforts underscored the links among campus collaboration, strategic planning, resource management, and achievement of campus goals.

The cultural competency that President Pauldine brought to her campus was rooted in her experiences as an enrollment consultant. In that role, she had mere days on a campus to diagnosis critical issues affecting enrollment and to suggest steps to take for positive change. When she arrived at Hunkering Down Community College, Pauldine quickly identified four financial problems and devised plans to address the bottom line. Student enrollment patterns were key to her solution. Pauldine noted, "Another interesting thing to me was that it was the campus practice to have students be full-time students, but at the lowest possible credit hour load." Given the state funding formula, this meant that the students were generating lower subsidies for the college. She added, "I did a series of educating that one way to help ourselves was to make sure students—I didn't want to overload students, that wasn't the goal, but we needed to be at maximum or closer to maximum [credit hours] for students to graduate on time. The parents don't like it when they think they're sending their students for a 2-year degree and it turns out to be three." This change in direction allowed the college to garner more resources without increasing the number of students on campus. Pauldine's focus on resource issues was a necessity, but it also allowed her to improve the educational environment for students. Pauldine reframed the resource issues so that campus members understood the scope of the issue and the need for it to change. She communicated with campus members on a regular basis and updated them regarding the status of outcomes. Presidents of campuses that are focused on survival need to rely on frequent communication and frame solutions in a way that celebrates successes.

## Systems Thinking

Leaders who view their campus from a systems perspective see the complexity of each decision as well as the underlying links between actions and reactions that are not always evident if they focus solely on one aspect of an issue. Generally, leaders gain this higher-order organizational perspective through years of experience. Past outcomes and observations help inform leaders about what to expect in similar circumstances. However, leaders must always be cognizant of the influence of new contexts, which can often result in unexpected outcomes.

President Jones bases Technology Community College's organizational strategy on a technology foundation. The campus was poised to employ technology to aid in student learning. Jones noted, "Unknown to me, faculty here had been to my campus in [another state] and had visited the campus to see what we were doing with laptops and the ThinkPad University concept. So there was a group of faculty here that were keenly interested, and that was one of the things I wanted to do and I was open about it." Jones's experience with the laptop program provided him with a way of understanding the various elements required to make this endeavor successful.

The first issues Jones needed to address were faculty buy-in and curricular support. The vice president of administrative services recounted, "We actually went out with an RFP to our own faculty and said, 'Who wants to be a part of the laptop program as a pilot?' So we chose five curriculums that were pilot laptop curriculums, by volunteer. We funded the laptops, even for the students. We loaned them to the students just to get things rolling. It worked out very well just as a pilot, and it demonstrated that we could do this. So we went out again with an RFP to faculty who were interested in converting to a laptop curriculum, so in addition to the original four or five, I think we added another seven or eight or nine that first year. Now I think we are up to almost 1,600 computers on campus in mandatory curriculums. So, in terms of consensus, if the faculty don't want to do this—no one made them do it, so they had to be aware of the fact that their teaching methods were going to change."

Next, Jones needed to address the issues of student access to laptops. The director of financial aid noted, "Laptops can be funded through student financial aid even if one is not in a laptop program. The financial aid started out only aiding those in a laptop program, but now so many courses [are] laptop involved. . . . I really thought a couple years ago when we started this that parents would really balk because anytime you raise money, anytime you say it's going to cost you more, we hear about it. With laptops it was the opposite. We had parents calling up saying, 'My son's not in the laptop major, but I want him to have a laptop.' They see the value of this in the workforce, having their children know about this." Planning and understanding the links between the new laptop program and financial aid—in other words, taking a systems perspective—was critical to the success of TCC's technology programs. Furthermore, Jones employed a systems perspective in thinking about building solid academic programs, instilling entrepreneurial goals in students and staff, and figuring out how to manage the entire process.

President Hammond also relied on systems thinking when he used the college's mission statement as a convening platform to bring campus members together in pursuit of a common goal. The mission statement states: "Strategic Community College offers educational, career, and lifelong learning opportunities through innovative partnerships which enhance the lives of people in [the nearby] counties." Several of the AACC competencies are evident in this statement, specifically those concerning advocacy, collaboration, and professionalism. Hammond's approach to leadership ensured that all faculty and administrators took a systems approach to campus decision making; campus members brought the strategic plan to every meeting and referred to it readily when discussing campus issues.

The vice president of information technology and learning resources reflected on one of President Hammond's first organizational initiatives at SCC. He stated, "From my perspective, one of the first things is he really pushed hard for the television channel, which is very important, not just as a communication tool but as a pathway for delivering instruction anywhere and anytime. It fit his [Hammond's] vision statement, and he really means it. Make it convenient for the people who are going to school here. So we brought that online and we started picking out information about the college and we also brought up telecourses in the very first year, which was a change in instruction. It changed the way we communicate with the outside world." Certainly this campus leader was attuned to a change that had great impact on his area of expertise, but the systematic changes resulting from the implementation of a TV channel were even more important. Hammond used his weekly television show to update stakeholders on campus progress and events. The channel also addressed another problem the college had: reaching students who lived within the college's large service area who could not readily commute to campus. By taking a systems perspective of how to address problems on his campus, Hammond effectively advocated for his institution, communicated with others, and ensured collaboration between the campus and the community.

## Role of Competencies in Multidimensional Leadership

An individual's multidimensional leadership model builds on the competencies that are most important to the individual and to his or her college context. As a particular competency cluster develops, the individual facets of the cluster merge in such a way that the singular "listed" items are no longer stand-alone competencies, but rather co-dependent on the other competencies within the cluster. Within each of the clusters is a continuum that represents a leader's expertise and comfort with enacting the overarching ideals of the cluster. Movement along the continuum ranges from a leader with this newly honed perspective to a seasoned leader who understands the nuances and interplay and can readily anticipate outcomes. Although leaders have a predilection for approaching ways to operationalize the individual competencies based on their underlying schema and leadership approach, the college context also affects how the particular cluster functions in practice.

By viewing leadership competencies in clusters rather than as individual traits, we gain a realistic understanding of how the skills play off one another and reinforce each other. We also begin to understand how leaders' multidimensional models change as they increase their competency in one or more clusters. As with all dimensions in the multidimensional model, seasoned leaders rely more on their past experiences and have a shorter learning curve on their new campuses. Newer presidents such as Fields and Pauldine, who were experiencing some key campus issues for the first time, had a steeper learning curve. Therefore, their multidimensional models grew and changed more slowly, but perhaps more dramatically than those of an experienced college leader. Thus, when thinking about how specific leadership competencies—or clusters of competencies—affect the multidimensional leadership model, one must consider different career stages. It is equally important to consider how these competencies (cultural competency in particular) may take on new meanings when they are viewed through a lens of race and gender.

# 6

# GENDER, LEADERSHIP, AND THE COMMUNITY COLLEGE

Some leaders are born women.

Unknown

C ommunity colleges are often singled out as good places for women to work (Townsend & Twombly, 2006), not only because they have large percentages of women working there but also because of their roots as "democracy colleges." The community college's open-door mission has provided many young women with access to higher education because programming is flexible, local, and less expensive than at 4-year institutions (Cohen & Brawer, 2008). Perhaps because these colleges are inclusive and supportive of women, they boast a greater percentage of women in faculty ranks and administrative leadership positions than 4-year universities (American Council on Education [ACE], 2007; National Center for Education Statistics, 2007; Townsend & Twombly, 2006). For instance, women compose 49.5% of the full-time faculty ranks at public 2-year colleges compared to only 30.1% at public research universities, 37.2% at public doctoral institutions, and 41.2% at public comprehensive colleges (U.S. Department of Education, 2007). Likewise, women hold the highest percentage of presidencies at public 2-year colleges at 28.8% relative to women at counterpart institutions (13.8% at doctorate-granting institutions and 23.2% at comprehensive baccalaureate colleges).

Leaders of color, however, sit in presidential offices at similar percentages in community colleges, baccalaureate colleges, and research universities—around 14%. Yet 36% of the students at community colleges are students of color relative to 26% at 4-year colleges, underscoring that leaders of community colleges are not representative of their student populations. A more limited discussion on the role of race and leadership is given here because this was not a specifically targeted area of research for the case site selection. For an excellent discussion of race and leadership, please see Edith Rusch's *Gender and Race in Leadership Preparation: A Constrained Discourse* (2004). Another good reference focused on issues specifically facing women of color is *From Oppression to Grace: Women of Color and Their Dilemmas within the Academy* (2006), edited by Theodorea Regina Berry and Nathalie Mizelle.

Despite the fact that women have a significant presence at community colleges, the leaders of these colleges are still mostly White men. Between 2001 and 2007, the number of women obtaining community college presidencies grew by a mere 2% to reach the current level of 29%. Pointedly, fewer than one in three community colleges have a woman as president. The pathway to the corner office is promising for women, however. Almost half (49.5%) of full-time community college faculty members are women (U.S. Department of Education, 2007). Although it is difficult to track the percentage of women in department chair roles because they often retain their faculty titles as well, one can assume that women are engaging in these positions in significant numbers.

As noted in previous chapters, perhaps the most critical position leading to the presidency is that of chief academic officer. In 2002, women held a mere 21% of chief academic officer (CAO) positions (Weisman & Vaughan, 2002), but women have made significant progress since then, and in 2009, 50% of CAOs at community colleges were women (ACE, 2009), but only 15% were leaders of color, indicating limited gains for these leaders. The increased number of pathways to the presidency relies heavily on an academic progression, though this route does not necessarily require beginning in the faculty ranks. Instead, leaders are also coming from other areas within the college, including student affairs, administrative services, workforce development, and continuing education (Weisman & Vaughan, 2007). Only 10% are coming to community college presidencies wholly from outside the 2-year college sector (Weisman & Vaughan, 2007).

Despite the increased routes to the presidency, women have not yet achieved parity in the president's office. The fact that 84% of current presidents are expected to retire by 2016 (Weisman & Vaughan, 2007), however, means that more and more presidencies will probably be awarded to women in the near future, especially if women seeking the presidency are mentored and supported as they move along their career pathway.

As several of the presidents in this study related, mentorship was often a significant factor that helped them achieve the presidency. However, in the past men were more likely to receive mentoring than their female counterparts (Hall & Sandler, 1983; Scanlon, 1997). Indeed, President Fields noted that she received much less mentoring than what she assumed her male counterparts were getting. On the other hand, all of the men in the study commented on the help they received from mentors during their careers. Two male presidents spoke specifically of the mentoring they received from women. In both cases, the mentorship they received from women helped them focus more on relationships and communication within the organization. President Simon reflected on what he learned from his female mentor: "I've been blessed with having pretty good bosses over the years and I did have a very, very good role model boss when I was at the [state agency]. I certainly learned a lot of things from her about how you relate to people. We went through a number of budget crises while I was with the state government, and state agencies usually get hit harder than educational agencies. I learned a lot about how to deal with budget cuts and how to come out the other end and survive, which was good because that seems to be kind of a recurring path." The fact that Simon referred to relationships in talking about his mentor is telling because this is a trait most often linked with women's ways of leading. Simon applied what he learned about relationships from his female mentor to his own leadership, underscoring that thinking about leadership simply as "men do this and women do that" is outdated.

Similarly, President Williams had a strong female mentor who looked out for opportunities for him to advance his career. As a result of the direction and support provided by his mentor, Williams learned new skills, including how to mentor junior faculty and administrators. To this day Williams maintains strong connections with his mentor and was quick to point out how many women he was mentoring for leadership. As he concluded, "I believe in inclusiveness." With more presidents like Williams, who focus specifically on mentoring women in the presidential pathway, and a greater number of women in CAO and other leadership positions, women may soon be accessing the community college presidency in never-before-seen numbers.

Nonetheless, any discussion of gender, leadership, and the community college is much more complex than statistics describing the percentage of women in top leadership positions. Indeed, to truly understand gender and leadership, one must first consider the social construction of gender, as well as gendered organizations and typical conceptions of the "ideal" worker. This chapter provides a brief introduction to the literature in these areas and then examines how gender affects communication and leadership styles. The chapter concludes with a discussion of how gender fits into a multidimensional understanding of community college leadership.

## Social Construction of Gender

The concept that gender is a social construction (i.e., the meaning of gender is developed through social interactions) can be traced to Berger and Luckmann's (1966) seminal work on the subject. As these scholars point out, social interactions take place on an individual level but are also part of larger organizational interactions. Thus, the construction of meaning and reality on college campuses occurs through social interactions at multiple levels along the structural hierarchy. It is tempting to characterize gender in a dichotomous fashion: men on the one hand and women on the other. Yet when we start from the standpoint that gender is socially constructed, we must acknowledge that gender is more complex than this simple duality.

Sex categories are evident at birth but are reinforced in different ways throughout life. As Lorber (1995) noted, "A sex category becomes a gender status through naming, dress, and the use of other gender markers. Once a child's gender is evident, others treat those in one gender differently from those in the other, and the children respond to the different treatment by feeling different and behaving differently" (p. 1). It is through these social interactions that gender is created, and with it, particular expectations for leaders. Lorber concludes, "Individuals are born sexed but not gendered, and they have to be taught to be masculine or feminine" (p. 4). Leaders, like all of us, act in gendered ways. West and Zimmerman (1987) refer to "doing gender" as the acting out of societal expectations based on gender.

All of the presidents in this study (five men and four women) acted in gendered ways. Some of the leaders spoke to their gender construction more directly than others; indeed, the women were more likely to note their gender and the issues associated with this categorization. President Fields's statement about her background as a physicist provides us with an opportunity to explore the social construction of gender. As she said, "I'm not a typical physicist either. Typical physicists would probably function more like chemists. I think I'm a little more right-brained than that. Maybe it's my femininity that I bring to that. I don't know. But every single one of us is a unique human being with a unique set of past experiences. There probably is no way to plot that out as a model of leader development." Embedded in

Fields's self-description are two distinct layers of gender roles. First, there is the social construction of what a physicist acts like and the expectations for that profession—which she defines as male and logical. Second, there is a recognition that gender is socially constructed through past experiences and individual characteristics. As Fields shows us, the social construction of gender does not happen along a straight line; it depends on one's individual background and his or her experiences in various roles.

Lorber (1995) noted that there is no essential femaleness or maleness, but that the constant reinforcement of institutional and societal norms reinforces gender. Individuals are socialized into their gendered roles and the ascribed expectations that follow through interactions with others: "In almost every encounter, human beings produce gender, behaving in the ways they learned were appropriate for their gender status, or resisting or rebelling against these norms. Resistance and rebellion have altered gender norms, but so far they have rarely eroded the statuses" (p. 6).

When individuals act in a manner that is inconsistent with the social construction and expectations of their gender, they can be penalized. For example, assertive or dominant women are often viewed as bitchy or aggressive (even though a man acting in the same way may be rewarded for his decisive leadership) because her actions are not part of her prescribed gender role. President Fields was penalized by her president (and called a bitch) when as the academic dean she tried to be assertive in an exchange with him and disagreed with his stance on an academic matter. Women are not the only ones who can be penalized for acting outside their prescribed gender roles. President Wilson had attempted to engage in a more relational, open leadership style in which he solicited input from many different people. However, not everyone appreciated his approach. As one faculty member commented, "We're waiting for someone to tell us what to do, and administrators are so scared of what faculty are going to think of them. They don't make decisions, or they tend to walk on eggshells." In this case, Williams was criticized for not being authoritative or "male" enough in his leadership.

When male norms serve as the measure for good leadership, women are placed in a bind. They must work to meet expectations of a president that are based on the experiences of men, but at the same time they are often penalized for acting in non-gender-appropriate ways. Gendered expectations also hold for men, but men are typically penalized less often than women when they act outside their expected roles (Eddy, 2008). How gender is constructed is influenced by the structures within gendered organizations.

## Gendered Organizations

The construction of gender does not occur in a vacuum. Acker (1990) coined the concept of "gendered organizations" to highlight the advantages that male norms bring to the distribution of power. Organizations are the "products and producers of gender-based power relations . . . masculine ways of doing things are inherent in structural, ideological and symbolic aspects of an organization, as well as in everyday interactions and practices" (Hatch & Cunliffe, 2006, p. 274). As gendered organizations, colleges often reinforce traditional gender expectations and place value on historic conceptions of leadership that are based on male norms. The ways in which work is divided among administrators can reinforce gendered ideals on campus. For instance, when data entry clerks are predominantly women and top administrators are men, there is almost certainly a gendered structure in place.

Acker (1990) posited that gendering in organizations occurs in at least five interacting processes:

- The construction of divisions along gender lines
- The construction of symbols and images that explain, reinforce, or oppose those divisions
- The interactions between women and men, women and women, and men and men that enact norms of dominance and submission
- The production of gendered components of individual identity
- The ongoing processes that create and conceptualize social structures

Within organizations, jobs are seen as separate from the individuals who hold them. Indeed, the concept underpinning the idea of gendered organizations is that jobs are best filled by "disembodied workers" (Acker, 1990) who can work full time and who have someone at home to handle their personal lives. Within colleges, hierarchies are constructed around the concept of the disembodied worker.

Although some may view the greater representation of women within community college leadership ranks as the beginning of the breakdown of gendered institutions, many of these female leaders act as disembodied workers in the same ways as their male counterparts might. Indeed expectations about what it means to be a leader are still based on the conception of the disembodied worker (or, as Williams [2000] terms it, the "ideal worker": one who is expected to be on the job in excess of 40 hours a week, with an unspoken understanding that the worker's personal and family responsibilities are met by someone else in the home, often a wife). Women in leadership positions are expected to meet ideal worker expectations in addition to any responsibilities they may have on the second shift (Hochschild, 2003).

Gendered expectations may be a barrier for women who desire to advance but also have responsibilities in caring for elderly relatives or young children. President Pauldine noted the tensions between her leadership responsibilities and her family responsibilities when she reflected on the difficulty of accommodating two-academic-career families. Pauldine struggled with the need to balance her career with her husband's because both required a full commitment of time and energy. For much of her career, she chose to put her job second relative to her husband's career. Only when her husband retired could she focus on her own career advancement to seek a college presidency. See vignette 6 for examples of the tensions inherent in seeking work/life balance.

---

### Vignette 6: Tensions Between Home and Work—Trying to Be "Ideal"

President Fields spoke most clearly about leadership issues resulting from her gender. As she noted, "It was just clear to me at that point when my son was just 3 or 4 years old that I could not take an administrative position and protect what was important to me, which was the stability of my marriage, my son's growing up in a stable environment." At this point, she left her administrative position and returned to teaching. A dozen years later, Fields returned to the administrative career path: "I did tinker with administration; I flirted with administration. You can do a division chairmanship or a department chairmanship without having to move. When I was division chair at [Community College A], my son was in junior high. And I took a couple of years as an associate dean when he was a toddler. Now that position I could've kept longer. I decided to get out of it because it was just obvious to me that (a) I wasn't giving my child the attention that he needed, [and] (b) at some point, there are fewer administrative positions at an institution. There are fewer opportunities to stay in administration at a given institution than there are opportunities to stay in a faculty. I mean the whole faculty is structured around stability. The tenure process, et cetera. In administration, the whole structure, if the institution is healthy, the administrative structure is not stable. There are constant changes."

---

Fields thus navigated her career path by putting her family first, knowing that an administrative job required time and energy that was not compatible with her concurrent roles of wife and mother. She was not willing to make the concessions to be "ideal" that she felt were required to take on higher-level positions.

When her son left for college, Fields pursued a position as chief academic officer in another town within her home state. Yet as noted previously, she didn't seek the presidency until her husband retired. In discussing the timing of this move, she said, "Well, I thought when I came here I thought this would be the first presidency and I would be president again. In fact, there was part of me that really wanted to come back to [Community College B]. But you know, I'm not a young person any more. I'm about to turn 60; in another year I'll be 60 years old. And frankly, I don't want to retire in the cold. And when we took this position, part of what pulled us here was that I love the area and [my husband] did too. As soon as I brought him out, he was really resistant, but as soon as I brought him out for the second interview, I rented a convertible, and we drove and it was a really short drive to the lake. And it was a beautiful weekend. . . . He just fell in love with it, the outdoors and the mild weather, and frankly, and we love our home, and we love being close to the kids, they'll just pick up and come up here in a couple of hours. . . . But it's really been a nice lifestyle for us." Clearly, Fields's family responsibilities acted as a barrier to career progression earlier in her life, and she waited until she felt her family responsibilities were manageable so that she could fulfill the responsibilities of the ideal worker.

All of the female presidents in this study were married, some with children, and all made choices about when to seek advanced positions based in large part on how well the new positions would fit with their home responsibilities. The experiences of the female presidents in this study are reinforced by national numbers. As Corrigan (2002) notes, 25% of female presidents had altered their career path at least once for their children, whereas only 2% of male presidents had done so. Furthermore, once they reached a point in their personal life where family expectations were less, these women ultimately had to embrace the ideal-worker norm in order to secure career advancement. In contrast, none of the male presidents in the study noted delays in seeking a promotion because of their partner's career or the ages of their children.

Indeed, the male presidents in this study rarely referenced their gender overtly. All of the men were married, but only President Simon mentioned his spouse in relation to his career—he commented that it was important that the position he chose was in an area that offered work opportunities for her. Furthermore, unlike the female presidents, none of the men noted any tensions between their work and home lives. Clearly, regardless of the increasing percentage of female leaders, community colleges are still gendered organizations, and leaders must contend with gendered expectations for career advancement, performance, and behavior. However, as Loder (2005) points out, as we become more comfortable with female leaders (and, in particular, when we can simply say that we have a president, rather than a *female president*), some of the tension inherent in balancing work and family life may lessen, and the concept of the ideal worker may lose some of its power.

## Gendered Communication and Leadership

The language used in studies of leadership at community colleges reinforces male norms because it is about and primarily conducted by a small cadre of White male scholars (Amey & Twombly, 1992). Over the past two  decades, the marked differences of a dichotomy are shifting, with more women entering leadership ranks and writing about 2-year college leadership. How we talk about leadership begins to dictate who feels included in the conversation.

### Women's and Men's Ways of Leading

As discussed in chapter 2 of this book, definitions of leadership are expanding. However, recent research shows that leaders still locate their power in the positions they hold. Thus, the higher the position, the more the person is a leader (Eddy & VanDerLinden, 2006). Understanding leadership simply as the achievement of a high-level position reinforces the idea that colleges are gendered organizations in which the hierarchy is valued. Yet as we move beyond a positional understanding of leadership, we can begin to dissect how women and men may differ in their ways of leading. Much literature exists showing that women have a more participatory orientation to leading and are more comfortable sharing power with others (Chliwniak, 1997; Townsend & Twombly, 1998). For example, traditional male leaders rely on transactions of rewards and punishments and are more direct and assertive in their demands. On the other hand, successful female leaders often operate within a "web of inclusion," rejecting traditional hierarchies and relying instead on a set of relationships (Helgeson, 1995). They may also focus on transforming individual self-interest into meeting institutional objectives via increased participation and power sharing (Rosener, 1990). As more scholars, leaders, and campus constituents express preferences for collaborative leadership, what we consider to be women's ways of leading are being increasingly valued and reinforced.

However, although some leadership scholars describe collaborative approaches to leadership as traditionally female (e.g., Sagaria & Johnsrud, 1988), other research suggests that leadership may not be so rigidly gendered. For example, in Gillett-Karam's (1997) study of male and female presidents at community colleges, she found that leadership actions were more strongly tied to specific situations, not gender differences. Similarly, Eddy (2003) found that, although campus members spoke about their presidents in gendered terms, perceiving that men exhibited authoritative leadership and women collaborative leadership, the actual leadership behaviors of the presidents were not stereotypically gendered. Finally, Jablonski (1996) found that, although female presidents believed that they led in more participatory and collegial ways, faculty members at their colleges disagreed.

Furthermore, as Jablonski (1996) showed, campus constituents are often conflicted about what they desire and expect in a leader. On the one hand, faculty members wish for more participatory leadership, but on the other hand, they also want strong, aggressive (i.e., traditionally male) leaders. Thus many female leaders face a dilemma: Adhere to traditional norms and expectations based on male ways of leading, or enact a more personally genuine, collaborative, and therefore more female construction of leadership (Amey, 1999).

Glazer-Raymo (1999) referred to women who opt to adapt to the male-normed system as ones who are "playing by the rules" (p. 157). Women may find it easier to attain leadership position by "playing by the rules," but doing so also reinforces strict male-female gender roles. Women are then constantly judged against a male norm and must attempt to meet these expectations, even if it means rejecting a sense of self. Women have options other than "playing by the rules," however. They can recognize the limitations of male norms but work within the system to change them (Tedrow & Rhoads [1999] call this "reconciliation"). Women can also resist the male norms altogether and work to break down the boundaries of gender roles.

In reality, female leaders often decide whether to play by the rules or test gender boundaries in relation to specific instances, or they combine different leadership approaches. In considering what it meant to lead, President Pauldine said, "The campus needed somebody who had some strong leadership, but also would be willing to be a team player." Acknowledging that her campus wanted her to engage in both traditional male and female leadership activities may have been daunting; in order for her to succeed, she needed to be a tough role model but also to act in a collaborative manner that fit gendered expectations for leadership. This was a difficult line to walk. As President Pauldine noted, when she walks around campus, "I frighten people. 'What's she here for?' 'What's she looking for?'" Although campus constituents desired a more collaborative approach to leadership, Pauldine's strong persona and approach to being a "team player" rubbed some people the wrong way because it did not align with being female.

Similarly to particular ideals being associated with women's way of leading, expectations are often associated with leaders of color. One of the additional women of color interviewed for this study noted her strong alignment with issues affecting students of color, in particular Latinos. As an immigrant in the 1960s, she noted, "I was schooled in deeply believing you have to be engaged, and yes, you could make a difference in life." She added that a challenge to the advocacy she embraces is that people underestimate her abilities. She mused, "Oftentimes folks think that's what I'm all about, and it surprises them that I have philosophical depth. They think maybe you are a lightweight or automatically make assumptions that the only issues I care about are women, immigrants, and race. They don't think I have knowledge on workforce development or curriculum or other key issues at the college. The risk one takes in being an advocate is that it might peg them in the eyes of others." In this case, the president's commitment to advocacy may limit how others conceive of her leadership, and others may align her leadership only with issues of race and color—dismissing her in other matters.

Research on the perceptions of male and female leaders shows that "leaders were viewed more positively when they used a leadership style that was typical of and consistent with their gender" (Griffin, 1992, p. 14). Thus, leaders are rewarded for "doing gender" (West & Zimmerman, 1987) in ways that reinforce historic assumptions of male and female leadership characteristics. As Nidiffer (2001) points out, in order to move beyond traditionally gendered leadership styles, leaders must blend gender-related leadership competencies and draw from the best elements of male norms (traits of power, decisiveness, assertiveness, etc.) as well as the best elements of female norms (e.g., generative, collaborative, or participatory leadership). This integrated model of leadership values both feminine and masculine proficiencies. Vignette 7 highlights the integrated forms of leadership demonstrated by the leaders in this research.

---

### Vignette 7: Integrating Gender and Leadership

Recognizing that many leaders are judged by how well they live up to both male and female leadership stereotypes provides opportunities for integrating the two leadership styles. Gender-integrated leadership moves past the notion that there is a right and wrong way of leading and combines traditionally female leadership traits such as collaboration, relationships, and cooperation with typical male leadership characteristics, including taking charge, making decisions, and focusing on individual, heroic actions.

All of the presidents in this study integrated gendered leadership roles to some extent. For example, President Fields talked about her desire to get things done and have the "right people" doing them: a more traditionally male leadership orientation. As she commented, "My self-image is I like to work through other people, but they've got to be the right people. [laugh] I know I have the same traits as all presidents do. I want to get things done. I know that there is a part of me that I always need to be very sensitive to. And that is the part that gets very offended when I see other people clearly looking at their own self-interests and not the institution's. . . . I always want to give people a chance to prove themselves. And so I don't like to form judgments about people. . . . But I don't know any other way to be." As this quote illustrates, Fields was more focused on product than on process. However, she did not altogether abandon traditionally female ways of leading because she stated her desire to nurture individuals and allow them an opportunity to perform.

Similarly, many of the male presidents incorporated traditionally female ways of leading into their leadership. More specifically, they expressed and acted on a desire to engage in collaborative leadership. Every one of the presidents held some type of forum to get to know campus members. Several even hosted coffee sessions, individual meetings, and small-group meetings. These sessions often resulted in additions to the strategic plans and change initiatives. However, the manner in which feedback from campus members was integrated into strategic plans often differed. For example, President Simon noted that he liked to develop a group decision-making process, but "you can't rely on them to make all the decisions. There are just some things that are not theirs to do. You don't want them to be the ones accountable to the board; *you* want to be accountable to the board. So they have to understand that." In this case, although Simon used collaborative leadership techniques to involve campus constituents, he acknowledged that some responsibilities that come with his position in the hierarchy should not be passed on to others. The notion that they were the person in charge on campus was evident in all of the interviews with presidents. Regardless of the levels of participation by campus members, there was a common sentiment that the buck stops at the president's desk. None of the presidents questioned this traditionally male conception of leadership; as the highest positional leader on campus, each one clearly understood his or her role as the final arbiter of decisions.

President Pauldine provides another example of a president who integrated traditionally male and female ways of leading, although in this case it was not always an effective integration of characteristics. Pauldine used information from small-group meetings she held on campus to inform the campus strategic plan. However, when she presented the plan to the campus or spoke about it, she referred to it as "my plan of work," not as the campus plan. Perhaps because of Pauldine's language choices when talking about the plan, campus members did not feel like they had any ownership of the plan; although they may have had some input, they did not consider it to be mutually developed. Thus, although President Pauldine engaged in collaborative leadership—a traditionally feminine trait—in creating the strategic plan, the language she used to discuss it put ownership for the plan firmly back into the traditional hierarchy.

How the presidents defined campus relationships and how they viewed their place in the college affected their leadership. Many of the female presidents talked about having personal ownership for the success of the college. This is a typically female leadership characteristic, which relies on relationships (among people and between people and the institution). President Pauldine exemplified this sentiment: "First of all, when you're a president, if you want to do a really good job, I believe you have to really become part of the institution." Pauldine's connection to the college was one of personal investment; she didn't just view her role as mere job functions.

Both the male and female presidents in this study valued their role in creating a sense of connection and community on campus. Interestingly, when the male leaders acted in collaborative ways, they were rewarded. But when the women assumed more assertive or directive stances, they were punished for pushing the boundaries of their gender roles. Thus it seems that, although integrating male and female ways of leading is a worthy goal on community college campuses, men who incorporate female norms may benefit more than women who take on male leadership characteristics.

## The Language of Gender

Gender schemas—the tendency to view people in terms of male-female dichotomies (Valian, 1999)—are prevalent in community colleges, as they are in many workplaces. "Gender schema assumes men and women are different based on a combination of nature and nurture and as a result, each gender manifests different behaviors in various aspects of life" (Nidiffer, 2001, p. 109). Language often reinforces the concept of gender in leadership. For instance, in describing President Pauldine, a campus member said, "The president is willing to use her authority, but she uses it fairly gracefully." The feminine descriptor of *gracefully* reinforces the gender of this president distinct from ways in which campus members described male presidents. The female presidents in this study also used language that reminded campus members of their gender—allowing these women to support traditional gender roles while assuming the presidency. As Pauldine reflected, "I spoke in my first convocation that I was particularly well suited to this challenge because we had raised a family on a single faculty member's salary, since I didn't work when our children were young. But I was always pinching pennies and managing—so I was well equipped for this job." As West and Zimmerman (1987) note, using feminine language is one way that individuals "do gender." In this instance, by reminding campus constituents that she fit the traditional gender role of a woman, Pauldine to some extent shaped the way in which others on campus would view her.

Much of the scholarship on communication asserts that women communicate in gendered ways, whereas men serve as the norm (Tannen, 1994).

Male norms of communicating allow for men to be directive, assertive, and in charge, whereas female norms expect women to be agreeable and nonconfrontational to allow for broader participation. For instance, women often speak in a manner that offers suggestions rather than absolutes, often doing so in the form of questions (Spender, 1981). During meetings with her cabinet, President Pauldine frequently asked "Why not?" in order to press cabinet members to give her reasons why some ideas may fail or others should be tried. As one vice president commented about the cabinet meetings, "She likes to throw out new ideas, likes to get feedback, and if she has an idea that she thinks is really good, if you say no, she'll ask you a million and one questions." Unlike the male norm of dictating solutions, Pauldine led by asking others to respond to her questions and think through their opinions.

Leaders are often perceived as successful when they adhere to expected gender roles and language. As noted earlier, when President Fields acted in an aggressive manner in her conversation with her then president, her supervisor called her a "bitch." As she related, "I never thought of myself as very pushy, and I still don't. I think I'm very frank." Nonetheless, Fields was penalized for acting assertively, which did not fit with her traditional gender role. In contrast, when President Jones arrived on campus, staff "were simply looking for someone to say, 'What should we do?' So there was receptiveness to any idea and a willingness to try things." In this case, Jones's direct commands and take-charge attitude were rewarded because they reinforced gendered expectations.

Others understand leadership through the use of language and discourse as the medium for building campus relationships. One of the additional interviews conducted with a woman of color pointed out how language also has a silencing effect. She related, "You are in a room at a meeting and speak up to contribute a point. No one says anything and the conversation moves on. Then about 10 to 15 minutes later, someone else makes the same point and they are acknowledged. You think to yourself, 'Maybe I didn't speak loud enough? Didn't I just say that?!'" In this case, this leader of color had her voice silenced and her contribution go unrecognized. Here, the leader was invisible despite her physical presence and actual contributions.

Language can also be used to break down gendered expectations. As an example, when President Simon first arrived on campus, he held individual meetings with campus members. In these meetings he focused on getting to know the people and asking their opinions about the direction the campus should take. As he stated, "A lot of conversations didn't even get into that [campus planning] at all; it'd just be about 'How did you get to be here?' or

'What drew you to teaching?' or 'Why are you doing that kind of work?' and I'd talk about my family, too." In this instance, Simon used language and conversations about his and others' families to move beyond a traditional male role. This conversational form and approach allowed President Simon to build a culture of collaboration on campus that was well received not only by campus members, but by the central office because the campus had previously been a rogue college within the system.

Language helps create reality and determine what is valued at the institution (Berger & Luckmann, 1966). Thus, an organization with male norms and language that reinforces those norms becomes a male-normed reality and ultimately defines success as a degree of congruence with male attributes. Thus, although more women are attaining leadership positions on community college campuses, unless more attention is paid to the language of gender, female leaders will be swimming upstream against the currents of male norms and language reinforcing those expectations on a daily basis.

## Gender and Multidimensional Leadership

In the early 1990s, when women first started attaining community college presidencies in more significant numbers, a number of predictions were made about how organizations would change as a result. Both DiCroce (1995) and Vaughan (1989) argued that the presence of female leaders would shift the culture of community colleges and help open the doors for other women. And indeed, one could effectively argue that the pioneering female leaders on community college campuses resulted in greater numbers of women entering high-level positions. The mere addition of women to the leadership ranks, however, does not ensure organizational change. In particular, no change in conceptions of leadership will occur if women attain the presidency by adopting male norms and displaying typically male leadership characteristics (Tedrow & Rhoads, 1999) or if men are bound by traditions to act in an authoritative and hierarchical manner.

Rather than seeking large organizational changes that have resulted from hiring female presidents, it may be more important to focus on the more nuanced ways in which female leadership has changed historic conceptions of what it means to lead. Instead of viewing gender, language, and leadership as dichotomies that pit male and female gender roles against one another, we have learned that it is important to view these ideals in a more complex manner. Indeed, Baca Zinn, Hondagneu-Sotelo, and Messner (2005) argue that there are more than 900 permutations of gender, making acting like a man or a woman more complex than a mere either-or response. Accepting that gender roles exist on a spectrum is key to breaking down the notion that there is only one way to lead. When leaders draw on both traditionally male and traditionally female ways of leading, they have a wider range of leadership options. Furthermore, when presidents—either male or female—model a gender-integrated approach to campus leadership, they may also increase the attractiveness of high-level positions for those who would like to move up the hierarchy but who do not want to conform to specific gendered ways of leading. Indeed, when leaders understand that they need not be completely bound by gender expectations, they may feel that a great burden has been lifted, regardless of whether they are male or female.

Leading in a way that integrates traditionally gendered leadership styles is an important way of building one's multidimensional leadership model. Historical conceptions of leadership that rely on preferences of an ideal worker (Williams, 2000) are no longer tenable because they limit the pool of those considered for and those who ultimately obtain leadership positions. First, current gendered constructs place value only on a male norm, thereby limiting how women can lead authentically and how men can lead in an integrated manner and likewise not be judged negatively. Second, recognition of the value that an integrated model of leadership brings (Nidiffer, 2001) acknowledges a broader array of competencies that are needed for leading today's complex organizations—namely, collaboration, participation, and generative leadership. The elimination of strict gender constructs removes the automatic advantage White men have held.

In practice, individuals can begin to incorporate more integrated leadership in their own multidimensional model by recognizing the assumptions they hold about leadership and the ways in which they themselves may inadvertently reinforce the concept of an ideal worker versus valuing an authentic orientation to leadership. One can begin by questioning personal practices that rely on positional authority and power versus more input from followers. Pointedly, this applies to both men and women. Individual modeling of gender-equitable leadership that values male and female attributes and contributions affects not only those formally mentored by leaders but also those observing leaders. Next, it is important to investigate the ways in which structural issues and power within the college have reinforced gendered practices for promotion, for job functions, and for access to development opportunities. Structural issues to investigate may include pay structures and job classification checks for instances of gender inequity and hiring and promotion practices that favor a male model. Clearly, these are in the purview of current presidents, but others may also have an impact on these structural issues regardless of position by raising concerns about inequity on campus, serving on campus committees to provide recommendations for change, and implementing campus policies that support equity on campus. As Eddy and Cox (2008) noted, "individuals can begin to change the micro-environments within their institutions" (p. 79). Changes on individual campuses begin to create a social construction of integrated leadership locally that can contribute to larger changes.

In considering the multidimensional model, individuals may find that they are initially bound by traditional social construction of gender based on how they "do gender" (West & Zimmerman, 1987). Here, what a leader should do is based on their gender and guides their leadership. On the one hand, a woman may socially construct her gender based on expectations for women and have this orientation reinforced by others, especially when she acts outside her prescribed role. On the other hand, a woman may feel compelled to buy into the historical norms of leading using a hierarchy, authoritative leadership, and directives. Here tensions are evident. As women question their own assumptions about leadership and begin to lead more authentically, they expand the ways in which they see leadership. This involves a movement along the gender continuum but also affects other elements of the model, such as ways in which they make decisions, how they use organizational frames, and the competencies that they use in practice.

Similarly, men may not question their leadership orientations from a gendered perspective because male norms have long been the benchmark for leadership. Once men reflect on the value of attributes traditionally deemed as women's ways of leading, a shift occurs in the norms of leadership. Value is now placed on an integration of what was previously conceived in a zero-sum manner. Individuals are located at different points on the gender continuum, both with respect to how they construct gender and also in what they value regarding integrated leadership. Expanded notions of gender are located at one end of the continuum, whereas singular concepts of gender (male/female) are located at the opposite end. In the more complex model of multidimensional leadership, men as well as women are rewarded for leading in an integrated manner.

# 7

# PLANNING FOR THE FUTURE

As for the future, your task is not to foresee it,
but to enable it.

Antoine de Saint-Exupéry

A variety of challenges face sitting leaders, potential leaders, and institutions as they prepare for the high levels of openings anticipated in the next decade in the leadership ranks in the nation's community colleges. The empirical findings presented in this book provide a backdrop for planning for the future, with the multidimensional model of leadership showcasing a theoretical framework to advance thinking about leadership and development. Key elements within the multidimensional model focus on how an individual's underlying schema provides the foundation for his or her leadership—what the leader knows and how he or she thinks about new experiences sets up the leader's approach to campus challenges and strategies for the future.

As has been showcased, leaders learn from their experiences, with mentors helping upcoming leaders gain knowledge as they model behavior, even if this may mean learning how not to lead. Formal training sessions and programs provide a way to learn new skills and to increase networking occasions with other leaders. Central to these learning opportunities are acquiring the competencies required to lead in the complex environments in which community colleges are located. In particular, cultural competency—the ability to read the traditions of the campus and the central ethos of operations and to align strategies to leverage change—provides a means to use the AACC competencies to the best advantage of the campus. Recall that the AACC competencies are organizational strategies, resource management skills, communication skills, a willingness to collaborate, advocacy skills, and professionalism.

From a multidimensional perspective, communication provides a mechanism that enacts a number of leadership skills. Communicating on campus provides leaders with a unique opportunity to frame their key messages and underpins a span of competency clusters. Viewing leadership from a multidimensional basis offers a view of the competencies that link skills with different foci of emphasis depending on a person's leadership orientation. The clusters outlined in this book are inclusivity, framing meaning, minding the bottom line, and systems thinking that highlight various competencies depending on the college context and the leaders' preferences.

Adding to the way we think of multidimensional leaders are gender and race. Gender and race affect the career pathways of leaders, affect how leaders are initially viewed, and contribute to leaders' identity. As conceptions of acceptable leadership expands beyond the historic White male model, a wider range of individuals will both consider advanced positions and be considered for openings. The anticipated turnover of college presidencies creates an opening to shift the composition of the leadership ranges and gives a chance to include a diversity of approaches to leading.

The flexibility of the multidimensional model provides a dynamic means of thinking about leadership at community colleges. First, it allows for a range of acceptable ways to lead and is malleable to indicate growth through experience and reflection. Second, the various elements of leadership interact via the connections between levels, allowing for communication, for example, to inform how a leader enacts an organizational framework on campus. Finally, the reliance of the model on the concepts of lifelong learning are underscored by the ways in which the model changes over time. This chapter begins with a review of the five propositions undergirding the multidimensional leadership model, then outlines critical issues of leadership development and succession planning, and concludes with a list of specific tools and resources that individuals, institutions, and the community college leadership profession itself can use to plan for the future.

## Revisiting the Propositions

In chapter 1, I identified five propositions that undergird the model for multidimensional leadership: (1) There is no single or universal model for leadership at community colleges; (2) leaders are multidimensional and multifaceted, relying on different skills and perspectives to address the complexity of their leadership challenges; (3) leaders are guided by their underlying cognitive schemas; (4) some central beliefs guiding leaders are less open than others to change; and (5) leadership development should be based on the tenets of adult learning theory, recognizing leaders as learners.

Each of these five propositions adds to the complexity of a multidimensional view of leadership and moves beyond traditional conceptions about what is required for successful leadership as well as simple lists of leadership skills or competencies. A multidimensional perspective of leadership provides for a range of ways to operationalize leadership and define success. Furthermore, by focusing on leaders as adult learners, a multidimensional perspective highlights the necessity of reflection and a commitment to life-long learning in the leading process. This orientation allows leaders to question their assumptions, identify new approaches to old problems, and create alternative solutions to nagging challenges facing their college.

### Proposition 1: There Is No Universal Model for Leadership

Key to understanding multidimensional leadership is accepting the premise that there is no single way for successful leaders to operate on campus. If hiring boards are to move beyond a cookie-cutter approach to hiring leaders, they need to end their reliance on a traditional model of how successful leaders look or act. More important in selecting a successful leader is an in-depth understanding of the organizational needs of the college, as well as a commitment to searching for a leader whose previous experiences and ideas will best serve the institution.

At its core, a multidimensional model of leadership assumes that a wide range of individuals can be successful leaders. This model challenges campus constituents and hiring boards to change their conceptions of what constitutes a "good" leader. As Leslie and Fretwell (1996) note, in difficult times, campus members often look to top leaders for solutions, endowing a type of "hero" status on the president. Yet these actions result in a narrow conception of leadership that, unlike a multidimensional perspective, overlooks the fact that successful leaders can and often do look and operate differently from historic conceptions of "great" leaders.

By focusing on the fact that there are multiple ways to lead, the multidimensional perspective allows for a wide range of role models who can help others along their own leadership pathway. As this book has shown, a mentor's encouragement often provides the necessary nudge for individuals to pursue leadership positions. By conceptualizing leadership in a multidimensional manner, we automatically create a wider pipeline leading to top-level positions in community colleges.

## Proposition 2: Multidimensional Leadership Is Necessary in Complex Organizations

The second proposition undergirding this book is the notion that leadership can be enacted along several dimensions and can consist of a wide range of approaches and styles, all of which may result in successful outcomes. Heifetz (1994) has argued that leaders need to view campus issues from "the balcony." In other words, they should strive to view specific issues in their overall context and rely on a broader systems perspective in developing solutions. When leaders take this bird's-eye perspective, they bring different aspects of leadership to bear, depending on the issue at hand and the contextual needs of the campus. This requires leaders to be multifaceted and multidimensional; leaders who seek to solve every problem with the same set of leadership actions will not succeed for long.

The presidents described throughout this book exemplify the notion of multidimensional leadership. For instance, President Pauldine was faced with major budgetary issues when she arrived on campus, and thus she relied greatly on her skills in resource management and organizational strategy. However, she also used a variety of communication methods to get her message across and to frame the financial crisis to her staff. President Burke, on the other hand, focused her attention on creating a college culture based on student learning. She focused on creating organizational processes, communicating a new shared vision for the campus, and developing new patterns for shared decision making. Each leader described in this book relied on different dimensions of his or her leadership to address the issues at hand. Not only is this a successful approach to campus management, but by relying on different aspects of their leadership, the presidents expanded their understanding of leadership, which resulted in leadership development and flexibility.

## Proposition 3: Leaders Rely on Their Underlying Cognitive Schema in Making Leadership Decisions

Leaders are guided by their underlying schemas and the way in which they see the world. Although leaders often rely on old mental models developed from previous experiences and beliefs, by engaging in reflection and continuous feedback loops, they can adjust their schema and allow for greater flexibility in their approach to problems on campus. For example, President Fields was forced to adjust her cognitive schema as she took in new information from her institution's self-study, which contained charges of nepotism and ethical concerns about decision making on campus. In adjusting her cognitive schema to take this new information into account, she became more cautious about whom to trust in new situations and more guarded about making initial assumptions about people and situations. She worked to increase communication venues on campus in order to prevent similar issues from occurring again.

### Proposition 4: Leaders Often Adhere to Their Core Belief Structure

As chapter 3 illustrates, community college leaders' cognitive schemas contain elements that are quite malleable, as well as others that are less open to change. Past experience and cognitive orientation often guides which elements are changeable. For example, President Jones brought a technical predisposition to his leadership. He focused on creating a vision for the college based on the infusion of technology and student learning, evident in the laptop initiative he brought to campus (which was based on the laptop initiative from his previous campus). Clearly, Jones preferred to implement organizational strategies via technical solutions. This mental map would be difficult to change, even in a different environment. Likewise, President Hammond brought a specific campus strategy when he arrived at Strategic Community College—the same strategy that he used at his last campus. Although Hammond's overall strategy and way to leading did not change much, he did tweak his strategic plan in response to the college's desire to place ethics at the center of the institution's vision statement. Past practice and actions serve as a blueprint for how leaders may approach new problems and situations and can serve as clues for hiring boards. Furthermore, the ways in which potential leaders speak about their plans for the campus during the interview process can give a glimpse into their core schemas and central leadership approaches.

### Proposition 5: Leaders Are Learners

As noted earlier, one way that leaders modify their mental maps of existing cognitive schemas is through reflection about their own leadership, the campus environment, and alternative approaches to campus issues. Chapter 3 describes Kolb's (1998) model of learning, in which adult leaders undergo a complex process that requires active reflection about the learning process. Not only can reflection and a commitment to continuous learning help leaders become more nimble and adaptable on their campuses, but by developing a clear understanding of their own learning strategies, they can be more effective in helping others within the organization along their learning process (Heifetz & Laurie, 1997). As Lave and Wenger (1991) have noted, learning does not occur in isolation. Rather, it takes place within a specific context. In this case, for community college leaders, authentic learning occurs through interaction with others, as well as reflection on the situation at hand, the surrounding campus context, and the leaders' own actions and beliefs.

This proposition is especially important to the leadership development process. Leadership development opportunities must be structured around authentic contexts and situations. This can be done through case studies, internships, and job shadowing. For sitting leaders, learning is ongoing. President Simon noted that the opportunity to work outside higher education provided him with a different perspective on his leadership approaches. President Hales's work on state boards similarly provided her with opportunities to observe how things were done on other campuses, which ultimately led her to conclude that the problems on her campus were not unique, that they were rather a part of a larger community college movement. Community college leaders and potential leaders should obtain wide and broad experiences that can expand their cognitive schemas, and leadership development opportunities should be structured around authentic and realistic campus situations to allow future leaders to strengthen their leadership instincts and capabilities. Leadership development opportunities must also take into account the problems and opportunities inherent in planning for leadership succession.

## Multidimensional Leadership Model

The propositions presented provide the framework for the multidimensional leadership model. The model is three-dimensional to underscore the dynamic nature of leadership as opposed to traditional conceptions of leadership historically illustrated in two dimensions (see Figure 2.1, for example). As leaders learn, their location within the model shifts, but because a key proposition is that there is no singular manner of leading, there is no preferred location within the model. Learning is represented by movement along the continua of each feature presented within the model. In general, each continuum represents a range of options for the various leadership concepts, with the endpoints representing the dichotomies often associated with the competencies. The levels of the model include the concepts reviewed in this book, namely, leadership schema, gender, communication, framing, and leadership competencies. (See Figure 7.1.) The model is not meant to be static; thus other specifics of leadership could readily be added as another level within the model to provide more lenses for deconstructing leadership. Expanded versions of this model may include levels for decision making, interpersonal relations, social capital, organizational perspectives, or partnership interactions, to name a few.

Leadership schemas provide the base for this multidimensional leadership model. How leaders see the world creates the platform for how they lead. Recall that schemas provide individuals with shortcuts of how to interpret new situations based on past experiences (Harris, 1994). As leaders develop, they acquire perspectives on the leadership approaches that best suit them, practices that worked in the past and they anticipate will continue to work, and specific thought processes used in coming to conclusions based on evidence at hand. Schemas are augmented as new experiences are added and critical reflection shifts long-held assumptions, but some elements of a leader's schema are less malleable. As noted, President Jones's view of the world involved using technology to address campus planning. He saw technical solutions for academic programming (initiation of the laptop program), student learning (the vignette of students walking across the graduation stage with laptops), and campus outreach (working with other institutions on technical programs with practical applications in agricultural science). No doubt, if Jones took a presidency at another institution, he would employ his technical perspective to address campus planning.

Another factor included in the model is gender. On one end of the continuum for gendered leadership are traditionally female forms of leadership, including generative approaches and collaboration, whereas on the other end of the continuum are male forms of leadership, marked by directives and assertive approaches. Integrated forms of leadership approaches are represented by points between these two extremes. Nidiffer (2001) posited that integrated forms of gendered leadership draw from the best of both absolute gendered leadership modes, which eliminates behaviors that traditionally favored men in the past and that discounted female forms of leadership. The integrated perspective values women's attributes equally. The location of leaders along the various points on the continuum illustrates the combination of ways that individuals favor more female or male ways of leading. Despite the perspective that an integrated approach can provide value for organizations, the language of gender often describes individuals using prescribed roles. The female leaders in this research noted occasions in which their gender made them voiceless or perceived unfavorably when too assertive. Men, on the other hand, did not reference their gender, reinforcing the notion that male leadership was the norm and did not warrant commentary or consideration. Even so, men used more traditionally female forms of leadership in collaborations and via participatory decision making. More integrated forms of gendered leadership value multiple approaches without favoring one approach at the expense of another.

Leaders use a variety of communication styles in their leadership. The continuum for this attribute shows the extremes of top-down communication styles versus participatory communication. The full range of communication styles outlined by Lunenburg and Ornstein (2007) may be found along the continuum. In this case, the most restricted form of communication in the chain model would be found on the end representing top-down interactions, whereas the star model and its reliance on dialogue and participation would be found on the other end.

Leaders may find that they operate using multiple communication patterns depending on the situation, individuals involved, and history with the audience for whom their remarks are intended. Thus, new leaders may first work primarily within their leadership cabinet to build rapport with this inner circle. In turn, the cabinet may relay information to their reports, thus initially using more of a top-down style. Public forums, on the other hand, may provide a mechanism for more participation by campus members, as do one-on-one conversations with the president. The level of communication involvement in these public interactions depends on the individual's approach because some public forums may be more formal and not structured for real interaction.

As campuses face budget cuts and create strategic plans to meet future challenges, leaders communicate information to stakeholders regarding these major campus changes. President Pauldine used small-group meetings to gather information for planning and then related these plans during a formal campus meeting. The formal presentation of the plan created the perception of a top-down delivery because campus members did not see their contributions to the project. President Burke, on the other hand, created a participatory process during her campus planning that created multiple opportunities for dialogue; she worked to reach consensus among various stakeholders.

Closely linked to forms of communication are the process leaders use for sensemaking on campus. How leaders frame information and situations for campus members takes on heightened importance as institutions become more complex and campus members attempt to figure out how to make meaning of ongoing changes. Leaders have a variety of ways in which to frame information. As outlined in chapter 4, sensemaking occurs in stages, often with retroactive sensemaking occurring. The thematic formats presented in the model include step-by-step framing, visionary framing, and connective framing. As is the case in forms of communication, each of these framing options relies on a particular approach by leaders.

In step-by-step framing, leaders frame by incremental advancement on plans. President Fields used this approach as she tackled campus problems, outlining for staff the next immediate step to address curriculum issues and community outreach. The sights of the campus were focused on the next step along the pathway versus the long-term destination for the college. Visionary framing, on the other hand, points campus members to the long-range goals and ideals of what the campus may become. President Hammond presented a vision for campus members at Strategic Community College that focused on a future based on efficiencies and ethical decision making. The physical strategic-bound plan symbolized the tactics to obtain campus goals and provided a road map to obtain these objectives. Key performance indicators allowed for alteration along the path. Finally, connective framing relies on the co-creation of the vision for the college through the use of group dialogue and decision making. President Burke used this form of framing as she worked with campus members to create a student-learning-centered environment at Cutting Edge Community College. Burke created opportunities in which dialogue occurred and multiple values were considered regarding future directions for the college. The types of framing employed may shift as campus needs develop. Leaders begin to read the environment and place value on different elements of meaning making as the situation demands.

The final level of the model represents leadership competencies. The cluster of competencies is rooted in the set of broad skills outlined by AACC (2005) as those most critical for community college leaders. Within each cluster, different sets of competencies receive more priority and are given heightened importance. The clusters include minding the bottom line, in which resource and management issues are central. Inclusivity focuses on blending communication with collaboration such that campus members feel that their voice is heard and incorporated into plans. The cluster of framing meaning incorporates communication and collaboration as well, but also attends to organizational strategy and advocacy to focus attention on the symbolic value of generating a particular campus saga. Building community occurs through storytelling and calling attention to particular campus elements. President Jones worked to create a campus saga around the notion of technology and advances using technology as a tool. Finally, the cluster of systems thinking relies on high levels of cultural competency in understanding the campus environment's influence on a variety of the college systems. Leaders in this cluster view more nuances within the organization and see the action-reaction sequence of events as changes are made. Heifetz (1994) argues that this "view from the balcony" moves thinking beyond a myopic view of understanding only what is directly in the focus of attention and instead broadens the perspective to see the larger implications inherent in the broader system.

The range of the elements within the multidimensional leadership model allows for a number of options to represent individualized leadership. Three examples (Leader A, Leader B, and Leader C) are shown in Figure 7.1 to highlight how various locations on the continua construct a unique leadership approach. Given the lack of judgment inherent in the model, no one compilation is privileged over another. The flexibility in the model also allows for movement along the continua as leaders learn and as they process feedback from their current actions. In general, the base location of leaders' schemas stay rooted, but other aspects become more malleable to change.

Linked to the location of leaders within the model are considerations of fit for institutions. For instance, Leader A may be the best fit for an institution facing critical budget decisions requiring a top-down decision-making process that allows for faster action as opposed to the time-consuming process involved in participatory decision making. Leader B, on the other hand, may be a better fit for an institution that needs to build a sense of community and a forward-looking direction. A leader using this set of attributes would focus on how to frame the future for campus members and would provide a blend of approaches using decisive leadership coupled with participation of campus members. Finally, Leader C would be a good fit for a college with open communication systems that allow for dialogue in decision making. A systems approach underscores a holistic organizational view in which leadership understands the links between actions and reactions throughout. More time is involved in the constellation of options for Leader C; thus this model may be most appropriate for mature institutions not facing an immediate crisis.

The multidimensional leadership model considers that leaders learn as they lead and can change their orientations. As well, institutions have different needs at different stages of their organizational development. The complexity of today's community colleges underscores the need to think more

**FIGURE 7.1**
**Multidimensional Leadership Model**

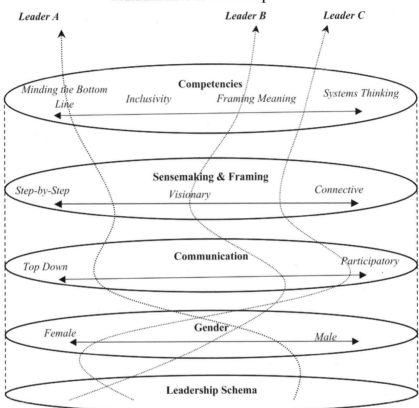

complexly about leadership. The cultural competency required of leaders showcases the need for fit.

## Succession Planning

Although business has a proven track record of leadership succession planning (Berke, 2005; Conger & Fulmer, 2003; Seymour, 2008), higher education does not (Bisbee & Miller, 2006; Fulton-Calkins & Milling, 2005). Historically, career trajectories leading to the presidency began in the faculty ranks and progressed through positions as department chair, dean, and vice president. However, these long-standing patterns have recently begun to change (Amey, VanDerLinden, & Brown, 2002), with leaders rising through other areas within the college and from outside higher education (American Council on Education [ACE], 2007; Weisman & Vaughan, 2007).

As colleges begin to think about leadership succession planning, it is useful to consider the areas in which many first-time presidents feel insufficiently prepared: fiscal responsibility for an entire institution and relationship interactions (ACE, 2007; Bassoppo-Moyo & Townsend, 1997). Interactions concern relationship dealings with staff, the board, and community stakeholders. According to ACE (2007), new presidents often feel unprepared for fund-raising, supervising capital improvements, managing risk, budgeting, and engaging in entrepreneurial ventures. Clearly, hiring boards and aspiring leaders must pay more attention to the AACC competency of resource management in order to ensure smooth succession-planning processes. Leaders also felt insufficiently prepared in the interaction skills of crisis management and governing board relations. The necessity of dealing with critical fiscal issues and the complementary need to find alternative funding through grants and development efforts may begin to shape the type of presidents needed in the future.

Community college boards of trustees and current leaders have begun to address some issues of succession planning with the implementation of grow-your-own (GYO) leadership development programs (Jeandron, 2006). GYO programs allow institutions to cast a wide net within their own campus community, especially at earlier stages in the career pipeline, to search for potential future leaders. Generally, these programs focus on providing on-site professional development sessions focusing on specific skills such as managing personnel, dealing with budgets, and community engagement strategies. Some programs require a formal application to participate, whereas others are less formal, with participants recommended by upper-level leaders. Because successful future leaders must possess a wide array of experiences and skills in order to lead effectively, GYO programs should recognize future leaders early on and prepare them with a diverse set of experiences, training, and mentorship. Guiding this preparation can be the competencies outlined in chapter 5, as well as areas of weakness commonly identified by incoming presidents.

Sometimes community colleges are reluctant to invest in training individuals who may take their talents elsewhere. This concern may be justified because aspiring leaders have noted that a barrier to their advancement was the unavailability of positions at their current institution (VanDerLinden,

2004). The structure of the community college hierarchy means that fewer upper-level positions are available to those seeking advancement from within. Furthermore, there seems to be a revolving door to the corner office. One quarter of presidents come to the position from a previous presidency (Amey, VanDerLinden, & Brown, 2002), and almost half of community college presidents have held two or more presidential positions (Weisman & Vaughan, 2007). Both President Hammond and President Jones came to their positions from previous presidencies. They hit the ground running because the scenarios and campus issues presented often were known to them from their previous leadership positions.

Hiring boards clearly prioritize experience on the job, but as a result, questions remain about how to bring new blood into these leadership positions. However, we also know that 35% of first-time presidents were hired from within the institution (Weisman & Vaughan, 2007). Internal hires have the advantage that the new president will have an in-depth knowledge of the institutional culture, an understanding of the direction and vision for the college, and an awareness of organizational practices, including hidden skeletons. Both President Burke and President Hales were hired from within the Large and Growing Community College District. However, a dilemma occurs because search committees may overlook outside candidates whose experiences and ideas may be more effective in addressing campus problems.

Clearly, community college leaders and boards of trustees need to think more consciously and proactively about succession planning. They may invest in leadership development opportunities for their staff, or they may mine nearby community colleges. Indeed, regional efforts to provide leadership development activities may allow institutions to share the costs for training and also provide opportunities for aspiring leaders to see leadership in action at other institutions, in the process gaining a broader view of the commonality of problems on community college campuses as well as potential solutions.

The increased mobility of community college presidents raises some serious issues for succession planning. In particular, the need to move to another city or state in order to obtain a presidential position may be a barrier for some potential leaders. In particular, women and leaders of color may be adversely affected by expectations that leaders need to be geographically flexible. The difficulties inherent in balancing one's career with the demands of raising a family may also preclude some aspiring leaders from seeking higher-level positions.

In summary, community college leaders and boards of trustees must treat succession planning as a critical issue. New leaders can be developed through grow-your-own leadership programs or by using outside development programs. Building mentorship opportunities into everyday life at the institution is also important and is also a way of transferring institutional history and knowledge to the next generation. Programs that support women and aspiring leaders of color help close the participation gap evident in high-level community college positions. Thinking critically about leadership succession is not something that should be put off for another day; many sitting presidents plan to retire in the next few years, and new leaders from various backgrounds who bring a wide variety of skills and competencies to the institution will be necessary if colleges are to successfully address community needs and educate students in a cost-efficient and equitable manner.

## Next Steps for Community College Leadership

The community college is a complex enterprise. Thus, preparing for a changing of the leadership guard and developing future leaders who are multifaceted and multidimensional are also complex endeavors. This section presents advice, tools, and resources that can help individuals, institutions, and the profession (defined as professional associations and individuals interested in community college leadership) as they seek to prepare for and promote effective community college leaders in the future.

### *Advice for Individuals*

As is clear from the stories and experiences of the community college presidents interviewed for this book, many community college leaders did not begin their careers with aspirations of being a president. Most found their way accidentally to these positions, a finding that is supported by the research literature (Garza Mitchell & Eddy, 2008). Nonetheless, their pathways often had several key features in common. First, the leaders had all developed a range of expertise in a community college setting. Their learning occurred on the job, as well as through participation in leadership training sessions or professional development workshops. Second, mentors played essential roles in helping them navigate their leadership career pathways— most often by opening doors to particular opportunities or by taking advantage of teachable moments. Just as important, however, were negative role models; in many cases, community college leaders learned from their predecessors how *not* to lead.

Leadership development programs helped the presidents in this study learn more about their own desires to advance, network with others in the field, and prepare for the challenges of the top-level office. Also, as one of the additional leaders of color interviewed for this book pointed out, leadership development programs can be helpful in reflecting on the demands of the presidency, as well as where one's leadership skills may be most effective within an organizational hierarchy. As this president pointed out, many aspiring leaders choose *not* to enter the presidency after engaging in a leadership development program, deciding instead to seek another type of leadership position. Thus, leadership training programs serve multiple functions. They help aspiring leaders acquire skills, but they also provide opportunities to reflect on how and where each individual can best contribute to his or her institution.

Aspiring community college leaders would be well served to create a career plan that maps out their desired path to a high-level leadership position. Given that community college leaders are often expected to move to a different city or state in order to find a position, career plans need to take timing and mobility into account, especially if the leader also has family responsibilities. In creating and carrying out a career plan, individuals should partake in the following activities:

- Engage in critical reflection of your core beliefs and values so that you can align these with potential leadership opportunities.
- Build relationships with mentors from whom you can learn the ropes and who can help open doors for you.
- Create a broad network both within your institution and in the larger community college field. These connections can help in a job search, but often more important, can provide you with advisers who may be able to help when you face issues as a new leader.
- Learn more about leadership by reading books and articles on leadership, by talking with leaders whom you respect, and by attending training workshops.
- Obtain a wide array of experiences. You may find leadership opportunities by volunteering for campus committees, engaging in professional associations or community groups, or doing a series of different jobs within your own institution.
- Acquire the credentials needed for high-level positions. The doctoral degree is a common prerequisite for a presidency, but it is increasingly necessary for other top positions as well.

- Participate in activities that give you an outside perspective. Serving on accreditation teams, working with state boards, or consulting at other colleges can provide unique learning opportunities that broaden your experience beyond what you can learn at a single institution.
- Prepare for role shifts. Taking on leadership positions involves a role shift whereby you become a novice again. Furthermore, your life becomes much more public; as president, you represent your campus 24 hours a day, 7 days a week, even when you think you are just getting a cup of coffee or buying the morning paper. This can be a difficult transition for new leaders and may create new relationship dynamics on campus and in the community. This role shift is made all the more difficult by the fact that presidents often have few peers on campus. Build your support network—both within and outside your college—and rely on those people to help ease your transition.
- Acknowledge the importance of effective communication and framing change for campus members. Creating and communicating a common vision can help achieve change.

Women and leaders of color should address additional items as they begin planning for advancement:

- Create a support network to help deal with sexism and racism you may face as you advance up the career ladder.
- Participate in training and development programs geared toward women and leaders of color to discover how others have navigated the career pipeline.
- Develop strategies to maintain a work-life balance that will support your career ambitions and also leave room for the other important things in your life.

### *Advice for Institutions*

Current leaders are often in a good position to identify leadership potential among their own staff and faculty. Early identification of promising leaders allows more time to foster leadership development and can help institutions be more intentional in their succession planning. Some future leaders will readily spring to mind, whereas others will become apparent through involvement in campus committees or programs. Including a broad range of individuals from many areas of the college can provide a rich environment to assess future leadership potential. Paying specific attention to groups who are often excluded from the leadership pipeline is key to creating a diverse upper administration. Involvement in grow-your-own leadership programming is increasing, but many colleges also provide less formal leadership development opportunities such as book clubs, mentoring relationships, and money or time off to allow individuals to participate in graduate leadership programs and acquire key credentials for advancement.

The board of trustees plays a critical role in promoting the leaders of the future, and therefore trustees need to broaden their concept of a community college leader to include those of different genders, races, and ethnicities. In advertising for open positions, trustees may be more successful in finding a leader who is a good fit if they articulate the particular needs of the college instead of listing a generic set of skills they would like to see in applicants (Drake, 2009; Leist, 2007). As this book has made clear, leaders who are better aligned with the problems, strengths, and issues of their institution are more likely to be successful at that college. Furthermore, by creating an ethos on campus that values leadership at all levels of the institution, trustees can take advantage of talent within their current employee base. Some individuals may opt not to seek an advanced position because of personal circumstances but may still contribute in substantial ways to the college. Providing challenging jobs that may not necessarily fit a traditional job description can help improve employee job satisfaction and stability at the college.

Institutional leaders and boards of trustees can help promote leadership transitions by engaging in the following activities:

- Establish an internal mentoring program to help develop potential leaders.
- Identify potential leaders early in their careers and provide opportunities for them to develop their leadership competencies, in particular by obtaining outside experiences.
- Create an induction program for new leaders. Providing leaders with support as they experience role shifts will help them navigate through this transition. Find ways to socialize the new leader to the campus and the community in order to improve his or her learning curve. Create and maintain links with statewide programs that oversee mentoring for new presidents in order to connect new leaders with peers throughout your state.
- Broaden your concept of who can be a leader, paying particular attention to women, leaders of color, and leaders who have unconventional career experiences.

- Establish and support a grow-your-own leadership program at your college. Smaller institutions may find it easier to do this on a regional basis or in conjunction with nearby 4-year colleges.
- Support staff attendance at state, regional, and national leadership trainings and conferences.
- Provide flexible scheduling and tuition support for individuals who wish to enroll in graduate leadership programs.

## *Advice for the Profession*

Those in the community college profession—including boards of professional associations, directors of graduate programs and leadership training programs, community college leadership scholars, and other interested parties—need to be engaged in supporting leadership development. Education is currently receiving a lot of national attention as a way of addressing the nation's economic and social needs. Community colleges have become increasingly popular as a gateway to higher education and as a linchpin in workforce development initiatives. However, this increased attention may lead to increased pressure on 2-year college leaders to be all things to all people. Tomorrow's community college leaders will be forced to take on diverse leadership challenges under unprecedented national scrutiny. As new challenges arise, and as new conceptions of multidimensional leadership take hold, leadership development programs must keep pace and provide learning opportunities and leadership strategies that are highly contextualized and adapted to the diverse array of potential future leaders.

The profession can help create leadership capacity in the 2-year sector and support aspiring leaders through engaging in the following activities:

- Create and foster regional, statewide, or national networks of community college leaders. By pooling resources these networks may be able to address a common set of issues facing community college leaders with increased efficiency.
- Share best practices in community college leadership at conferences, meetings of professional associations, online, and in a wide array of publications for scholars and practitioners.
- Identify graduate leadership programs that do an exemplary job of meeting practitioner needs and institutional requirements. The best programs incorporate a focus on lifelong learning and link theory and practice.

- Assess the need for different types of leadership development programming at all stages of the career pipeline. New leaders and seasoned leaders require different types of support and may benefit from different types of training or other opportunities.
- Expand research on community college issues and leadership dilemmas in order to help leaders better understand the issues they face. In particular, using methodologies that highlight voices that are not traditionally heard in leadership literature can shed more light on how to support community college leadership in the future.

## Key Resources for Individuals, Institutions, and the Profession

Several resources can help individuals and institutions engage in or support community college leadership development. Many universities offer graduate programs for future leaders, and some focus specifically on the community college. The Council for the Study of Community Colleges maintains a list of such programs (see http://www.cscconline.org/gradprogs.htm). Additionally, the Association for the Study of Higher Education provides a searchable database of all higher education programs (see http://www.ashe.ws/?page=187). Furthermore, statewide community college associations or coordinating boards often host leadership training programs, seminars, or certificate programs. A check with state association directors can determine what resources are available locally.

As noted in chapter 3, several community college professional associations and leadership development programs exist. Many of these are listed here.

- American Association of Community Colleges
  (http://www.aacc.nche.edu)
  Future Leaders Institute for Midlevel Administrators
  Presidents' Academy
  American Association for Women in Community Colleges
  National Community College Hispanic Council
  National Council on Black American Affairs

- American Council on Education (http://www.acenet.edu)
  Presidential Seminars and Roundtables
  Women Presidents' Summits
  Summits for Presidents of Color
  Presidents' Consultation Network

Institute for New Chief Academic Officers
The Internationalization Forum for Chief Academic Officers
National Leadership Forums for the Advancement of Women Leaders
Advancing to the Presidency: A Workshop for Vice Presidents
ACE Fellows Program
ACE National Network for the Advancement of Women Leaders
Women of Color Summits
Department Chair Workshops

- The Chair Academy (http://www.chairacademy.com)

- Higher Education Resource Services (HERS)
  Sponsors institutes for female midlevel and senior administrators at
  Bryn Mawr, the University of Denver, and Wellesley College (http://
  www.hersnet.org/Institutes.asp)

- Institute for Community College Development (http://www.iccd
  .cornell.edu)

- League for Innovation in the Community College (http://www
  .league.org)
  Executive Leadership Institute
  Expanding Leadership Diversity

- National Institute for Leadership Development (http://www.pc.mari
  copa.edu/nild)
  Focuses on leadership development for women

In addition to these leadership development programs, a plethora of
research exists on issues facing community college leaders. Some of this is
presented in academic journals and conference programs, and more can be
found in practitioner-oriented publications. It is critical for leaders to understand the wider issues facing leaders in higher education and to explore how
others have opted to meet these challenges. Following are resources focused
on the community college, as well as some that cover general higher education issues. Finally, there is a list of community college research centers.

- Journals
  *Community College Enterprise*

*Community College Journal of Research and Practice*
*Community College Review*
*Journal of Applied Research in the Community College*

- Magazines and newspapers
  *Change*
  *Chronicle of Higher Education*
  *Community College Journal*
  *Inside Higher Education*

- Community college centers
  Center for Community College Policy
  Community College Research Center, Teachers College, Columbia University
  Office of Community College Research and Leadership, University of Illinois at Urbana-Champaign
  Office of Community College Research and Policy, Iowa State University
  UCLA Community College Studies

## Conclusions

In re-envisioning community college leadership, we must move beyond a single type or model of how a leader looks and acts. As increasingly complex institutions, community colleges require multidimensional leaders from a range of backgrounds and experiences who can be flexible and adaptive as they approach new challenges. The voices and experiences of presidents interviewed for this book show that community college leaders rely on underlying cognitive schemas or mental maps to initially help them make sense of challenges and opportunities their institutions face. However, as they acquire new knowledge, gain different experiences, explore alternative perspectives, and take new contexts into account, their leadership styles and skills evolve, resulting in more flexible, thoughtful leadership. In the process, various elements within their multidimensional models expand and become more malleable. Leaders are, at their core, adult learners. As such, they improve their leadership through continuous reflection on their own actions and on their surrounding environment. Through reflection, leaders can question their assumptions and long-held beliefs, which provides opportunities for both personal and organizational change.

The ability to see problems and situations from multiple perspectives allows leaders to move beyond strict adherence to tactics that worked in the past if they are no longer effective in the current context. Therefore, a critical aspect of multidimensional leadership is cultural competency—the ability to scan an environment and determine strategies that best fit the culture, traditions, and practices of the institution and its constituents. Effective communication with faculty, staff, and students is also important to multidimensional leadership, as is the ability to frame information and strategies for change for campus members. Effective framing allows leaders to highlight the aspects of a given situation that they would like the campus to focus on, while downplaying others. Not only does this allow the leader to help construct the perceived reality on campus, but it also pulls campus constituents together to pursue strategies for change. Because information framing is such a powerful tool, however, leaders must continuously reflect on their actions in order to ensure that they are ethical and aligned with the campus mission and vision.

The multidimensional model of leadership put forth in this book, as well as the five propositions undergirding it, provides a new platform for understanding leadership. This book has relied primarily on the voices and experiences of community college presidents to illustrate multidimensional leadership in action, but the model can apply to leaders at all levels within the organization. Formal titles and hierarchical positions do not necessarily qualify one as a leader, and thus the model applies equally to presidents and other administrators as to faculty members and staff who are working for change and who are willing to reflect on their experiences and leadership styles in order to build their leadership capabilities and effect positive change on campus. Understanding that leadership is a dynamic and ongoing process that occurs on multiple dimensions allows a much broader range of individuals to be considered for leadership positions and ensures that tomorrow's leaders will bring a wide array of attributes and competencies to the nation's community colleges.

Community colleges are currently at a crossroads. Although they have gained a great deal of national attention and praise for providing postsecondary education and training to all who seek it and are viewed by many as vital to the future strength of the nation, they are also chronically underfunded. Twenty-first-century community college leaders thus face numerous challenges, but there are also a great many opportunities and rewards. For example, shifts toward more collaborative decision making on campus will allow tomorrow's leaders to rely more extensively on the experience and judgments of those around them and may be more enjoyable as well. In order to attract a diverse set of individuals to community college leadership positions, we must recast how these positions are operationalized. Making changes that allow for a better work-life balance, creating a supportive campus climate, and building relationships and collaborative opportunities within the college and the broader community may ensure more attractive work environments. Community colleges are complex, multidimensional institutions, and if they are to live up to their core mission of ensuring access to high-quality education and training, they require diverse, multidimensional leaders.

# EMPIRICAL AND THEORETICAL FOUNDATIONS FOR MULTIDIMENSIONAL LEADERSHIP

This appendix provides more detailed information on the methods used for data collection and expansion on the theoretical underpinnings for the leadership model. Readers interested in more of an academic discussion of leadership may find this information useful. Likewise, faculty members using this text for classroom discussion can build lesson plans around the content, in particular when used in conjunction with the case studies in this volume.

## Case Study Methods

The propositions and leadership model outlined in this book draw from findings from comprehensive qualitative interviews from case studies of presidential leadership at nine community colleges and include information provided from three additional minority leaders from across the country. Because shifts in leadership often provide opportunities to enact change initiatives on college campuses (Birnbaum, 1992), I based my examination of community college leaders at colleges that had recently hired a new president. In addition, the nine colleges were selected because they were undergoing some form of organizational change at the time—either in response to external pressures or resulting from the new president's internal motivations and understanding of the campus community. The additional minority participants were selected based on the diversity of their career paths, different institutional experiences, and unique career pathways.

Sites were purposefully selected to cover various regions of the country and to represent the contextual issues facing the broad range of community colleges. The site colleges were located in rural, suburban, and urban areas and ranged in size from small to large. The interview methods involved semistructured interviews using a hermeneutic phenomenology (Van Manen, 1990) approach in the case studies. Interview questions focused on uncovering how leaders defined their leadership and the way they led their campuses through change efforts. Of particular interest was the communication process regarding change on campus, decision making for the change efforts, and leadership training that informed the ways leaders acted on their campuses.

The framework for analysis used the AACC competencies and the concepts developed for the multidimensional leadership model. According to Merriam (1998), "By concentrating on a single phenomenon or entity (the case), the researcher aims to uncover the interaction of significant factors characteristic of the phenomenon" (p. 29). In this instance, the focus within each case site was to better understand community college leadership. Data analysis involved looking for patterns using categories and interpretation of the participant interviews (Stake, 1995). Relational patterns were most obvious when presenting the data in tabular form. The use of multiple case sites allowed for cross-case analysis, which in turn led to a better understanding of the influence of local conditions on findings. Detailed case studies are found in Appendix B. Pseudonyms have replaced the names of all colleges and college presidents.

## Leadership Theory

Initial conceptions of leadership based solely on traits are shifting. As we move from a postindustrial to a knowledge-based era (Dolence & Norris, 1995), new ideas such as collaboration, common good, global concern, diversity, pluralism, participation, client orientation, civic virtue, freedom of expression, critical dialogue, qualitative language and methodology, substantive justice, and consensus-oriented policy making have become more important (Kezar, Carducci, & Contreras-McGavin, 2006; Rost, 1991). A shift from thinking about leadership as a list of desirable traits to consideration of influence of leaders provided the first expansion of leadership theory.

Consideration of interactions with followers took on heightened importance in leadership theory as organizations grew more complex and shifts in organizational theory moved beyond bureaucratic structures. Social power theory and transformational leadership theory both accept that leadership is a social construction and therefore focus on how leaders influence and are influenced by followers (Bensimon, Neumann, & Birnbaum, 1989). Kelman (1961) notes three processes of social influence: compliance, identification, and internalization. Compliance occurs when members accept the influence of the president because they hope the president will view them favorably. A member is often compliant only when the influencing agent (i.e., the community college president) is present. Identification, on the other hand, occurs when campus members seek to emulate the behavior of the leader and are concerned with meeting a leader's expectation for role performance. The process of internalization occurs when campus constituents accept the influence of the leader because it is congruent with their value system. Similarly, Weber (2009) identified three sources of power for leaders: that which is conferred because of their position, that which can be attributed to charisma, and finally, the legitimate power a leader possesses because of his or her expertise. In both Weber's and Kelman's theories of leadership, a leader's power is enhanced or constrained by follower expectations and behaviors (Morgan, 2006).

Burns's (1978) idea that there are transactional and transformational leaders also relies on the notions of power and influence. As he writes, just as followers comply with a leader to garner favor, transactional leaders meet follower expectations by exchanging things of value. Therefore, follower compliance is ensured through the receipt of rewards. Transformational leaders, on the other hand, seek to change follower expectations, building on the followers' internalization of values. Followers of a transactional leader do not change their underlying beliefs. Rather, their behavior reverts to past patterns once an exchange with the leader stops. Transformational leaders, however, are concerned with higher-order "end values such as integrity, honor, and justice that can potentially transform followers" (Kuhnert & Lewis, 1987, p. 653).

New ideas about leadership focus on the role of relationships and a focus on cognitive theories of meaning making. In this case, as in conceptions of leadership throughout the organization in higher education (Peterson, 1997), the role of followers takes on increased importance (Avolio, 2007). Collective cognition is constructed through social exchanges and interaction (Lord & Emrich, 2001). Focusing on interactions and dependencies of both leaders and followers results in heightened importance of relationships (Beatty & Brew, 2004; Burns, 1978; Kelman, 1961). Several recent cognitive theories of leadership emphasize a flatter leadership structure rather than the traditional organizational hierarchy (Bensimon & Neumann, 1993; Helgeson, 1995). From these perspectives, leadership is collective and relational. A leader shares information and power and regularly includes others in decision making. Effective leaders are described as participatory, flexible, authentic, team oriented, and collaborative.

Leaders of the future must learn to deal with uncertainty and a constantly changing organizational context (Alfred, Shults, Jaquette, & Strickland, 2009). The adaptive leader obtains a view from the balcony, allowing for introspection of the movements on the dance floor below (Heifetz, 1994). The act of reflection and contemplation provides a site for learning about what works in practice, what doesn't, and how to change actions. This sense of heightened awareness is a critical component for current and future leaders.

## Communication Theory

How leaders communicate on campus contributes to how campus members understand events. Gioia and Thomas (1996) determined that during strategic change, the perceptions leaders put forth regarding an image of future outcomes were key to helping people make sense of the changes. The process of sensemaking and influence were interdependent (Gioia, Thomas, Clark, & Chittipeddi, 1994) and served as a lever for change. The ability of leaders to act as the front-runner to paint the picture of change and the future depends on the relationships the president has with campus members. Thus, the intentional use of framing to make sense for campus members can help create the reality envisioned.

Transactional leaders view communication as a top-down venue in which the leader gives information out to the organization. Transformational leadership, on the other hand, finds leaders viewing leadership as dialogue, concentrating on the meaning-centered view of communication. The transformative leader uses conversational practices to help in framing meaning for the organization. Campus members at Technology Community College were quick to point out how President Jones used personal conversations. One department chair recalled Jones's first year. He noted how Jones came around to department meetings and hosted open meetings to chat with campus members. This chair recalled, "[Chris] talked a little bit about some of his vision, but more so asked questions, trying to get to know our thoughts, feelings. He asked for reactions to his thoughts in e-mail or writing, so he encouraged feedback from the faculty." Personal conversations occurred with campus members when the president walked around campus, attended campus sporting events, or had interactions off-campus. One campus member also serves with the president on a community board of directors; after one of the meetings, the president stopped this person and asked for advice about a campus issue. The campus member reflected, "[Chris] is out there actively seeking influence." Systems thinkers reject the individual notion of leadership and look rather at interactions. In this case, conversational interactions create a jointly constructed meaning for the organization.

To further emphasize the links between leadership and communication, it is helpful to review Kelman (1961). As noted earlier, Kelman created a theoretical framework for looking at how attitude and opinion data provided the basis for how different people infer meaning by reviewing the antecedents of the importance of the induction, the source of power of the person trying to influence, and the manner of achieving the response. His three levels of process are compliance, identification, and internalization. Kelman also discussed the consequences of the processes with each antecedent. This research provides a way of thinking about leadership as transaction (mutual trade-offs for the leader and the follower) and as transformation (as associated with a change in the follower that corresponds with the ideal of a change in the individual's meaning schema). Thus, how the leader frames and communicates the change to campus members ties back to leadership style. The attempt to use opinion data for the prediction of subsequent behavior is useful in thinking about how leaders may use this information to create a framework of meaning on campus.

Leaders can also use symbols to draw attention to specific versions of the campus story they are creating. "Symbols assume principal significance as constructs through which individuals concretize and give meaningful form to their everyday lives" (Morgan, Frost, & Pondy, 1983, p. 24). The use of symbols by the leader focused attention on aspects of reality that the leader wished to highlight for others to incorporate in their meaning making or to draw attention away from historical items of importance. Responses from campus members to items of framing may differ based on a variety of individual factors, such as time at the institution, area of study, or gender (Kezar, 2000; Neumann, 1995).

When considering communication and framing by leaders, it is important to consider that female leaders bring different knowledge creation to their positions (Gilligan, 1982). Gender does not solely characterize a different voice; rather, the basis for voice is on a continuum that contributes to the multiple dimensions of leadership. Even though men and women do not necessarily follow the prescribed styles for their gender, there are often assumptions and norms from others based on gender. West and Zimmerman (1987) point out that men and women are rewarded for acting within their gender stereotypes; thus men may communicate in "assertive" ways, but women may not for fear of being viewed as dominating.

Gilligan's (1982) research suggested that men and women may speak different languages that they assume are the same, using similar words to encode disparate experiences of self and social relationships—systematic mistranslation—creating misunderstandings that impede communication and limit the potential for cooperation and care in relationships. For example, one leader may say he is open to feedback on an issue, but merely use this as an input as he makes the final decision, whereas another person may say she is open to feedback and then makes clear how the feedback was considered in the decision making. In each case, the leaders noted their openness, but had different meaning attached to ultimate actions.

## Organizational Perspectives

A useful tool when investigating leadership is the understanding of the organizational context in which leaders operate. Bolman and Deal (2008) presented a topology of organizations using four different frameworks: structural, human resource, political, and symbolic. Likewise, Morgan (2006) reviewed organizations using metaphors to understand the various contexts. It is important for leaders to understand the type of organization in which they work in order to determine effective tactics and to anticipate areas of support and barriers. Additionally, leaders must understand their own orientation to organizations. Bensimon (1991) pointed out that given the complexity of higher education, a president using more than one organizational lens to view operations may hence "fulfill the many, and often conflicting, expectations of the presidential office more skillfully than the president who cannot differentiate among situational requirements" (p. 423). Seeing issues from multiple perspectives likewise enhances leaders' ability to see multiple solutions to pressing issues.

The structural frame draws on the ideals of bureaucracy. Weber (2009) outlined several key factors within bureaucracies: that there is a fixed division of labor, a hierarchy of offices, set rules for performance, a separation of personal from official property and rights, and technical qualifications to distinguish jobs. The focus of this frame is on efficiency and how to obtain targeted outcomes. Key to this is the allocation of work and the means by which this work is coordinated. The structure of the organization is shifted to best meet goals within the environment.

The role of people is central to the human resource frame. Individual needs and feelings are emphasized in this frame. Instead of a focus on the structure, the fit between individuals and the organization is paramount. An underlying assumption here is that organizations exist to serve human needs rather than the reverse (Bolman & Deal, 2008). There is a symbiotic relationship between people and organizations—they need each other. A poor fit means that both suffer, whereas a good fit benefits both. In this frame, leaders believe in and trust people, are accessible and visible, and empower others (Rost, 1991).

The consideration of organizations as political systems draws attention to the conflict inherent in institutions when taking consideration of multiple interests. "Conflict arises whenever interests collide" (Morgan, 2006, p. 167). Understanding that organizational activity is interest based and that interests may diverge, resulting in conflict, provides a context for the theater of activity taking place on campus. Critical to the political systems metaphor is the role of power. The use of power to resolve conflicts highlights the function of influence in an organizational system. "A strong case can also be made for the idea that, although everyone has access to sources of power, ultimate power rests with the people or forces that are able to define the stage of action on which the game of politics is played" (Morgan, 2006, p. 213). The negotiation involved in the political frame depends on the various levels of power that individuals hold and how they leverage this power with respect to others.

Leaders can use a cultural lens to enact their style (Bolman & Deal, 2008). In this case, they create theaters in which actions transpire. Heifetz (1994) discussed how the leader can create a holding environment and a sense of urgency to accomplish an agenda. As discussed, how the leader uses this theater to create meaning often dictates progress. Tierney (1991) outlines the importance of the organizational culture in higher education and how leaders need an awareness of this. He goes on to point out that part of an understanding of culture includes a sense of use of time, space, and communication. Deal and Kennedy (1982) use the metaphor of "tribes" to discuss different types of cultures present in organizations and how awareness of the particular culture by the leader is imperative to enabling change. Part of the emphasis for leaders using a cultural lens is the creation of the organizational saga (Clark, 1972). How the leader tells the story and develops the saga can shift the focus of the institution.

The role of cognition for college presidents depends on the number of cognitive frames they use (Bensimon, 1991), whether they are "old" or "new" presidents (Neumann, 1989), and what type of institution they serve. Neumann and Bensimon (1990) generated four presidential types dependent on the context of their institution of higher education (financial stability, faculty morale) along three dimensions relating to the presidents' target of attention, mode of action, and relatedness to the institution. They posit that viewing the relative position of the leader on these dimensions leads to corresponding prototypical "personal theories" of the college presidency (Neumann & Bensimon, 1990, p. 696). This topography allows for a means of analyzing presidential thinking at a given moment in time. A difficulty, however, results from the inability to precisely locate any one college president precisely in one domain of type given the complexities faced by colleges and, in turn, by those that govern them.

Positionality theory investigates the impact of the role of experience on what an individual knows (Alcoff, 1988; Berger, 1963). "Positionality theory acknowledges that people have multiple, overlapping identities and thus make meaning from various aspects of their identity, including social class, professional standing, and so forth" (Kezar, 2000, p. 724). Therefore, investigating community college leadership assumes an interrelationship between the leader and campus members that may influence the ultimate frame chosen by the leader for a particular issue.

As leaders gain experience, they add to their understanding of organizational operations. Working toward viewing organizations from multiple perspectives should be a goal for leaders. The ways in which individuals view the various frames is also influenced by an individual's philosophical approach. Hatch and Cunliffe (2006) discuss the differences among a modernistic, symbolic-interpretive, or postmodern approach. A modernistic view focuses on structure, systems, and the environment. A symbolic-interpretive approach, on the other hand, is concerned with the meaning making that individuals construct within an organization; a postmodern approach questions the structure itself and argues for different forms of positionality. Bess and Dee (2007) provide a comprehensive overview of organizational theory using the additional perspectives of these philosophical perspectives.

## Summary

The brief review of some basic theoretical concepts underpinning organizations and leadership helps provide ways for leaders to understand better the issues they face. In reviewing the cases that follow, consider how the use of these various theoretical concepts can help create solutions and alternatives for the problems presented. Different insights may be gleaned from analysis using a theoretical framework based on communication theory versus organizational frameworks. Important learning insights can occur when these analyses are intersected to determine what communication tendencies align with particular organizational frameworks. Investigation into individual philosophical approaches can also shed light on rationales for decision making and leadership.

# CASE STUDIES IN LEADERSHIP

C ase studies can provide a useful learning tool for aspiring leaders, graduate students, faculty, and leadership development trainers. Nine case studies informed the concepts presented in this book. This section provides further details on each of the sites, ultimately posing questions at the end of each case to aid in application to classroom exercises or leadership development training. The American Association of Community Colleges proposed six competencies to support the development of future leaders: organizational strategy, resource management, communication, collaboration, community college advocacy, and professionalism. The additional concept of cultural competency is relevant to all the cases because leaders' approaches are influenced by their ability to read the environment and use this information in their leadership. Each of the competencies is highlighted in the following cases to provide examples of the ways experiences may be gained in each area. Table 1 presents a guide to links among the cases, leadership topics, and the leadership competencies.

There are several means for using cases to apply theory to practice. Typically, a quick read first occurs to obtain an overarching idea of the context and identification of some of the main issues within the case. On a closer second read, the central problem of the case and any associated secondary issues should be identified. An important element in case analysis is the identification of evidence from the case to support the arguments put forth regarding the central and secondary issues. Once readers are confident in their assessment of the main issues of the case and the evidence to support these claims, alternative solutions are generated. A wide net should be cast at this stage to brainstorm a variety of forms of action for the central players involved. Once this larger list is generated, the best alternatives should be chosen. For classroom use, the alternatives should have clear links to theory being studied, whereas for individual use, plausible alternatives should be

**TABLE 1**
**Case Context, Issues, and AACC Competencies**

| Case | Site | Leadership Issue | AACC Competency |
|---|---|---|---|
| **New World College** | Technology Community College | • Business influence<br>• Student learning<br>• Technology | Organizational strategy, communication, collaboration, advocacy |
| **Nose to the Grindstone** | Hunkering Down Community College | • Communication<br>• Relationships<br>• Planning<br>• Decision making | Organizational strategy, resource management, communication |
| **Us Versus Us** | Bifurcated Community College | • Career planning<br>• Relationships<br>• Organizational structure | Communication, collaboration, advocacy, professionalism |
| **Creating a Vision** | Strategic Community College | • Learning systems<br>• Planning<br>• Culture<br>• Symbolism | Organizational strategy, communication, advocacy, professionalism |
| **Building Bridges Through Curriculum Alignment** | Don't Make Waves Community College | • Collaboration<br>• Faculty work<br>• Student learning<br>• Remediation | Organizational strategy, communication, collaboration |
| **Changing Image and Culture** | Rogue Community College | • Culture<br>• Faculty governance<br>• Communication | Organizational strategy, communication, professionalism |
| **Learning in the Center** | Cutting Edge Community College | • Culture<br>• Collaboration<br>• Student learning | Organizational strategy, communication, collaboration, advocacy |
| **Moving Too Fast? Too Slow?** | Tradition-Bound Community College | • Communication<br>• Decision making<br>• Leadership | Communication, collaboration, professionalism |

explored based on what you know from your own practice. Finally, an outline of an implementation plan is created. This process may show holes in thinking regarding the alternatives and may require tweaking of the solutions.

Each of the following cases is presented in a variety of formats throughout this book. This version brings together several pertinent points of the cases and presents additional information that fleshes out the scenarios and highlights specific areas of tension evident for leaders. Table 2 provides an overview of all the presidents and colleges included in the cases; readers can use it to best match their own personal situation or college contexts to see what may be learned by this exercise in comparison. Likewise, cases may be chosen based on the issues they present. Individual leaders may refer to the cases to find a different perspective on issues they are currently facing and

### TABLE 2
### Participant and Institutional Demographics

| President* | Campus* Location | Year Presidency Began at This Campus | Number of Presidencies** | Annual Student FTEs |
|---|---|---|---|---|
| Jon Hammond (White male) | Strategic CC (suburban) | 1996 | 2 | 4,000 |
| Christopher Jones (White male) | Technology CC (rural) | 1998 | 2 | 3,000 |
| Karen Fields (White female) | Bifurcated CC (suburban, rural branches) | 1999 | 1 | 2,100 |
| Lynne Pauldine (White female) | Hunkering Down CC (rural) | 1999 | 1 | 2,500 |
| *Part of a suburban five-college district—Large and Growing Community College District* | | | | |
| Brenda Hales (White female) | Don't Make Waves CC | 1999–2008 | 1 | 8,000 |
| Jennifer Burke (White female) | Cutting Edge CC | 2000 | 2 | 15,000 |
| Shawn Williams (Black male) | Tradition-Bound CC | 2000–2007 | 2 | 11,000 |
| Michael Garvey (White male) | Me-Too CC | 2001 | 2*** | 7,800 |
| James Simon (White male) | Rogue CC | 2002–2008 | 1 | 8,000 |

*All participant and institutional names are pseudonyms.
**Includes current presidency.
***Also served in five interim presidencies.

work through some potential solutions or use the variety of scenarios presented to "practice" how they may anticipate their reaction in a similar situation. As noted, a key learning opportunity for leaders is reflection. The cases can be used in training situations to reiterate points made in leadership workshops to develop professional competencies. Small groups may analyze each case and then reconvene as a larger group to compare reactions and solutions. This level of sharing not only allows for the opportunity to work on group processing of problems within a smaller unit, similar to a leadership cabinet, but also provides a chance to hear how other groups address the same issues in different ways. Case study analysis allows a safe format for application of solutions that may be useful to individual practice and learning and to group processing.

## New World College: Technology Community College

Technology Community College (TCC), located in the Northeast, is a residential 2-year technical college that serves as the de facto community college for the region. The main campus is in a rural part of the state, and there is a branch campus 35 miles away. Despite its rural location, the campus is more diverse than the local population given the draw of students across the state. Before taking the helm at TCC, President Chris Jones was president of a 2-year college in the Midwest. Before that, Jones taught in and led a community college manufacturing engineering technologies department as well as a computer-aided design department. He also brought to TCC experience as a business consultant, designer, small-business owner, and Vietnam veteran. Jones's main focus since arriving at TCC was the initiation of ThinkPad University at the college, a college program in which each entering student was required to purchase a ThinkPad computer for use in his or her college program. TCC has received national recognition for its use of technology, most recently implementing the use of cell phones for student access to faculty and classes, for use as an entry to residence halls, and as a student identification system for food services and the bookstore.

President Jones had two leadership offers on the table when he decided to come to TCC. In summing up his first impressions, he stated, "The campus had gone a long time without an investment in physical plant, which from my perspective represented an incredible opportunity." He inherited a large senior staff of faculty but knew this group would be retiring over his first 5 years, giving Jones an opportunity to develop new programs and new views within traditional programs—"to bring in some new blood!" He felt the campus was ripe for change and was "simply looking for someone to say, 'What should we do?'" Campus members from TCC had actually visited the midwestern campus when Jones was president there, looking at the ThinkPad University concept. On his arrival at TCC, Jones replicated this same program.

To obtain buy-in to proposed changes, Jones initiated a strategic planning process. He reviewed the input from campus members and presented the results. Jones commented, "I engaged the college in a strategic planning process, from which these ideas emerged—not in purely the way I thought of them, but in expanded ways." This group processing provided more universal ownership than one dictated solely by the president. At this point, "the bandwagon became crowded."

Undergirding the college plans was an emphasis on applied business and entrepreneurialism and an integration of technology. The picture painted by the president and several campus members was the same—"Our goal is to graduate students who not only have a very valuable degree, but walk across the stage with a degree in one hand, their laptop loaded with software in the other, and their own business waiting for them when they walk off the stage." The focus on entrepreneurship meant that the president was constantly scanning for new ideas. Jones related how a student pitched the idea of growing vegetables in the horticulture program and selling them to the cafeteria. The dairy already has a storefront where it sells milk and cheese. The president also established an Equine Institute, which operates as an auxiliary business separate from the college.

The president was constantly on the prowl for new ventures and partnerships, drawing from his experience to find new applications for the programs at the college. Several dog-eared technology magazines were strewn across his desk. He readily spoke of how facial recognition software for surveillance could be used for animal identification systems and had been on the phone with a company in California as a potential partner. Similarly, he looked for transferable technology to apply to the dairy industry. He stated, "It's a parallel kind of thing—taking things that apply over here and applying them to the academic world." All of the new activity focused on ways in which to augment the college budget—chasing after the most lucrative deals.

President Jones described himself as a visionary, a view several campus members supported. He hosted the beginning-of-the-year meeting in the new automotive center to highlight the progress the college had made, all the while distracting campus members from the bleak state budget situation and the remaining decaying infrastructure. Jones was quick to add, "The problem I've had everywhere I've been is that others will say, 'Chris, we have more ideas than we have money or time to deal with so, slow down!' And that's a very fair concern."

## Questions

- What risks are inherent for the college with its reliance on its rapid shifts to implement new initiatives based on entrepreneurial demands?
- How might academic programming be impacted by the business ventures?
- What needs to occur at the college to provide for sustainability of programs when President Jones leaves?

## Nose to the Grindstone: Hunkering Down Community College

Hunkering Down Community College (HDCC) is a residential 2-year campus located in a rural area of a northeastern state. The college was formed in 1913 and currently serves 2,500 students. The college offers baccalaureate degrees in addition to traditional associate programs and certification programs, as well as online program offerings. HDCC's premier academic programs include veterinary technology, hospitality, and golf management curricula. A feature of the campus is an 18-hole golf course for student training and for community use. There are 19.5 students for every faculty member on campus, and students of color represent 25% of the student body, creating a diverse community. President Lynne Pauldine is in her first presidency, coming to HDCC in 1999. Previously, she served as vice president of enrollment at a midwestern community college, and she continues to consult for a national enrollment management firm and teach online courses in strategic planning. She holds a doctorate in higher education administration and a bachelor's degree in communications. Early in her career, she taught in communication departments at both 2- and 4-year colleges.

On her arrival on campus, Pauldine identified several key financial problems. The first dealt with low enrollment; the second was that the auxiliary unit (food service, the bookstore, etc.) was losing $300,000 a year; the third was a desire to build a residence hall—the first in 40 years; and finally, the campus foundation that owns the golf course was losing money. Pauldine commented, "Financially, the college had been hit over and over and over. And I did not begin to understand the staggering financial challenges here." She explained to the campus that there weren't sufficient resources to continue expanding or to maintain at the current level. According to Pauldine, "We would have to let go of some things if we wanted to add new things. . . . There are no sacred cows. We put everything on the table." A structured review procedure was instituted for all academic programs, with an associated rating system. On one end of the rating system were "star" programs, whereas struggling programs on the other end of the continuum were placed "in jeopardy." Pauldine's perception was that this process was clear and fair. At the end of the first year, she eliminated 14 programs, but no faculty members were terminated. Instead, they were moved to areas in which they had teaching competencies.

Pauldine noted, "The program review and changes helped me because there was kind of a campuswide buy-in that 'Oh! She's really going to do what she said she would do!' And that process has been repeated." One of the programs initially put "in jeopardy" was the nursing program. Typically, nursing programs are resource intensive, and HDCC's degree was no different. Adding to this scenario were low enrollments in the nursing program. The faculty and chair of the department worked hard during the year to institute a strong weekend/evening program, resulting in increasing enrollment. Additionally, they partnered with a regional pharmaceutical company in which the company guaranteed employment for participating students, with the company providing scholarship money for tuition. At the end of this recognized stellar year, the department asked, "Can we get off jeopardy?" The response from Pauldine was, "We want to see another year of solid performance." Predictably, the staff was disappointed.

A constant refrain from campus members was being asked to do more with less. One faculty in the humanities noted, "People feel very thinly spread at times. And we in our division have to offer a fair number of electives for the bachelor's degree students, and we also have a new statewide general education program which is housed in this division, and all but one of the classes is through this division. So it certainly has increased class size. So there is, I think, a legitimate sense that if we are really agreeing to be stressing the 4-year programs, then some of the certificate programs probably are going to be eliminated. It's a question of how much can we do very well."

Tough choices were being made in the name of resource savings. This situation exacerbated a growing divide between longer-serving faculty and newcomers.

QUESTIONS

- What type of decision making was in operation at HDCC?
- As a leader, if you were faced with dire resource issues, how might you plan to make up shortfalls in the budget?
- What type of communication plan would you institute to disseminate information regarding your organizational plan?

## Us Versus Us: Bifurcated Community College

Bifurcated Community College (BCC) opened in 1971; in addition to its main campus, it has two branch campuses and five outreach centers in the western United States. It is one of four community colleges in a relatively large state; its service area encompasses 18,000 square miles. In order to increase full-time enrollment, one of the college's current goals, BCC has targeted outreach to area high schools and instituted bridge and dual-enrollment programs in order to introduce students to the college. BCC also serves as a cultural resource for the city in which it is located, hosting community theater events and lectures. Tensions exist at the college with the branch campuses seeking more autonomy, which runs counter to the current push for centralization of functions and standard operating procedures across the campus.

BCC President Karen Fields followed a traditional path of leadership ascension within community colleges. She taught physics at a community college for nearly 20 years and occasionally held administrative leadership positions within the division. She then worked for 4 years as vice president of academic affairs at a college in the East before assuming her first presidency at BCC. One of Fields's initial goals when arriving on campus was to create a ladder curriculum in which students could easily move from a certificate to an associate degree and ultimately either earn a baccalaureate of technology from BCC or transfer to a university 4-year program. In 2007, the college officially dropped *Community* from its name to better reflect its expanded mission, which included baccalaureate of technology degrees.

In reflecting on her first days at BCC, President Fields mused, "If you're looking at new presidents, you're looking at people that haven't had much experience looking for presidential positions. Based on my own experience, I went in not knowing the whole story." She commented that she felt the board of trustees should have sent clearer signals regarding the needs of the college; it was not until midway through the first semester that she understood some critical issues. Fields received a copy of the self-study report the college steering committee had created in anticipation of its regional accrediting agency 10-year review. She stammered, "I nearly died—it was a shocker!" The chapter on institutional integrity proved to be the "zinger" with allegations of violation of the college nepotism policy, misleading advertising, unreliable course scheduling, and cancellation of elective courses needed for graduation because of low enrollment.

One of the first changes Fields made was to the organizational structure. She commented, "Well, the organizational structure was terrible. There were a number of serious problems. The most serious was that I had deans that I did not trust." On her arrival on campus, she had 12 direct reports, all with the title of dean. Fields created two vice president positions with areas grouped under each, stating, "I couldn't get breathing room. I had people at my door constantly." From a faculty perspective, the change to a more hierarchical organizational structure was a feeling of loss of empowerment. The smaller circle of immediate contacts closed off communication routes to larger groups of the campus.

Fields commented, "All these deans had carved off their little fiefdoms and they were all fighting one another; there was no collegelike cohesion. . . . the institution was at war with itself." Even after the restructuring, elements of hostility remained between the areas of arts and sciences and the occupational program. Despite this, Fields thought, "I can see some light at the end of the tunnel." Given the wide service area, there are few opportunities for the campus to come together as a group, making e-mail announcements the biggest source of communication. Several times a year, Fields hosts a series of faculty forums to provide access. Nonetheless, a senior director added, "I just don't think she'd got the buy-in that she could have because of the new VP structure, but it may still come anyway, but it'll probably take longer because people don't feel empowered."

## QUESTIONS

- How might the college staff have retained a sense of empowerment within the new, more hierarchical organizational structure?

- As a new leader, what change process would you initiate when you discovered your new institution was at war with itself?
- What responsibility does a hiring board have to alert prospective candidates of potential issues? How might a presidential candidate best prepare for a campus visit to avoid "surprises"?

## Creating a Vision: Strategic Community College

Strategic Community College (SCC) is a Hispanic-serving institution in the Southwest, where most students are the first in their family to attend college. The district serves a 10,000-square-mile district spanning two counties and has 13 remote sites. The college also has a branch office out of which one of the state's 4-year public universities offers courses leading to certificates and select bachelor's and master's degrees. The college actively engages in strategic planning, annually updating its 5-year plan. Furthermore, administrators and faculty revisit the planning document on a regular basis, carrying printed copies to meetings and working toward attainment of specific performance outcomes.

Before taking over the presidency at SCC, Jon Hammond was president of a midwestern community college, which he led out of bankruptcy and successfully rebuilt. Hammond quipped, "I'm what they call a change agent, what they call the savior president." In considering the presidency at SCC, he added, "This college was in good shape, so what do you do with that? Change can come in huge increments when things are broken or in refinements—I've really come to enjoy the refinement of a mature institution in terms of planning." In contemplating changes, Hammond wanted to honor the traditions on the campus and not "inflict" change. The first step the president took to bring the campus community together was the creation of a mission statement. The resulting statement was succinct, 25 words, and is printed on the back of all campus business cards and posted on the back of all outdoor building signs. The president uses college meetings, the web, and his own television talk show on the college's station to reinforce the vision for the college.

According to Hammond, "Learning systems must facilitate change." A video was created to reinforce the vision for the college. The video supports the notion of lifelong learning and creates a picture of what the college will look like in 5 years. A vice president shared more about the process to create the 5-year planning documents: "We work on this as a staff that identifies all of our activities and who's responsible for the year. And we use the lists at our monthly president's council meeting to review everything that we as a college staff should be doing. I really like this visual; it captures all of our activities, all of our key activities, and who's responsible and we discuss this every month. It's a 5-year planning process document that we update as needed [and] that we use every month."

The document has a red cover and is spiral bound, allowing for quick access to the current month's spreadsheet of activities. Campus members readily accessed this document, pulling it out as they referred to how it was used in area and campuswide meetings, as opposed to the strategic-planning documents that often sit on the shelves on most campuses. One tactic of President Hammond was to repeat his change message over and over—he noted, "I want people to know what I stand for." Campus members reinforced that they felt up to date on the issues facing the college and the goals the college as a whole was striving to meet. President Hammond's plan was straightforward; he recounted, "You get a vision of what you want to do, you define the expectations, and then you reward the people."

Part of the vision was a six-stage decision-making model that supported the learning platform. Guiding all decision making were the following:

1. Excellence—the decision provides for high quality, outstanding educational results.
2. Equity—the decision allows for reasonable participation from target populations in the service area.
3. Efficiency—the decision produces the desired results within defined organizational resources.
4. Effort—the decision will be maintained by staff commitment.
5. Effectiveness—the decision implementation can be successfully measured by outcomes and/or results.
6. Ethics—the decision supports behavior congruent with college values, principles, and morals.

QUESTIONS

- How might a cut in the college budget impact the vision for the campus?
- What impact might there be when a "savior" president comes into a mature college?

- How could you get buy-in to implement the decision-making model in operation at Strategic Community College?

## Building Bridges Through Curriculum Alignment: Don't Make Waves Community College

Don't Make Waves Community College was established in 1972 as one of the first two colleges in the Large and Growing Community College District; the community college serves 8,000 students and has distinct offerings in interior design, respiratory care, and dental hygiene. The challenge currently facing the college was to coordinate curriculum with regional high schools to help connect high school preparation of graduates with college readiness. Additionally, a goal for the college was to smooth out problems created by previous midlevel administrators and to align the organizational structure within the college.

President Brenda Hales initially held a central office position at the Large and Growing Community College District and took over the presidency in 1999, retiring in 2008. Her move to this position was a surprise for many and, as Hales noted, "one of the best-kept secrets." As a result, it took Hales the better part of a year to build campus trust. She reflected, "On the campus here, everybody wanted to have some say as to who their president is, and they didn't get any." Before her work at DMWCC, Hales held districtwide positions that provided her with a big-picture perspective of leadership. She commented, "It's interesting [that] you're going to see a lot of people here that have never been anywhere else. They don't realize that these same issues are some other places." The president who took over after Hales's retirement, Lisa Stewart, had been a long-serving member of the DMWCC team and a member of the founding faculty but had left the district in 2005 to assume a presidency of her own in another state. Of note, Stewart was the lead administrator working with Hales on an initiative addressing college readiness. Stewart described Hales's start as "a year of permanent white water."

Faculty were asked what it would take for students to be successful in their classes, in particular looking at evidence of what level of reading was required and how much math competency was required. The push to establish these prerequisites was the college's accreditation study. When compiling the information, incongruence became evident because some faculty in content areas felt that students did not need to be college ready, instead arguing that students would gain those skills during the class. Stewart recalled, "When all the reports were compiled, it was really a mismatch. There were some technical problems, like automotive required that students have college-ready reading, writing, and math, whereas economics didn't have any prerequisite skills and that's an upper-level course." Ultimately, the executive decision was made to require college readiness in reading and writing, with math readiness levels determined by the course of study. There were faculty grumblings over why they were asked for their recommendations only to be trumped by what the executive staff decided.

Obviously, key stakeholders regarding this change in college prerequisites are the feeder high schools for the college. Stewart wrote a letter to the assistant superintendents, who serve as their districts' curriculum directors, and to the high school principals within the schools in these districts, inviting them to a luncheon forum to review the changes. Included in the mailing was a statistical summary of the levels of college readiness of students entering from their district based on the state's end-of-high-school testing report. This report allowed the public school leaders to see the percentage of their graduates that might be impacted by the new requirement for college readiness prerequisites at the college.

The meeting provided for some rich dialogue. Stewart posed the following question to the group: "What do you need from us to prepare your graduating seniors who are coming to us for college readiness, and then what can we do to help your juniors who have another year?" The college offered to have English and math faculty serve as consultants to the districts to work on vertical alignment of the curriculum to make for seamless transition between the high schools and the college. Given that most of the college's students require developmental math, strategies proposed were to test students at the end of their junior year in high school to try to remediate students while still in high school and to brush up their skills.

## QUESTIONS

- How might the planning process have been organized differently to determine what prerequisites would be required for classes to avoid faculty frustrations?
- The open-access mission of community colleges and their reputation of second-chance opportunities often results in incoming students lacking basic skill levels. What impact will the new program of prerequisites have on access?

- Finger-pointing of blame between high school and college leaders often occurs when addressing college readiness. Analyze the plan put forth by DMWCC, pointing out strengths and weaknesses and offering suggestions for implementation. What are you assuming about decision making and communication?

## Changing Image and Culture: Rogue Community College

As part of the Large and Growing Community College District, Rogue Community College (RCC) enrolls 8,000 students and has one of the highest rates of transfer students in the system, with more than 70% of its students transferring to 4-year programs. James Simon is the second president of the college, which is still relatively new in the district, having opened its doors in 1995. One of Simon's first actions was to bring together the campus to develop a plan to increase occupational programs and to increase access. Simon noted, "We don't have the same kind of graduation rate for lower income students, and I just have this feeling that we're not serving those students." Simon worked on consensus decision making, but also noted that the buck stopped with him because he was accountable to the board on college outcomes.

According to Simon, "This was the rogue campus before I came. That's why I'm here and that person [previous president] is not. So that adds a certain dimension to your job if you know you were hired because someone didn't want that kind of problem to exist anymore." The chancellor of the district wanted the individual campus presidents to support the centralized goals of the district but also to have a unique culture that allowed each campus to meet community needs. RCC's previous president had been known for his innovation, but his practices often ran counter to the chancellor's plans for the district. The previous president at RCC did not believe in hosting annual events to draw campus members together. Thus, one of Simon's actions was to instill more opportunities for faculty and students to intermingle. Simon started an online newsletter to share information and sent out campuswide e-mails with updates.

The vice president of students noted, "Our president before was very just intense, energetic, and James is not like that. He's a little bit more methodical, more thoughtful in what he says but really knows what's going on." The VP added that he thought the hiring of Simon was "getting this campus back with the folds." The "maverick" ideas of the previous president were in line with the needs of the new campus at the time. Now, with the swing back to a centralized system, a wild-card campus was no longer appropriate. One example of this difference was the fact that the campus supported a Macintosh computer platform, whereas the rest of the college district system used IBM personal computers. This first test of the new president began to send the message that the president was gentle but firm—the campus would switch to IBM.

Under the previous president, the feeling was that goals were targeted based on innovations and technology, whatever might be a tactic to put the college on the map and mark it as new and innovative. New ideas were being constantly generated by the president's office. One vice president mused, "[The previous president] said, 'That is what I want to see happen (snap, snap)—make it happen.' James's approach is very, very different." A change was evident when President Simon took over, with more processes in place. A vision statement was established for the college and a campus team selected to put together a strategic plan. One initiative that was added was a balance between occupational and technical programs and transfer programs.

Communication venues were one way in which the culture evidenced a change. A person on the leadership team reflected, "Simon is excellent at getting us to communicate, so the basic message is that he pushes communication, not just with programs and initiatives, but with change also." Not only did the president keep the leadership cabinet in the loop, he encouraged the other campus leaders to keep one another in the loop as well. The president's democratic style made him open to other viewpoints, concerns, and questions from campus members. A campus member noted of Simon, "He's an excellent listener."

In the past, the maverick culture meant, "We're going to do our own thing come hell or high water, man the torpedoes, full speed ahead, we're better than you are!" The feeling of "arrogance" added a level of tension to staff meetings. One tension was the need to "play nice" with the district, while blazing a trail that in reality did not match the central district ideology. Simon's mission was to align the campus more closely with the district philosophy and overall goals. Some of the founding faculty members were reluctant to lose their maverick identities.

## Questions

- New presidents face the challenge of getting to know their campus and honoring previous traditions but at the same time needing to place their own mark with their leadership. As a new president, what steps would you take to shift the "maverick" culture?

- What steps are necessary to bring together the founding faculty members, who may miss the shoot-from-the-hip style of leadership? What is the role of governance in the change process?
- How would you develop a communication plan to support your change in focus?

## Learning in the Center: Cutting Edge Community College

Cutting Edge Community College (CECC) opened its doors in 2003 because of advocacy by the community to have a 2-year college in its region. CECC quickly enrolled students—increasing to its current enrollment of 15,000—without significantly impacting the enrollment at the other colleges within the district. Helping to serve the community, the college has several facilities for the arts including a 500-seat theater, a black box theater, an art gallery, and music facilities. The campus is located on a 200-acre site and is dedicated to saving the local flora of the surrounding community. Additionally, a major need for water retention exists in the area, resulting in 18 acres of lakes and waterways on campus to act as sources of irrigation and campus atmosphere.

CECC was built around the concept of a learning college, with a focus on student-centered education. President Jennifer Burke stated, "We started with a blank page—a totally blank page." Best practices in the field guided planning and development of the new college. To tie into the existing culture within the district, the system chancellor mandated that at least 50% of the CECC hires come from within the district. Several faculty and staff made lateral moves to be part of the new venture at the ground up. One was the new vice president of student success. The VP related, "I was so excited about what I was seeing being developed here. . . . I thought, 'I'll put my name in the hat.' And it was a parallel move for me, but I have discovered that building new things like this, developing things from the start, changing the way we serve our student population, is what drives me; that's what it's all about."

The college was built around learning engagement, taking from the research and best practices to create a new culture focused on enhancing student learning. Burke reflected, "Students have better outcomes if they're fully engaged in the learning process, and so everything was built around building an organization, building a staff profile, building a physical site, and the pedagogy all around learning engagement—collective learning, to try to get a different outcome." Organizational reporting and policies were created by the small leadership in place during the developmental stage.

As the faculty hiring expanded the ranks, tensions began to develop. The president noted, "We've already gotten some criticism from faculty, saying decisions are made from [the] top down. And it's because the senior team is holding on to that vision, saying, 'Well, no, you don't understand, this is what we know from research.' . . . but we've never communicated that in a way that let them have some ownership over it, so how would they know? So I think that's something we're going to really have to pay attention to, or else all this talk about collaboration will have been for naught. You can't be a learning college if we as a group don't make decisions that way."

The strong tradition of bureaucratic hierarchies was difficult to shed. The head of the faculty senate pointed out, "Depending on what the issue is, sometimes there's no arguing through it—no matter how tight your proposal or rationale." Breaking with tradition to a more learner-centered approach meant hiring faculty with innovative and progressive practices committed to student learning. A dilemma resulted because many of the new hires had no real community college teaching experience, resulting in a huge investment of personal time for class preparations. On the other hand, the faculty leader pointed out, "It's difficult to get aligned with the vision and find people with years of experience because they're more entrenched and married to what they're used to doing." Key was keeping the student-centered vision alive and collaboration in practice versus just the idea of collaboration. The vice president of student success mused, "I keep reminding our team here that if we believe in what we're starting here, we need to revisit and say, 'Does that play into what we originally planned?' When that happens 2 or 3 years down the road, you see some continuity in what you started."

## QUESTIONS

- Creating a student-centered culture requires rethinking teaching roles. As new faculty join the ranks of the college, what issues might arise? How might a learning culture be reinforced?
- What type of communication and leadership would best support continued use of collaborative decision making at CECC?

- Enrollment increased at CECC from zero to 15,000 in just 3 years. Discuss the organizational and governance issues that may result from such a drastic expansion.

## Moving Too Fast? Too Slow? Tradition-Bound Community College

Tradition-Bound Community College (TBCC), founded in 1973, was one of the charter colleges in the district. For 40 years, TBCC had the largest enrollment at 11,000 students, but it was eventually surpassed as the largest college in the district when Cutting Edge Community College opened. The college's enrollment has stabilized after a slight dip in student admissions and is now slowly growing. Over time, the setting for the college shifted from a suburban college to an urban campus with a mostly minority student body. The college continues to provide cultural events for the community and has a small international student body.

Shawn Williams, the only president of color in the case sites, led TBCC for 7 years but left the college in spring 2007 for another presidency in the Midwest. At that time, John Smith was named interim president and, after a failed presidential search, was promoted to president. Smith has a long work history with a variety of roles in the district. He was president of Don't Make Waves Community College from 1991 to 1999, then worked in the district central office until joining TBCC.

When Williams first arrived on campus, he stated that he was going to do three things: "Look, listen, and learn." Typical of most new presidents, Williams met with various campus members to learn more about the college. In the end, he retained the strategic plan developed by the previous president, stating, "I did not want to throw it out—I wanted to respect all the work that had been done here." Williams viewed his role as that of a "cheerleader" by being visible on campus, while encouraging staff and faculty to make decisions with one question in mind: "How does it benefit students?"

According to the vice president of instruction, "Shawn cares about people deeply. And he always tries to do what's in the best interest of the individual and the institution." Williams was noted for his dynamic energy and for being visible on campus. The VP also mused, "I would love to tell you everybody loves administration; we do have faculty that believe that administrators are the enemy." The president commented, "I genuinely want input, until I've said I'm doing this or it's done. But if you don't participate and the train leaves, it's not always possible that you can stop the train when it goes and so they have the opportunity to provide enough input." He saw the college as operating as a team, but stated if there were a fire in the room, he'd put it out before talking with others. He spoke with passion about his commitment to participatory leadership.

Another perspective on Williams's decision to retain the existing strategic plan was noted by a faculty member, however, who stated, "The president doesn't impress me as a change type person . . . he certainly didn't have a template in his head when he came here, which I appreciated." The initial perspective was that Williams would honor the traditions of the campus and maintain the status quo. Williams was noted to be conservative on change, treading the line between tradition and new change lightly. The recent state budget-cutting situation pressed the college to keep up enrollment and at the same time cut expenses. Added to this was a shifting student demographic given its urban location. Now, some type of change needed to occur. A faculty member bluntly stated, "My reading of this is they [the faculty] feel there is a leadership vacuum at this campus. They don't feel Dr. Williams is taking charge and getting us the direction that we need." One of the issues was the perception by faculty that decisions were not being followed through. On the campus there was angst that the college did not have a sense of vision or articulated goals.

One former administrator who was now back as a classroom faculty had a long history at the college. He said, "I think Dr. Williams's laissez-faire style of leadership is probably not appropriate to a college that's used to patronizing leadership and authority leadership." Faculty perceived that communication contributed to a sense of malaise on campus as well with Williams's lack of an overall message to the campus. Feedback loops with the external environment also were not always evident to faculty.

QUESTIONS

- Leaders run a fine line between being perceived as an autocratic leader versus one who is not leading at all. As a new leader, how would you tread this line?
- How would you analyze President Williams's decision to retain the existing strategic plan?
- How should the leadership team prepare for the shift in student demographics to a population made up of minority students? How should faculty prepare?

## Second Best: Me-Too Community College

Me-Too Community College (MTCC) sought charter status when the Large and Growing Community College District was established in 1972, but the last-minute withdrawal of a school district's support meant MTCC was excluded. Persistent community efforts, however, eventually secured the support needed for creation of the college. The college's location farther from the urban center meant that the student body of 8,000 was more homogenous than those of other campuses. The late entry into the district meant that the growth of the campus infrastructure was haphazard and cobbled together as pressing space needs demanded. Perhaps as a result of the college's late entry into LGCCD, interviewees at MTCC noted a continuous lack of resources at the college and a need to fight for equity among the other colleges in the district.

Michael Garvey has been president of MTCC since January 2001. Garvey was involved in community colleges for almost 40 years, serving in the state community college office, as president of another college in the state, and recently as a consultant and interim president at five different colleges throughout the state. This variety of positions provided Garvey with a rich array of experiences to draw on. Indeed, Garvey initially started at MTCC as an interim president, at which time the chancellor told him that if things "worked out," he would be named president. A mere 3 months after his start at MTCC, Garvey was named president, and as the current president of the faculty senate pointed out, "I was part of the group initially not happy that we did not do a nationwide search, but we said, 'Why do this if you've already got a good person? He's been here for a while, we know him, he knows us. So, he's excellent.'" A key goal for Garvey was to obtain financial resources for the college. He obtained significant increases in the operating budget and an additional $20 million dedicated to building construction on campus. In his first months on campus, Garvey engaged the campus community in a visioning process to eliminate what he referred to as the "hangdog attitude" he witnessed when arriving at MTCC.

There was a sense on the campus that the college was not getting its fair share of resources compared to other colleges within the district. One of the founding faculty said, "We could have grown even more if we had facilities—we have been crying for classroom space." The college runs classes back-to-back from 8 a.m. to 10 p.m. during the week. Garvey recalled, "The feeling of the faculty leadership was that MTCC was the poor third cousin who had always been shortchanged in facilities and in budget and in personnel." The president and his newly hired vice president of instruction worked diligently to turn funding around. The need existed not only to change attitude, but to demonstrate that the campus could garner the resources to do the job. Campus members felt overworked, underfunded, and underappreciated.

The game of catch-up was beginning to pay off. The funding allocation model among the district colleges shifted, which gave MTCC a significant boost of $6 million to its operating budget, a growth of 37% in 2 years. The extra funding allowed for the hiring of new faculty. A vision workshop was conducted to help the campus think about where the college should be in 5 years. The open sessions allowed for venting of frustrations and ultimately the creation of a road map of where to go. Yet people were skeptical. Long-serving faculty did not feel they had a say in many of the decisions impacting their work, whereas many of the newer faculty were not as vested in old processes. The influx of funding, however, allowed for some resources to support proposed changes.

Despite these positive changes, the president stated, "We've turned the corner on some of the issues, but I feel like we're a ship that's dead in the water." The vice president used a boat metaphor as well, relating, "My associate deans and I got on the boat and then two people left for better positions. Two new people got into the boat; they were experienced. So we were ready to set sail and just got off shore and reorganization came. The way that change occurred was like waves." Recent state budget cuts have undermined campus momentum and threaten to push us back into old patterns so that we may lose ground. Garvey added, "It's a bittersweet time for us because we're a growing, dynamic institution, and it's like somebody put the handcuffs on us and said, 'Time out.'"

## QUESTIONS

- How can college leaders frame the current budget cuts to avoid the culture reverting to the feeling of second best?
- What issues are present as a result of the college being part of a larger district, and how can the leaders manage this dynamic?
- How might President Garvey's past leadership experiences influence his current approach to the campus's challenges?

# REFERENCES

Acker, J. (1990). Hierarchies, jobs, bodies: A theory of gendered organizations. *Gender and Society, 4*(2), 139–158.

Acker, J. (2006). *Class questions: Feminist answers.* Lanham, MD: Rowman & Littlefield.

Alcoff, L. (1988). Cultural feminism versus post-structuralism: The identify crisis in feminist theory. *Signs: Journal of Women in Culture and Society, 13,* 405–436.

Alfred, R., Shults, C., Jaquette, O., & Strickland, S. (2009). *Community colleges on the horizon: Challenge, choice or abundance.* New York: Rowman & Littlefield.

American Association of Community Colleges. (2001). *Leadership 2020: Recruitment, preparation, and support.* Washington, DC: American Association of Community Colleges.

American Association of Community Colleges. (2005). *Competencies for community college leaders.* Washington, DC: Author.

American Association of Community Colleges. (2008). *Leading forward report.* Washington, DC: Author.

American Council on Education. (2007). *The American college president: 2007 edition.* Washington, DC: Author.

American Council on Education. (2009). *The CAO census: A national profile of chief academic officers.* Washington, DC: Author.

Amey, M. J. (1992, November). *Cognitive constructions of leadership.* Paper presented at the annual meeting of the Association for the Study of Higher Education, Minneapolis, MN.

Amey, M. J. (1999). Navigating the raging river: Reconciling issues of identity, inclusion, and administrative practice. In K. Shaw, R. A. Rhoads, & J. Valadez (Eds.), *Community colleges as cultural texts: Qualitative explorations of organizational and student cultures* (pp. 59–82). Albany: State University of New York Press.

Amey, M. J. (2005). Leadership as learning: Conceptualizing the process. *Community College Journal of Research and Practice, 29*(9–10), 689–704.

Amey, M. J. (2006). *Breaking tradition: New community college leadership programs meet 21st-century needs.* Washington, DC: American Association of Community Colleges.

Amey, M. J., Eddy, P. L., Campbell, T. G., & Watson, J. L. (2008, April). *The role of social capital in facilitating partnerships.* Paper presented at the annual conference of the Council for the Study of Community Colleges, Philadelphia, PA.

Amey M. J., & Twombly, S. B. (1992). Re-visioning leadership in community colleges. *Review of Higher Education, 15*(2), 125–150.

Amey, M. J., & VanDerLinden, K. E. (2002). Career paths for community college leaders. *American Association of Community Colleges (AACC) Research Brief, 2,* 1–16.

Amey, M. J., VanDerLinden, K., & Brown, D. (2002). Perspectives on community college leadership: Twenty years in the making. *Community College Journal of Research and Practice, 26*(7), 573–589.

Argyris, C. (1980). *Inner contradictions of rigorous research.* New York: Academic Press.

Argyris, C. (1990). *Overcoming organizational defenses. Facilitating organizational learning.* Boston: Allyn & Bacon.

Argyris, C., & Schön, D. (1974). *Theory in practice: Increasing professional effectiveness.* San Francisco: Jossey-Bass.

Avolio, B. J. (2007). Promoting more integrative strategies for leadership theory-building. *American Psychologist, 62*(1), 25–33.

Baca Zinn, M., Hondagneu-Sotelo, P., & Messner, M. A. (Eds.). (2005). *Gender through the prism of difference.* New York: Oxford University Press.

Bailey, T., Jenkins, D., & Leinbach, T. (2005). *What we know about community college low-income and minority student outcomes: Descriptive statistics from national surveys.* New York: Columbia University, Teachers College, Community College Research Center.

Baker, G. A., & Associates. (1992). *Cultural leadership: Inside America's community colleges.* Washington, DC: Community College Press.

Bassoppo-Moyo, S., & Townsend, B. K. (1997). The effective community college academic administrator: Necessary competencies and attitudes. *Community College Review, 25*(2), 41–56.

Beatty, B. R., & Brew, C. R. (2004). Trusting relationships and emotional epistemologies: A foundational leadership issue. *School Leadership and Management, 24*(3), 329–356.

Belenky, M. F., Clinchy, B. M., Goldberger, N. R., & Tarule, J. M. (1997). *Women's ways of knowing: The development of self, voice, and mind.* New York: Basic Books.

Bensimon, E. (1991). The meaning of "good presidential leadership": A frame analysis. In M. Peterson (Ed.), *Organization and governance in higher education* (pp. 421–431). Needham Heights, MA: Simon & Schuster.

Bensimon, E., Neumann, A., & Birnbaum, R. (1989). *Making sense of administrative leadership: The "L" word in higher education* (ASHE-ERIC Higher Education Report No. 1 ED 316 074 MF-01; PC-05). Washington, DC: George Washington University, Graduate School of Education and Human Development.

Bensimon, E. M. (1989). The meaning of "good presidential leadership": A frame analysis. *Review of Higher Education, 12*(2), 107–123.

Bensimon, E. M., & Neumann, A. (1993). *Redesigning collegiate leadership: Teams and teamwork in higher education.* Baltimore: Johns Hopkins University Press.

Berger, P. L. (1963). *Invitation to sociology: A humanistic perspective.* New York: Doubleday.

Berger, P. L., & Luckmann, T. (1966). *The social constructivism of reality: A treatise in the sociology of knowledge.* Garden City, NY: Doubleday.

Berke, D. (2005). *Succession planning and management: A guide to organizational systems and practices.* Greensboro, NC: Center for Creative Leadership.

Bernard, C. (1938). *The functions of an executive.* Cambridge, MA: Harvard University Press.

Berry, T. R., & Mizelle, N. (2006). *From oppression to grace: Women of color and their dilemmas within the academy.* Sterling, VA: Stylus.

Bess, J. L., & Dee, J. R. (2007). *Understanding college and university organization: Theories for effective policy and practice.* Sterling, VA: Stylus.

Birnbaum, R. (1988). *How colleges work: The cybernetics of academic organization and leadership.* San Francisco: Jossey-Bass.

Birnbaum, R. (1992) *How academic leadership works.* San Francisco: Jossey-Bass.

Birnbaum, R. (2000). *Management fads in higher education.* San Francisco: Jossey-Bass.

Birnbaum, R., & Umbach, P. D. (2001). Scholar, steward, spanner, stranger: The four career paths of college presidents. *Review of Higher Education, 24*(3), 203–217.

Bisbee, D. C., & Miller, M. T. (2006). *A survey of the literature related to executive succession in land grant universities.* Washington, DC: ERIC Clearinghouse on Higher Education. (ERIC Identifier No. ED491565)

Blake, R., & Mouton, J. (1964). *The managerial grid: The key to leadership excellence.* Houston, TX: Gulf.

Boggs, G. R. (1993, September). *Community colleges and the new paradigm. Celebrations.* Austin, TX: National Institute for Staff and Organizational Development. (ERIC Identifier No. ED366363)

Bolman, L. G., & Deal, T. E. (2008). *Reframing organizations: Artistry, choice and leadership.* San Francisco: Jossey-Bass.

Burns, J. M. (1978). *Leadership.* New York: Harper & Row.

Cherry Commission. (2004). *Final report of the Lt. Governor's Commission on Higher Education and Economic Growth.* Lansing: Michigan Department of Education.

Chliwniak, L. (1997). Higher education leadership: Analyzing the gender gap. Washington DC: ERIC Clearinghouse on Higher Education. (ERIC Identifier No. ED410846)

Clark, B. R. (1972). The organizational saga in higher education. *Administrative Science Quarterly, 17*(2), 178–184.

Cohen, A. M., & Brawer, F. B. (2008). *The American community college* (5th ed.). San Francisco: Jossey-Bass.

Conger, J. A., & Fulmer, R. M. (2003). Developing your leadership pipeline. *Harvard Business Review, 76*, 1–11.

Corrigan, M. (2002). *The American college president 2002 edition.* Washington, DC: American Council on Education Center for Policy Analysis.

Davis, J. (2003). *Learning to lead.* Westport, CT: Praeger.

Deal, T., & Kennedy, A. (1982). *Corporate cultures: The rites and rituals of corporate life.* Reading, MA: Addison-Wesley.

Dever, J. T. (1997). Reconciling educational leadership and the learning organization. *Community College Review, 25*(2), 57–63.

DiCroce, D. M. (1995). Women and the community college presidency: Challenges and possibilities. In B. K. Townsend (Ed.), *Gender and power in the community college. New Directions for Community Colleges,* vol. 89 (pp. 79–88). San Francisco: Jossey-Bass.

Dolence, M. G., & Norris, D. M. (1995). *Transforming higher education: A vision for learning in the 21st century.* Ann Arbor, MI: Society for College and University Planning.

Drake, E. (2009). *Searching, selecting, and appointing a president: A multi-site case study of rural-serving community college board of trustee perceptions of the presidential selection process.* Unpublished dissertation, Central Michigan University, Mt. Pleasant, MI.

Eagly, A. H. (2007). Female leadership advantage and disadvantage: Resolving the contradictions. *Psychology of Women Quarterly, 31*(1), 1–12.

Ebbers, L. H. (1992, July). *LINCing: Creating a regional consortium for leadership development.* Paper presented at the annual international conference of the League for Innovation in the Community College and the Community College Leadership Program, Chicago, IL.

Eddy, P. L. (2003). Sensemaking on campus: How community college presidents frame change. *Community College Journal of Research and Practice, 27*(6), 453–471.

Eddy, P. L. (2005). Framing the role of leader: How community college presidents construct their leadership. *Community College Journal of Research and Practice, 29*(9–10), 705–727.

Eddy, P. L. (2008). Reflections of women leading community colleges. *Community College Enterprise, 14*(1), 49–66.

Eddy, P. L. (2009a). Changing of the guard in community colleges: The role of leadership development. In A. Kezar (Ed.), *Rethinking leadership in a complex, multicultural, and global environment: New concepts and models for higher education* (pp. 185–212). Sterling, VA: Stylus.

Eddy, P. L. (2009b). Leading gracefully: Gendered leadership at community colleges. In D. R. Dean, S. J. Bracken, & J. K. Allen (Eds.), *Women in academic leadership: Professional strategies, personal choices: Vol. 2. Women in academe* (pp. 8–30). Sterling, VA: Stylus.

Eddy, P. L., & Cox, E. (2008). Gendered leadership: An organizational perspective. In J. Lester (Ed.), *Gendered perspectives on community colleges. New Directions in Community Colleges,* vol. 142 (pp. 69–80). San Francisco: Jossey-Bass.

Eddy, P. L., & VanDerLinden, K. (2006). Emerging definitions of leadership in higher education: New visions of leadership or same old "hero" leader? *Community College Review, 34*(1), 5–26.

Evelyn, J. (2004). Community colleges at a crossroads. *Chronicle of Higher Education, 50*(34), 34A.

Fairhurst, G. T. (2001). Dualisms in leadership research. In F. Jablin & L. Putnam (Eds.), *The new handbook of organizational communication: Advances in theory, research, and methods* (pp. 379–439). Thousand Oaks, CA: Sage.

Fairhurst, G. T., & Sarr, R. A. (1996). *The art of framing: Managing the language of leadership.* San Francisco: Jossey-Bass.

Fiedler, F. E. (1967). *A theory of leadership effectiveness.* New York: McGraw-Hill.

Floyd, D. L., Skolnik, M. L., & Walker, K. P. (2005). *The community college baccalaureate: Emerging trends and policy issues.* Sterling, VA: Stylus.

Frost, P. J., & Morgan, G. (1983). Symbols and sensemaking: The realization of a framework. In L. R. Pondy, P. J. Frost, G. Morgan, & T. C. Dandridge (Eds.), *Organizational symbolism* (pp. 207–236). Greenwich, CT: JAI Press.

Fulton-Calkins, P., & Milling, C. (2005). Community-college leadership: An art to be practiced 2010 and beyond. *Community College Journal of Research and Practice, 29*(3), 233–250.

Garza Mitchell, R. L., & Eddy, P. L. (2008). In the middle: A gendered view of career pathways of mid-level community college leaders. *Community College Journal of Research and Practice, 32*(10), 793–811.

Gillett-Karam, R. (1997). *Administrators in North Carolina community colleges: A comparative study by gender. Preliminary report.* Raleigh, NC: American Council on Education, Women Administrators in North Carolina Higher Education. (ERIC Identifier No. ED409073)

Gilligan, C. (1982). *In a different voice: Psychological theory and women's development.* Cambridge, MA: Harvard University Press.

Gioia, D. A., & Thomas, J. B. (1996). Identity, image, and issue interpretation: Sensemaking during strategic change in academia. *Administrative Science Quarterly, 41*(3), 370–403.

Gioia, D. A., Thomas, J. B., Clark, S. M., & Chittipeddi, K. (1994). Symbolism and strategic change in academia: The dynamics of sensemaking and influence. *Organization Science, 5*(3), 363–383.

Glazer-Raymo, J. (1999). *Shattering the myths: Women in academe.* Baltimore: Johns Hopkins University Press.

Gratton, M. (1993). Leadership in the learning organization. In R. L. Alfred & P. Carter (Eds.), *Emerging roles for community college leaders. New Directions for Community Colleges,* vol. 84 (pp. 93–103). San Francisco: Jossey-Bass.

Green, M. (1997). No time for heroes. *Trusteeship, 5*(2), 6–11.

Green, V. (2008). Reflections from one community college leader. *Community College Journal of Research and Practice, 32*(10), 812–821.

Griffin, B. Q. (1992, March). *Perceptions of managers: Effects of leadership style and gender.* Paper presented at the annual meeting of the Southeastern Psychological Association, Knoxville, TN.

Gronn, P. (2000). Distributed properties: A new architecture for leadership. *Educational Management and Administration, 28*(3), 317–338.

Gumport, P. J. (2003). The demand-response scenario: Perspectives of community college presidents. In K. M. Shaw & J. A. Jacobs (Eds.), Community colleges: New environments, new directions. *Annals of the American Academy of Political and Social Science, 586,* 38–61. Thousand Oaks, CA: Sage.

Hall, R. M., & Sandler, B. R. (1983). *Academic mentoring for women students and faculty: A new look at an old way to get ahead.* Washington, DC: Association of American Colleges.

Halpin, A. W., & Winer, B. J. (1957). A factorial study of the leader behavior descriptions. In R. M. Stogdill & A. E. Coons (Eds.), *Leader behavior: Its description and measurement* (pp. 140–152). Columbus: Ohio State University, Bureau of Business Research.

Harris, A., & Spillane, J. (2008). Distributed leadership through the looking glass. *Management in Education, 22*(1), 31–34.

Harris, S. G. (1994). Organizational culture and individual sensemaking: A schema-based perspective. *Organization Science, 5*(3), 309–321.

Harvey, W. B., & Anderson, E. L. (2005). *Minorities in higher education 2003–2004: Twenty-first annual status report.* Washington, DC: American Council on Education.

Hatch, M. J., & Cunliffe, A. L. (2006). *Organization theory: Modern, symbolic, and postmodern perspectives.* New York: Oxford University Press, 2006.

Heifetz, R. A. (1994). *Leadership without easy answers.* Cambridge, MA: Harvard University Press.

Heifetz, R. A., & Laurie, D. L. (1997). The work of leadership. *Harvard Business Review, 75*(1), 124–134.

Helbel, S., & Sellingo, J. J. (2009). Obama's higher-education goal is ambitious but achievable, college leaders say. *Chronicle of Higher Education, 55*(26), A21.

Helgesen, S. (1995). *The web of inclusion: A new architecture for building great organizations.* New York: Currency/Doubleday.

Hellmich, D. M. (Ed.). (2007). *Ethical leadership in the community college: Bridging theory and daily practice.* San Francisco: Anker.

Hochschild, A. R. (2003). *The second shift.* London: Penguin Books.

Hockaday, J., & Puyear, D. E. (2008). *Community college leadership in the new millennium.* Washington, DC: American Association of Community Colleges.

Horner, M. (1997). Leadership theory: Past, present, and future. *Team Performance Management, 3*(4), 270–287.

Hull, J. R., & Keim, M. C. (2007). Nature and status of community college leadership development programs. *Community College Journal of Research and Practice, 31*(9), 689–702.

Jablonski, M. (1996). The leadership challenge for women college presidents. *Initiatives, 57*(4), 1–10.

Jeandron, C. A. (2006). *Growing your own leaders: Community colleges step up.* Washington, DC: Community College Press.

Johnson, H. H. (2008). Mental models and transformative learning: The key to leadership development? *Human Resource Development Quarterly, 19*(1), 85–89.

Katz, D., & Kahn, R. L. (1952). Some recent findings in human relations research. In E. Swanson, T. Newcombe, & E. Hartley (Eds.), *Readings in social psychology* (pp. 650–655). New York: Holt, Reinhart & Winston.

Kelley, R. E. (1998). In praise of followers. In W. Rosenbach & R. L. Taylor (Eds.), *Contemporary issues in leadership* (4th ed., pp. 96–106). Boulder, CO: Westview Press.

Kelman, H. (1961). Process of opinion change. *Public Opinion Quarterly, 25*(1), 57–78.

Kezar, A. J. (2000). Pluralistic leadership: Incorporating diverse voices. *Journal of Higher Education, 71*(6), 722–743.

Kezar, A. J., Carducci, R., & Contreras-McGavin, M. (2006). Rethinking the "L" word in higher education: The revolution of research on leadership. *ASHE-ERIC Higher Education Report, 31*(6). San Francisco: Jossey-Bass.

King, J. E. (2008). *Too many rungs on the ladder? Faculty demographics and the future leadership of higher education.* Washington, DC: American Council on Education.

Knowles, M. S. (1970). *The modern practice of adult education: Andragogy versus pedagogy.* New York: Association Press.

Kolb, D. A. (1998). Learning styles and disciplinary differences. In K. A. Feldman & M. B. Paulsen (Eds.), *Teaching and learning in the college classroom* (pp. 127–137). Needham Heights, MA: Simon & Schuster.

Kuhnert, K. W., & Lewis, P. (1987). Transactional and transformational leadership: A constructive/developmental analysis. *Academy of Management Review, 12*(4), 648–657.

Lave, J., & Wenger, E. (1991). *Situated learning: Legitimate peripheral participation.* Cambridge, UK: Cambridge University Press.

League for Innovation in the Community College. (2008). *About the League.* Retrieved May 9, 2008, from http://www.league.org/league/about/about_main.htm

Leist, J. (2007). "Ruralizing" presidential job advertisements. In P. L. Eddy & J. P. Murray (Eds.), *Rural community colleges: Teaching, learning, and leading in the heartland. New Directions in Community Colleges,* vol. 137 (pp. 35–46). San Francisco: Jossey-Bass.

Leslie, D., & Fretwell, E. K., Jr. (1996). *Wise moves in hard times: Creating and managing resilient colleges and universities.* San Francisco: Jossey-Bass.

Levin, J. S. (1998). Presidential influence, leadership succession, and multiple interpretations of organizational change. *Review of Higher Education, 21*(4), 405–425.

Levin, J. S. (2005). The business culture of the community college: Students as consumers; students as commodities. In A. Kezar (Ed.), *Organizational learning in higher education. New Directions in Higher Education,* vol. 129 (pp. 11–26). San Francisco: Jossey-Bass.

Lewin, K., Lippitt, R., & White, R. K. (1939). Patterns of aggressive behavior in experimentally created 'social climates.'" *Journal of Social Psychology, 10,* 271–299.

Lewis, M. D. (1989). *Effective leadership strategies for the community college president.* Long Beach, CA: Long Beach City College. (ERIC Identifier No. ED307948)

Loder, T. L. (2005). Women administrators negotiate work-family conflicts in changing times: An intergenerational perspective. *Educational Administration Quarterly, 41*(5), 741–776.

Lorber, J. (1995). *Paradoxes of gender.* New Haven, CT: Yale University Press.

Lord, R. G., & Emrich, C. G. (2001). Thinking outside the box by looking inside the box: Extending the cognitive revolution in leadership research. *Leadership Quarterly, 11*(4), 551–579.

Lunenburg, F. C., & Ornstein, A. C. (2007). *Educational administration: Concepts and practices* (5th ed.). Belmont, CA: Wadsworth.

McKenney, C. B., & Cejda, B. D. (2001). The career path and profile of women chief academic officers in public community colleges. *Advancing Women in Leadership, 9*(1). Retrieved January 21, 2010, from http://www.advancingwomen.com/ awl/summer2001/cejda_mckenney.html

Merriam, S. B. (1998). *Qualitative research and case study applications in education.* San Francisco: Jossey-Bass.

Mezirow, J. (1997). Transformative learning: Theory to practice. In P. Cranton (Ed.), *Higher education: A global community. New Directions for Adult and Continuing Education,* vol. 74 (pp. 5–12). San Francisco: Jossey-Bass.

Morgan, G. (2006). *Images of organization.* Thousand Oaks, CA: Sage.

Morgan, G., Frost, P. J., & Pondy, L. R. (1983). Organizational symbolism. In L. R. Pondy, P. J. Frost, G. Morgan, & T. C. Dandridge (Eds.), *Organizational symbolism* (pp. 3–38). Greenwich, CT: JAI Press.

Myran, G. (1995). *Community college leadership in the new century: Learning to improve learning.* Washington, DC: American Association of Community Colleges.

National Center for Education Statistics. (2007). *Digest of Education Statistics: 2007* (NCES No. 2008–022). Washington, DC: U.S. Department of Education. Retrieved August 30, 2008, from http://nces.ed.gov/programs/digest/d07/

Neumann, A. (1989). Strategic leadership: The changing orientations of college presidents. *Review of Higher Education, 12*(2), 137–151.

Neumann, A. (1995). On the making of hard times and good times. *Journal of Higher Education, 66*(1), 3–31.

Neumann, A., & Bensimon, E. M. (1990). Constructing the presidency: College presidents; images of their leadership roles, a comparative study. *Journal of Higher Education, 61*(6), 678–701.

Nidiffer, J. (2001). New leadership for a new century. In J. Nidiffer & C. T. Bashaw (Eds.), *Women administrators in higher education: Historical and contemporary perspectives* (pp. 101–131). Albany: State University of New York Press.

O'Banion, T. (1997). *A learning college for the 21st century.* Phoenix, AZ: Oryx Press.

Peterson, M. (1997). Using contextual planning to transform institutions. In M. Peterson, D. Dill, L. A. Mets, & Associates (Eds.), *Planning and management for a changing environment* (pp. 127–157). San Francisco: Jossey-Bass.

Quinton, R. (2006). Daytona Beach Community College's leadership development institute: Cultivating leaders from within. *CUPA-HR Journal, 57*(1), 28–32.

Rhoads, R. A., & Tierney, W. G. (1992). *Cultural leadership in higher education.* University Park, PA: National Center on Postsecondary Teaching, Learning and Assessment.

Rosener, J. B. (1990). Ways women lead. *Harvard Business Review, 68,* 119–125.

Rost, J. C. (1991). *Leadership for the twenty-first century.* New York: Praeger.

Roueche, J. E., Baker, G. A., III, & Rose, R. R. (1989). *Shared vision: Transformational leadership in American community colleges.* Washington, DC: Community College Press.

Rowley, D. J., & Sherman, H. (2001). *From strategy to change: Implementing the plan in higher education.* San Francisco: Jossey-Bass.

Rusch, E. A. (2004). Gender and race in leadership preparation: A constrained discourse. *Educational Administration Quarterly, 40*(1), 14–46.

Sagaria, M. A. D. (1988). Administrative mobility and gender: Patterns and processes in higher education. *Journal of Higher Education, 59*(3), 305–326.

Sagaria, M. A. D., & Johnsrud, L. K. (1988). Mobility within the student affairs profession: Career advancement through position change. *Journal of College Student Development, 29*(1), 30–40.

Sawyer, J. O. (2008). *The impact of job satisfaction on the career trajectory of community college administrators in Michigan.* Unpublished dissertation, Central Michigan University, Mt. Pleasant, MI.

Scanlon, K. C. (1997). Mentoring women administrators: Breaking through the glass ceiling. *Initiatives, 58*(2), 39–59.

Schön, D. (1983). *The reflective practitioner: How professionals think in action.* London: Temple Smith.

Senge, P. M. (1990). *The fifth discipline: The art and practice of the learning organization.* New York: Doubleday.

Seymour, S. (2008). Boost your business value with succession planning. *Human Resource Management International Digest, 16*(4), 3–5.

Shults, C. (2001). *The critical impact of impending retirements on community college leadership.* Leadership Series Research Brief no. 1. Washington, DC: American Association of Community Colleges.

Smircich, L., & Morgan, G. (1982). Leadership: The management of meaning. *Journal of Applied Behavioral Science, 18*(3), 257–273.

Spears, L. C., & Lawrence, M. (Eds.). (2003). *Focus on leadership: Servant-leadership for the twenty-first century.* San Francisco: Jossey-Bass.

Spender, D. (1981). *Man made language.* London: Pandora Press.

Stake, R. (1995). *The art of case study research.* Thousand Oaks, CA: Sage.

Stogdill, R. M., & Coons, A. E. (Eds.). (1957). *Leadership behavior: Its description and measurement.* Columbus: Ohio State University, Bureau of Business Research.

Tannen, D. (1994). *Talking from nine to five: How women's and men's conversational styles affect who gets heard, who gets credit, and what gets done at work.* New York: Morrow.

Tedrow, B., & Rhoads, R. A. (1999). A qualitative study of women's experiences in community college leadership positions. *Community College Review, 27*(3), 1–18.

Thayer, L. (1988). Leadership/communication: A critical review and a modest proposal. In G. M. Goldhaber & G. A. Barnett (Eds.), *Handbook of organizational communication* (pp. 231–263). Norwood, NJ: Ablex.

Tierney, W. (1991). *Culture and ideology in higher education.* New York: Praeger.

Townsend, B. K., & Ignash, J. M. (Eds.). (2003). *The role of the community college in teacher education: New Directions for Community Colleges,* vol. 122. San Francisco: Jossey-Bass.

Townsend, B. K., & Twombly, S. B. (1998). A feminist critique of organizational change in the community college. In J. S. Levin (Ed.), *Organizational change and the community college. New Directions for Community Colleges,* vol. 102 (pp. 77–85). San Francisco: Jossey-Bass.

Townsend, B. K., & Twombly, S. (2006, April). *The community college as an educational and workplace site for women.* Paper presented at the 48th annual conference of the Council for the Study of Community Colleges, Long Beach, CA.

Twombly, S. B. (1995). Gendered images of community college leadership: What messages they send. In B. K. Townsend (Ed.), *Gender and power in the community college. New Directions for Community Colleges,* vol. 89 (pp. 67–77). San Francisco: Jossey-Bass.

U.S. Department of Education. (1980). *National Center for Education Statistics: Digest of education statistics.* Washington, DC: Author.

U.S. Department of Education. (1995). *National Center for Education Statistics: Digest of education statistics.* Washington, DC: Author.

U.S. Department of Education. (2006). *A test of leadership: Charting the future of U.S. higher education.* Washington, DC: Author.

U.S. Department of Education. (2007). *National Center for Education Statistics: Digest of education statistics.* Washington, DC: Author.

Valian, V. (1999). *Why so slow? The advancement of women.* Cambridge, MA: MIT Press.

Van Manen, M. (1990). *Researching lived experience: Human science for an action sensitive pedagogy.* Albany: State University of New York Press.

VanDerLinden, K. (2003, April). *Career advancement and leadership development of community college administrators.* Paper presented at the annual meeting of the American Educational Research Association, Chicago, IL.

VanDerLinden, K. E. (2004). Gender differences in the preparation and promotion of community college administrators. *Community College Review, 31*(4), 1–24.

Vaughan, G. (1990). *Pathway to the presidency: Community college deans of instruction.* Washington, DC: Community College Press.

Vaughan, G. B. (1986). *Community college presidency.* Santa Barbara, CA: Oryx Press.

Vaughan, G. B. (1989). *Leadership transition: The community college presidency.* New York: Macmillan.

Wallin, D. L. (2006). Short-term leadership development: Meeting a need for emerging community college leaders. *Community College Journal of Research and Practice, 30,* 513–528.

Walton, K. D., & McDade, S. A. (2001). At the top of the faculty: Women as chief academic officers. In J. Nidiffer & C. T. Bashaw (Eds.), *Women administrators in higher education: Historical and contemporary perspectives* (pp. 85–100). Albany: State University of New York Press.

Weber, M. (2009). *From Max Weber: Essays in sociology.* New York: Routledge.

Weick, K. E. (1995). *Sensemaking in organizations.* Thousand Oaks, CA: Sage.

Weisman, I. M., & Vaughan, G. B. (2002). *The community college presidency, 2001. AACC Research Brief.* Washington, DC: American Association of Community Colleges.

Weisman, I. M., & Vaughan, G. B. (2007). *The community college presidency 2006.* Washington, DC: Community College Press.

West, C., & Zimmerman, D. H. (1987). Doing gender. *Gender and Society, 1*(2), 125–151.

Williams, J. (2000). *Unbending gender: Why family and work conflict and what to do about it.* New York: Oxford University Press.

# Also available from Stylus

**The Community College Baccalaureate**
*Emerging Trends and Policy Issues*
Edited by Deborah L. Floyd, Michael L. Skolnik and Kenneth P. Walker

". . . an important contribution to our understanding of what is sure to become a major policy issue . . . a must read for state policy makers and community college leaders contemplating adding the baccalaureate."—*Journal of Applied Research in the Community College*

"This book is clearly valuable to policy makers, state legislators, faculty in community college or higher education programs and their students, and the community college constituencies of trustees, administrators, and faculty...This book...will contribute greatly towards future research and policy decisions regarding the mission and role of the community college." — *Community College Journal of Research and Practice*

(Forthcoming)
**A Gateway to Opportunity?**
*A History of the Community College in the United States*
Josh M. Beach

**Understanding College and University Organization**
*Theories for Effective Policy and Practice*
James L. Bess and Jay R. Dee
Foreword by D. Bruce Johnstone

**Volume I: The State of the System**
**Volume II: Dynamics of the System**
This two-volume work is intended to help readers develop powerful new ways of thinking about organizational principles, and apply them to policy-making and management in colleges and universities. It is written with two audiences in mind:

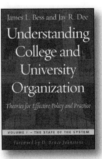

administrative and faculty leaders in institutions of higher learning, and students (both doctoral and Master's degree) studying to become upper-level administrators, leaders, and policy makers in higher education.

"This will be seen as a landmark work in the field. It should be required reading for all who claim to understand higher education institutions and the behavior that goes on inside and around them."—*David W. Leslie*, *Chancellor Professor of Education, The College of William and Mary*

"I highly recommend this textbook to master's level instructors who seek to foster critical thinking about theory and practice."—*Cheryl J. Daly*, *director, College Student Personnel master's program, Western Carolina University*

22883 Quicksilver Drive
Sterling, VA 20166-2102

Subscribe to our e-mail alerts: www.Styluspub.com